BE THE
BEST
BOSS

Empower your people so they don't flee, fail or get fired

John Pennington

An Accela Book

Accela is an Australian owned company that specialises in high impact sales performance improvement. We're passionate about helping people to be their best and to achieve their sales goals. What differentiates Accela is our commitment to people first and foremost by helping them leverage a treasure trove of resources to easily solve their challenges.

Accela was founded by John Pennington, a sales executive with over 20 years' sales excellence with blue chip Australian and international organisations. For more information about how Accela can boost your sales performance:

+61 2 9368 7969
info@accela.com.au
www.accela.com.au

CONTENTS

To my wife and best friend Kylie, and my beautiful daughters Madeleine and Samantha, who constantly remind me that dreams really do come true.

John Pennington

OVERVIEW

In over ten years of creating, delivering, and bolstering successful management training, we have built an accelerated and efficient competency building program which successfully addresses the four major pitfalls of even the best development strategies:

1. Failing to consider the **context** in which the skill is performed. For example, when a curriculum teaches methods of communication that fail to take into account organisational preferences or corporate policies. Some offices might prefer phone to email, so teaching a strict communication method that preferences email won't be helpful.

2. Misjudging current levels of **proficiency**, or having unrealistic or unclear expectations for the level of proficiency that can be acquired through training. For example, most people will rate themselves "above average" drivers, but of course it's impossible for everyone in a given cohort to be "above average." In the workplace, sometimes this means that the person who needs training the most won't necessarily be able to recognise that need in themselves. Often, the lack of proficiency can also lead to a lack of understanding about what level of skill can be acquired, leading to a vague and ineffective training process that won't be beneficial in the long run.

3. Ignoring **motivational drivers**. People seek out training, or are required to complete training by managers or companies for a wide variety of reasons. Impactful training not only acknowledges these differences in motivation, it uses them to inform lessons and increase potential for competency development. For example, someone who is motivated to complete training by intrinsic interest will have a very different approach to learning than someone who needs to complete a course to receive a promotion. Taking these different motivators into account means it is far more likely that both people will achieve what they want to achieve without getting bored or burnt out.

4. Providing inadequate or ineffective **support**. Ongoing holistic training should aim for a 70:20:10 support model: that is, 10% formal learning, 20% learning from others, and 70% learning by doing the work itself. If a subject is practical, like management, reading about it is not the only activity that will be necessary in order to achieve tangible improvement. Providing opportunities for practice is crucial to helping anyone develop their skills, especially in practical areas.

Be the Best Boss is the manual to help 21st century managers and their organisations pursue the training they need without falling prey to these issues. Over the past ten years, we have identified 52 of the most critical competencies necessary to propel managers forward in a world of accelerating innovation. Be the Best Boss provides the flexibility necessary to help managers learn new skills in ways that are appropriate for their context. We provide a proficiency assessment to accurately assess areas where growth is needed, so that managers start at the right level for each competency. We then guide managers through the program based on their specific motivational drivers so that they can tailor the program to their specific interests and needs. Finally, we provide holistic learning support by building practice opportunities into Be the Best Boss, so that managers have clear, consistent ways to add to their skills in the real world and track their progress.

The ultimate goal? It's in the title. We want all managers to Be the Best Boss they can be, using a proven, multi-dimensional, team-oriented approach. By focusing on improving managers, we make it easier for managers to support their teams, and prevent anyone on their team from fleeing, failing or getting fired.

Our management strategies are so powerful because of our clear focus. We help managers deal with the things that are within their control, and we provide a practical, applied program that is designed to be adaptable to any context. We acknowledge that there are plenty of things in the business world that managers have no control over. Managers who focus on what they can do rather than what their teams, bosses or organisations need to do better, will be able to clarify which actions and changes will make a difference, and avoid wasting time and energy trying to fix unfixable problems. As it turns out, when the focus is limited to the ways in which we can change ourselves, it becomes easier to adapt to change and find opportunities where previously there were only challenges visible. By narrowing the focus to managers and what they can change, Be the Best Boss helps managers impact the entire ecosystem of their organisations.

By providing practical applications within the lessons of Be the Best Boss, managers will be able to use what they have learned immediately, and tweak their behaviour, responses and ideas as necessary to their situation.

You wouldn't expect someone to be able to play tennis well just by reading about it; therefore managers shouldn't expect themselves to manage well until they have opportunities to practice their skills and use them in the real world. Because *Be the Best Boss* can be adapted as necessary to a manager's or organisation's needs, managers will not find themselves having to start from scratch if one part of a module doesn't apply to them, or a practice session reveals that they were moving in the wrong direction. Instead, by returning to the manual, managers can restructure their own learning and adapt to their new knowledge about their needs.

The book is divided into three sections.

Section 1: Competency Development Loops

We set managers up for success by grouping each module into a specific **Competency Loop**. Each module within a loop is designed to maximise the manager's learning potential through goals in line with the theme of the loop. The Competency Loops are:

Competency Loops	Self
	Leadership
	Collaboration
	External Relationships
	Business

The organisation of *Be the Best Boss* provides a framework for assessing managers' development gaps. Within each Competency Loop, we provide competency assessment tools for the subjects within that loop, as well as real-world indicators of weak competencies, no matter the score on the assessment tool.

We include explanations and foundational material for the 25 key Motivation Drivers. Each individual will have a different set of motivational drivers and these may change depending upon which Competency Loop they are developing. We provide information on the most common motivators across all Competency Loops, as well as motivators that work best within an individual Competency Loop. We map these out for you and explain how to use them.

Finally, we provide the programatic support necessary for managers to promote 70:20:10 Holistic Learning and embed rapid development seamlessly within everyday worklife.

Section 2: Competency Development Modules

By grouping similar Competency Modules together within each loop, managers can ensure they are progressing towards their goals more efficiently and effectively, and can monitor their overall progress more easily.

Within each Competency Module, we focus on accelerated competency development for faster, clearer results. We do this by breaking down each Competency Loop into single skillsets, and then outlining each skillset in a single module designed to give managers an overview of the skillset to be acquired, detailed information to help them learn the skillset, and practical applications for the skill in their work lives. Each module links the defined skillset back to the main Competency Loop, and allows managers to use their relevant Motivational Drivers as they work through the modules. By keeping the modules action-oriented and clearly defined, we give managers the best opportunity possible to meet their development goals in measurable, meaningful ways.

1. Self	Module 1.1. Demonstrate Efficiency and Resourcefulness
	Module 1.2. Take Responsibility
	Module 1.3. to 1.10

Each Module is structured in the following format:
- Competency Name
- Definition
- Competency Context
- Motivation Driver Emphasis

11

- Development Actions
- Coaching Tips
- Holistic Learning Emphasis

Be the Best Boss avoids being too prescriptive in order to create broad utility for managers in a variety of settings. By providing concrete definitions and explicit instructions for practice, without forcing managers to pursue a particular plan that won't work for their industry or needs, we avoid sending managers down unproductive professional development routes that won't add value to their day-to-day activities.

Section 3: Development Case Study

Here we provide a typical example of how a competency development intervention is applied for each Competency Loop. The aim here is to provide a tangible example of how the information in this book can form part of a comprehensive strategic plan to achieve best-practice business results through the application of elegant people management skills.

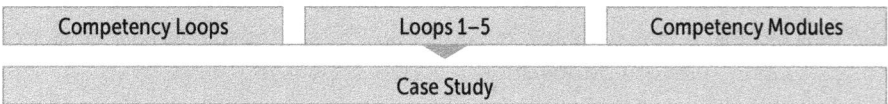

Competency Loops	Loops 1–5	Competency Modules
Case Study		

The case study provided focusses heavily on the personal interactions this specific "best boss" has with a key new hire. It outlines the leadership disciplines she is able to pass on using her advanced planning skills, willingness to role-model and her passion to achieve great outcomes through her people.

For managers, organisations and teams, *Be the Best Boss* is a comprehensive approach to management that benefits everyone.

This book is for ambitious people who want to approach their work life from a big picture perspective. Great managers are able to manage the details while also keeping their eye on the ball, and the format of *Be the Best Boss* favours this "forest and the trees" approach. For managers and organisations who care about people and their careers, *Be the Best Boss* provides opportunities for development that are often left out of manuals that see management as a science rather than an art. From a business perspective, *Be the Best Boss* will help managers and their teams solve problems and align their work with organisational goals by taking a holistic approach to management. We see managers as an integral part of the organisational ecosystem. No one operates in a vacuum, so why should managers attempt to learn to manage more effectively without outside input or real-world conditions? *Be the Best Boss* addresses the entire work environment through the lens of management training. We encourage managers to find possibilities for collaboration and coordination, rather than focusing on pain points and dissonance. In this way, managers not only learn how to do their work more effectively; they learn how to help their teams and organisations work more effectively as well.

Our approach makes management simpler, by breaking down big questions into manageable action items. We believe there is already enough complication in leaders' work lives. A management manual should always strive to make the complex issues present in most leaders' day-to-day environments clearer, less abstract, and more approachable. Leaders usually aren't looking for more theories about why things are going wrong; they are searching for practical solutions that can help them solve persistent issues in real ways. While we encourage formal and informal reflection in each module, *Be the Best Boss* does not allow for much navel-gazing; the approaches managers will find here are deeply practical and action-oriented, designed to work in the real world and not just on paper, and the goal of reflection should be to create new modes of operation, not just thinking.

Understanding how the entire system works is key to leaders understanding their part in that system. Once managers understand what they can control, what they can influence, and the places where they have neither much control nor much influence, they will be able to focus their energy in the places where it will make a difference and let go in areas where their impact is negligible. In doing so, leaders will likely find they have significantly more power than they realised. When a leader unlocks their own potential, they will be able to see clearly where others are under or over-utilised, and help their teams redirect their energies more efficiently as well. When everyone on a team is functioning at a higher level, organisations will see a systemic difference beyond pure efficiency; morale increases and people become not just more productive, but more effective.

Great management is the foundation on which great organisations are built.

How sturdy is your foundation?

BONUS

Free 360 Degree Feedback Survey, usually USD59!

Gain valuable insights as to how your skills are perceived by conducting our online 360 Degree Feedback Survey based on the competencies within Be The Best Boss.

Goto www.btbboss.com.au and enter in promocode BTBBoss.

View a sample 360 Degree Feedback Report and other supporting tips and tools to Be The Best Boss.

1

SELF DEVELOPMENT

INTRODUCTION

Great leaders know themselves as well as they know their business. When someone is promoted to management, they may find themselves struggling under the weight of new responsibilities. They may have gotten by with bad working habits or problematic ideas about business before they were a manager, but with the additional responsibilities, the façade has begun to crack.

Personal qualities of great managers are often widely felt by everyone who works around them. These qualities are also at work in their personal lives, and management transitions can sometimes reveal ways in which the manager's goals are not aligned even between their personal and work life. Certain derailers they were able to work around before, like a predisposition to a negative attitude or a lack of resourcefulness, can cause them to fail in one or both areas of their lives as their environment changes, or the complexity of their role increases.

By providing new leaders with the support and space they need to develop personally and encouraging them to do the work, organisations can help leaders not only manage, but thrive. A healthy, happy leader is far more likely to do and inspire great work. By taking the time to build a solid foundation at the level of the self, leaders will be better prepared to do the work and take on the responsibilities expected of them by the organisation.

Red Flags to Look For

Indicators that a new leader might be struggling:

- **They come up with problems, but not solutions.** This could be an indicator that the manager is not working efficiently or using their resources well (Efficient and Resourceful 1.1). More likely, however, it is an attitude issue that will require a perspective shift (Maintain a Positive Attitude 1.8).

- **They seem like they are always on the edge of an emotional breakdown.** Sometimes, the pressure of a new role is just too much to handle. Emotion is not a bad thing, but if the manager's emotions seem to be running high most of the time, they may need to develop more resilience (Be Resilient 1.5), more emotional intelligence (Display Emotional Intelligence 1.6), or both.

- **Things just aren't getting done when they should be.** The load of new responsibility can bring out unproductive coping skills in many people. Sometimes, these coping skills actively get in the way of productivity (Make Things Happen 1.3). Other times, it can be an issue of prioritisation in the face of so many responsibilities (Produce Results 1.4).
- **They blame someone else when something goes wrong and seem surprised when something fails.** If a manager finds a new scapegoat for every failure, or they seem surprised by failures even if they acknowledge the issue, they are likely not taking full responsibility for their team yet (Take Responsibility 1.2).
- **They've made it to management...and now they've stagnated.** Motivation issues can even happen to great managers if they've been ignoring their personal goals (Set Personal Goals 1.9) and development needs. Managers who avoid learning will likely lose momentum quickly: one of the biggest responsibilities of any manager is to ensure they are constantly learning how to manage more effectively (Rapidly Self Develops 1.7).

Preparation

When you start developing leadership talent, it is important to assess where everyone is starting from. What problems and challenges do key leaders exhibit? What skills do they have that can be better utilised? The questions below can help you assess where an employee may experience problems as they move into leadership roles.

Negative attitude	Extremely	Very	Moderately	Slightly	Not At All
1. Assumes the worst will happen.					
2. Has a fixed mindset (not a growth mindset).					
3. Avoids managing upward.					
4. Poor empathy skills.					
5. Is reactive (not proactive).					
6. Goals are vague, unachievable, or misaligned.					
7. Has trouble prioritising.					

Motivating Drivers

Everyone is motivated differently and understanding yourself is the first step towards understanding others. When a leader knows their own motivations, they are then able to explore the individual motivational drivers for each person on the team. This knowledge can completely change how team leaders interact with their teams and drive team success, so this is where we start.

Each motivational driver comes with its own set of "triggers" – concrete ways to jump-start motivation for someone with that driver. Below, we discuss the four main drivers.

Growth for growth's sake: People who enjoy learning purely for the sake of self-improvement are constantly striving to improve because they believe they can always be better. These people typically embody a growth mindset and are extremely hardworking; however they can veer into perfectionism territory if their growth mindset isn't directed properly.

Relationships: People motivated by relationships want to be their best selves because it improves their relationships with others. They tend to be highly self-sacrificing and outwardly oriented, resulting in excellent teamwork and high empathy levels. However, they can sometimes ignore their own needs in the service of others to the point that it negatively impacts their career, or physical or emotional health.

Ambition: People motivated by ambition thrive when they have clear goals to achieve and a position that allows them to work towards those goals. They love working towards those goals with clear, decisive action and plans. They tend to be highly organised and productive, but they can be lower in empathy and have a hard time slowing down and prioritising relationships.

Balance: People motivated by balance seek to prioritise holistically in all areas of their lives. They feel best when they know their lives are working smoothly and they have created systems that allow them to be highly effective in all areas of their lives. These people are usually great at knowing themselves and often have high levels of empathy and a great capacity to see the big picture. However they may not deal well with large changes in their external environment, and may avoid handling the responsibilities they find unpleasant or unnecessary to their personal vision.

1.1.

DEMONSTRATE EFFICIENCY AND RESOURCEFULNESS

Overview

It can feel like the pace of business gets faster each year. Ten years ago, returning an email the next day was considered a fast reply; now, people often expect responses within minutes. How does someone manage the increased volume of work without becoming completely overwhelmed? Becoming a more efficient worker will certainly help, because if they are working on the right thing at the right time, they can manage that feeling of falling behind before it reaches an overwhelming level. Resourcefulness, or the ability to find creative solutions using limited resources is also key to sustainable success.

66
Great things are done by a series of small things done together.
Vincent van Gogh

Setting the Scene

Their phone won't stop ringing. Their email inbox is always full. They have five meetings today and their colleague just asked them to attend a business lunch. What do they do?

If they had infinite time, money and help, their days would probably be simple. They could move forward at a comfortable pace, do everything perfectly, and still get eight hours of sleep every night. Of course, none of us actually lives in that world. What we lack in time, resources and money we must make up for in efficiency and resourcefulness. We need to use the time we have available, the resources we can afford and the money we can spend to their fullest potential to produce the best results we can.

In India, resourcefulness is such an essential part of daily life that the idea of "jugaad" (the closest English translation is to "McGyver" or "jerry-rig" a solution) is an integral part of both everyday life and the board room. "Jugaad" is not just for making do; it's often the best path towards achieving great results.

Resourceful leaders are perceived by their people, peers and managers as being able to "get it done". They think clearly, create minimum fuss and are able to solve quite complex problems with apparent ease. The secret? It's not a secret, it's simply maximising the use of available resources to greatest effect.

Those who are yet to master this skill will often appear stressed, fall behind on deadlines and often make sub-optimal decisions due to time and workflow pressure.

Development Instructions

1. Develop effective daily plans.

If they don't know what's coming, they won't be prepared to handle it. Making effective calendars, daily agendas, schedules and sticking to them is key to increasing their productivity. If they are working on a complex project, creating a calendar with all important due dates, and breaking the project up into smaller tasks can help them figure out more quickly what resources they truly need and how much time they require to complete the project as a whole. Scheduling their time more efficiently (and sometimes, more intensely) can actually help them find more time in their day.

2. Maintain focus on highest priorities.

What is a high priority for them? Usually, our highest priorities are tasks that are both urgent and important. Urgent tasks are things that must be done very soon on a strict deadline. Important tasks are things that are essential to our jobs. Sometimes, these things overlap, but often, they don't. Being able to judge which tasks fall into which categories is a skill they can develop, which will help them understand their priorities clearly and decide which to do first.

3. Prioritise tasks for maximum results output.

Start with a to-do list. What things on that list are urgent and which are important? Making these judgment calls early helps them focus on the tasks that truly matter that day, and schedule other important tasks so they're not missed. If they tackle tasks based on the order of their email inbox, they are likely to accomplish lots of urgent tasks, but very few important ones: This will lead to feeling overwhelmed.

4. Complete tasks within deadlines.

If someone on the team is constantly missing deadlines, other people can find it hard to plan to their own time efficiently and resourcefully. Learning to meet deadlines can also help them manage their own work more efficiently by telling them which tasks to prioritise. Deadlines aren't there to make their life more difficult: They are tools they can use to decide how to organise their work day. If they are finding it hard to complete tasks within deadlines, it could mean that something needs to change about how they allocate time within their work day.

5. Allocate resources within budget.

Like deadlines, budgets can be seen as tools to help them prioritise, rather than obstacles to overcome. They plan their budget the same way they plan their time: by breaking down the whole into smaller individual parts, and being honest about both the priority and the amount of time and energy required to complete each part. Are there people who aren't using their full potential? Learning to recognise who can do more can help them avoid asking for a bigger budget. Are there ways to accomplish a less-important task with less money, or to simply cut it out entirely? Learning how to cut their budget where they can will let them spend more money on the most important goals that ultimately affect the outcome of the project. In a similar vein, can they accomplish the same task with additional resources other than money? Learning to consider all of their available resources, not just their budget, can help them find creative solutions and use the resources they have at their disposal with intent, rather than allocating the most funds to the loudest problem. After all the planning in the world, they may still come up short on resources. This is where negotiation skills can be critical: Learning to negotiate for scarce resources, or trade less important resources for critical ones, can be key to helping them accomplish their goals and meet their deadlines.

6. Apply a proactive approach to complex and challenging tasks.

"They can't plan for everything, or they never get started in the first place" –Jim Butcher. Too often, it feels so much easier to manage a simple problem rather than tackle the elephant in the room. We procrastinate and avoid complex and challenging tasks until we are up against a deadline, leaving us with no choice other than the most expensive and time-consuming solution. By that point, it is too late to do the planning and budgeting that would have made the problem manageable. Instead, start by planning for the most complex and challenging tasks so that they can allocate their time, money and resources most effectively. Proactively tackling these problems earlier in the process prevents them from wasting their resources on easier tasks. Taking even one first step can make the remaining parts of a challenging task seem more doable.

7. Manage contingencies via effective communication.

Unfortunately, all the planning in the world won't help when something changes in the middle of a project, or even in the middle of their day. So how do they plan for the unexpected? Learning how to plan extra time and resources for the most likely contingencies can prevent total disaster. When things do go wrong, starting with effective communication makes the recovery process smoother. Making important players aware of interruptions, changes and roadblocks as they happen and having back-up plans which are effectively communicated can help the project stay on track. No one works in a vacuum, so they use their resources and help others to help them when they get stuck. Good communication helps maintain their professional image: if teammates, bosses, clients or other stakeholders only find out about major changes or problems after the deadline has passed, it is already too late.

8. Avoid mental multitasking.

Multitasking can be a huge tax on mental energy, even if they are just thinking about multiple tasks at once. Learning to mindfully focus can help them get better at staying focused on one thing at a time, even under pressure and despite interruptions. This doesn't mean that they avoid working on multiple parts of a project at the same time – sometimes, this is what will make them most efficient and effective. However, when doing deep work on a particular task, learning to focus on the task at hand is far more efficient than worrying about the other things they also need to be doing.

Coaching Suggestions

1. Understand what the current planning process looks like. Is there one?
2. Have coachee self-prioritise current tasks
3. Follow up small milestones and reward

Training Suggestions

1. Have groups consider all tasks in current job role
2. Work as a team to find solutions to common prioritisation, resource and time management issues
3. Have each participant walk away with tailor-made planning template

Challenge Level: 2 – Difficult

Resourcefulness is not an ability that comes naturally to many. People generally operate well in an environment where clear and precise instructions are given at micro level.

Resourcefulness challenges people to deliver desirable outcomes using creative means, while still acting within organisational values, policy and risk management frameworks. It is a skill which can certainly be learned and enhanced given expert tools, guidance and sufficient mentoring.

1.2.

TAKE RESPONSIBILITY

Overview

We rarely get to see strong responsibility in leadership except when something bad has happened. This is unfortunate, because at the end of the day, much of what we are seeing is not actually the leader's demonstration of responsibility but of accountability. They may think of a university vice-chancellor who responds to the needs of students by changing a policy that is creating problems for them, or an employee who accepts feedback from their manager graciously and works to change problematic behaviour when they think of responsibility. These actions are both good examples of accountability, but responsibility is more than responding well to negative feedback.

What is the difference between responsibility and accountability? Accountability is contained within responsibility, but responsibility is more than holding themselves accountable for their actions and the   of the team after the fact. Responsibility is a mindset: responsible managers believe that they are not only accountable for their team's performance and the end product, but that they are the person responsible for making things happen in the first place. Accountability happens after the action; responsibility is part of the action.

What does that look like for a manager? Instead of simply owning up to their team's mistakes at the end of a project or after feedback, a responsible manager feels the importance of their role in their team's success throughout the lifetime of a project. They look for areas where they can assist before they receive negative feedback. This doesn't mean that they take over their employee's tasks or micromanage. Instead, they are constantly looking for ways that they can help their team succeed, and they are ready to jump in when their team needs them. It also means holding team members accountable for their actions, even when the process is uncomfortable.

> **"** I'd rather regret the things I've done than regret the things I haven't done.
> Lucille Ball

Setting the Scene

So how does a manager demonstrate responsibility if they don't even know what their responsibilities at work are? While their job description is a good place to start, it may be more helpful to think of it as the baseline, not the full scope. Managers who are able to discern the full extent of their responsibilities have a much better chance of avoiding accountability issues in the future, and maintaining a strong, supportive relationship with their teams. Managers who truly understand and respond to their responsibilities are able to provide more value to their organisations and maintain a strong focus on results. Having a responsible outlook also improves managers' chances of self-improvement: if they are constantly scanning their environment for ways in which they can be of service, or issues they may have missed, they are more likely to find opportunities for growth as well.

Development Instructions

1. Understand current responsibilities.

Let's start with their current role. Can they describe the responsibilities of their job to someone else clearly? Where does their role overlap with other roles? Are these lines clear, or are the roles within their organisation fuzzy and ill-defined? Teach them how to identify their own responsibilities, discuss them clearly and concisely, and map them in relationship to their colleagues' and employees' responsibilities. Additionally, create and apply strategies and techniques for working effectively when responsibilities are unclear.

2. Demonstrate positive behaviour.

It's easy enough to ask someone to demonstrate "positive behaviour," but positive is a qualitative term. Different people see their own behaviour and the behaviour of others in different ways, and no one is totally correct or totally wrong. Instead, we should provide them with strong models to use in order to understand what responsibility in the workplace looks like. This will include models like "above vs below the line behaviour", and values modelling based on their company's particular profile, their position and their personal values. We will also look at how their mindset and thinking patterns can fit into these models, in addition to their actions. Are their values motivating their behaviour, or is their behaviour influencing their values? Aim to put their values back in the driver's seat.

3. Admit to mistakes and errors.
Organisations often develop feedback processes partly by accident: it might start informally, and as the organisation grows to where all the members can't know each other well, the company realises a feedback process is necessary. These processes don't always take into account the current needs of the company, the employees or the managers, because they were developed at an early stage and haven't been updated regularly. What is their feedback process like? Are there twice-a-year formal performance reviews, and little informal or formal feedback throughout the year? Do they know with 90% certainty how their boss feels about their work at this very moment? If not, it might be time to update their feedback process.

4. Create a listening culture.
Do their employees feel they can challenge them respectfully, and that they will take what they say seriously? Do their feel they can approach their boss with criticism and their boss will take what they said to heart and act on it? If not, the management team probably needs to take steps to talk less and listen more. Even more important than how much they listen is how they listen. Coach them through practice of techniques for improving the listening culture in their office, and make it easier for them to respond well to feedback so that their colleagues and employees feel comfortable approaching them. We will also discuss how to make that approach, and foster the willingness to speak up in themselves and their employees, while maintaining clear boundaries and a respectful office environment.

5. Report on events and outcomes.
At a basic level, being responsible for their team's activities means they must have a method of tracking workflow. If they have no idea what their team is doing, or what anyone is supposed to be working on, how can they either answer for their work, or make sure everything is on track? Use proven workflow monitoring methods to help them keep themselves and their team on track.

Workflow monitoring is the process that allows them to report well on their team's progress at the end of the day. When they are asked to relay what they or their team are doing, can they do so with data? If not, their reporting standards likely need a tune up. Adopt clear, concise, valuable reporting to deliver news about outcomes in a way that both keeps them accountable and allows them to progress in a positive fashion.

6. Display ownership.

When teaching presentation skills, coaches often have their students walk into the space like they own it. It's a technique to help students develop the confidence to speak well, even when they are nervous. But to create the actual feeling of ownership? It translates even better into confidence when they actually own the place (or in this case, the work they are doing). Teach them what taking true ownership of a project means and how to own their work even when they are working in collaboration with others. Specifically, develop a feedback loop among themselves and their collaborators and team, so that everyone involved feels fully responsible for their contribution, without losing the flexibility necessary to work together as a group.

7. Give and accept feedback.

Workplaces and employees have started to recognise the importance of nearly constant feedback. Millennials are often cited as having the biggest appetite for feedback, but the truth is, we all want to know where we stand. We can't learn or do better if we don't know where we stand, and in a vacuum of information, some of us may change good behaviours because we sense, falsely, that they aren't necessary or wanted. However, this doesn't mean all feedback is appropriate at all times, or that all feedback actually helps us do our jobs better. Help them create and apply models for constructive feedback, timelines for appropriate feedback, and how to deliver feedback in a casual, constant way that allows their team members to know where they stand without fear or judgment.

The feedback culture at some companies can make it feel like every time feedback is given, HR needs to be involved, and they should deliver the feedback on a Friday afternoon so that everyone has a chance to cool off over the weekend. Firstly, the feedback experience does not need to be negative. Secondly, if feedback is being done well, it shouldn't be a surprise to anyone. If an employee finds themselves in a situation where their work performance or behaviour requires improvement, they should already have had conversations with their boss about the issue, as well as an explanation of the consequences if they don't improve. If the first time an employee receives feedback on problematic behaviour or work performance happens in a formal setting, there are bigger problems to address within the company culture. Therefore, apply methods for giving constructive and direct feedback with kindness and respect on a regular basis. Also, teach them how to balance positive and constructive feedback, so that employees know what they are doing well, and are able to hear, respond to and act on the constructive feedback without damaging their sense of self-worth or the positive aspects of their work.

Accepting feedback, especially constructive but critical feedback, can be difficult, especially when it isn't delivered well. Unfortunately, just because necessary feedback might come in a less-than-perfect package doesn't mean it can be ignored. In order to effectively act on negative feedback, there are certain steps people can take, including taking care of themselves emotionally so that they remain receptive to criticism without damaging their workflow. Coach them on how to receive feedback, including body language and appropriate responses, creating a mindset of gratitude around feedback in general, practicing emotional self-care without avoiding acting on the feedback, and setting up a strong support network to help them continue to make progress.

8. Know project and work status.
In the aerospace industry, it is typical for a jet aircraft to be assembled in several different countries, depending on what each country can offer the company. For example, the body of the plane might be made in Germany, but the seats are made in Canada, and the electronic systems are assembled in the UK from parts produced in China. On top of that, the experts who know how to assemble these systems within the physical plane body might be based in France, the US and the Netherlands, and not every factory has the space to store multiple jetliners while the engineers work on them. Therefore, a plane literally must travel all over the world to be assembled. How does an aerospace company keep track of this world-traveling work-in-progress plane? WIP tracking and reporting systems may have started as a logistics and manufacturing technology,

but teams with complex systems in many other fields are now using these systems to help track workflow. Teach them to adapt the principles of WIP tracking and reporting to their needs and use the system to improve their ability to manage their responsibilities. Practice using these systems as triggers for proactive communication around their responsibilities, and help them develop the communication skills they need in order to take responsibility in the moment, not just hold themselves accountable when something goes wrong.

Coaching Suggestions
1. Draw out key workplace goals and accountabilities
2. Focus on strong ownership and remediation processes for errors
3. Use case studies

Training Suggestions
1. Have groups consider how to define and prioritise their responsibilities
2. Brainstorm gaps in their feedback systems
3. Role play feedback situations

Challenge Level: 1 – Very Difficult
While it seems intuitive to "take responsibility" for one's work performance and outcomes, very often workplace responsibilities can be poorly articulated or understood at the outset. This is then exacerbated as some people may look to shift blame when errors or other unexpected results occur.

At leadership level, the complexity is multiplied by several factors, including number of direct reports, level of seniority in the organisation and the increased organisational and potentially personal consequences of defect or failure.

The importance of establishing clear frameworks and methodology for taking and assigning responsibility and accountability cannot be overstated. Often an external view at macro or micro organisational level can assist in putting together clear roles, responsibilities and business contingency planning.

1.3.

MAKE THINGS HAPPEN

Overview

If demonstrating strong input is no longer sufficient to be considered a good employee, how can managers increase the effectiveness of their output? If a manager already feels that they are at or near their maximum level of input, there is a good chance that they are working hard, but not in ways that serve their output. Therefore, they must find ways to increase their output without increasing their input.

Planning is the first step. Once a manager has a plan, acting on that plan thoughtfully and rapidly will move them from the category of people who watch things happen to people who make things happen.

Setting the Scene

In the workplace, we often reward people for the time, effort and devotion they show the company, rather than the value they produce for that company. In some ways, we may be rewarding the wrong thing: the person who is always busy, who stays late at the office, and always comes to company events but achieves nothing important can go further under this kind of reward system than a high-achieving worker who can get twice as much done in half the time, creates tangible value for the company, and then takes the appropriate amount of scheduled leave to feel well rested. Some companies are beginning to realise this is costing them valuable resources and employees, and are restructuring their HR policies to reward output rather than input. One of the most notable examples, Netflix, leads the pack with a PowerPoint presentation that has become legendary in Silicon Valley. One of the slides on this presentation simply reads: "Hard work = not relevant." Netflix grants their employees unlimited vacation time and exceptionally high salaries, even for the tech industry, but at a cost: Employees know that they must continue to achieve if they want to keep their jobs, no matter what they have accomplished in the past.

Netflix is an extreme example, but all indicators point to a future world in which employee output matters much more than employee input. The ability to act quickly, decisively and deliver desired results will likely matter more than long hours, delayed vacations, tenure or attendance at company events.

_____

"There are people who make things happen, there are people who watch things happen and there are people who wonder what happened. To be successful, we have to be people who make things happen.
Jim Lovell

Development Instructions

1. Recognise and avoid procrastination.

Procrastination is putting off anything that needs to be done until later. More than the dictionary definition, however, procrastination is a mindset. Postponing an important phone call until the office is quieter is reasonable, but putting off that phone call indefinitely when the office is never perfectly quiet puts managers in dangerous territory. Sometimes, we can get so good at procrastinating, we don't even realise we are doing it: Our brains automatically justify delaying the activity.

"I can't submit the report until my boss checks it, so there's no reason to start working until they are back from leave."

"It's quarter to twelve, they've probably already left for lunch. I'll just try phoning tomorrow instead."

Sometimes it's even simpler – rather than putting off specific tasks, some people generally have trouble staying on track at all. Most desk workers have a computer that's connected to the internet, and a phone with data. A few minutes break surfing the web can easily turn into a deep dive into cat videos or research on the temperature in Townsville. A co-worker stopping for a coffee break can easily bleed into half an hour of unproductive time between coffee, chatting and easing back into work. Some people use work itself to procrastinate by working on less important things to avoid tackling more difficult but necessary tasks.

Chronic procrastinators sabotage their own ability to get strong results. Work with managers to identify procrastination mentality, triggers that make procrastination more likely and strategies for avoiding those triggers. Managers should also consider strategies for maintaining momentum, even as focus and willpower wains.

2. Recognise and avoid perfectionism.

Perfectionism can make people feel like they are being extra productive and efficient. They just want to get the job done right, how could that be a problem? At the end of the day, however, finishing something on time is far more important than completing something "perfectly" (an unachievable goal in any case because "perfect" is a relative term that means different things to different people). Refusing to accept that something is "good enough" and allowing others to do their jobs without interference only creates problems in the work place, and worse, it can be a truly self-defeating behaviour.

As managers climb the career ladder, their responsibilities will only increase, leaving them with less time and, therefore, less room to let perfectionist tendencies run wild. Managers should learn strategies for how to let go when a task is complete. Identifying underlying causes of perfectionism and methods for managing perfectionist tendencies can create a great deal of efficiency and reduce stress levels in many managers.

3. Set priorities.

Good planning starts with prioritisation. The question then becomes: What should be prioritised? Checking email might be important because it's the way your boss communicates urgent requests, but there is also a project that affects the company's entire business that's been waiting in the background for months. Classify tasks within an Urgency-Importance matrix to help managers decide which to do first.

Help managers quickly sort and manage conflicting priorities, and develop communication strategies for ensuring that they are on the same page with other people involved in these priorities. Without buy-in from other parties, a manager's priorities may not be taken seriously, or may be out of alignment with the rest of the organisation.

4. Assess risks and trade-offs.

Risk management in the workplace doesn't always need to involve an actuary and complicated accounting: it can also mean simply taking into account the possible risks and rewards before acting on a decision. Sometimes, people work hard but not smart by acting on their first instincts or limited information, rather than taking the time to learn more about the problem. Help managers deal with risk in a systematic way by using a Risk vs Return matrix to identify the best possible lines of action, learn to think more creatively about solutions and look for alternatives.

5. Access resources and people.

Sometimes a willingness to manage the human side of relationships can be much more effective than following the technically perfect path forward. Learning how to use contacts, and both formal and informal networks, can save a great deal of time. Help managers make full use of all of their connections by learning the best moments to tap their networks. Managers should also think about how to utilise networks ethically, and how to think about business politics as a useful tool for management, rather than a hinderance to progress.

6. Establish and report on milestones.

Are the manager's goals specific? Does their daily work relate substantially to their long-term goals, or are their output objectives mostly unrelated to the work they do every day? Setting clear, specific, relevant objectives with strict timeframes is a necessary skill for all managers. A vague goal prevents managers from keeping themselves accountable, or being able to report well on what they accomplished. Teach managers how to set these kinds of goals, and how to communicate their progress. If someone can't talk about their own work effectively, how will anyone else be able to?

7. Change direction when required.

Maybe the manager is not a procrastinator nor a perfectionist, but they still find themselves getting very little done, no matter how many hours they put in. Is the manager being flexible enough in their approach to work? For some people, the ideal job is one where they can show up, do the same thing every single day, and then go home knowing that they've done a good job. These people rarely become managers – the diversity of the work is part of the appeal for most people in management positions.

With diversity of work needs to come diversity of approach: Does the manager tackle every problem the same way? Do they have trouble finding a way to manage without the resources, support or timeframe expected? Managers should strive to increase mindset flexibility. Equally important, learning to deal with "no," and designing workflow so that they can be flexible and creative when necessary will help them accomplish what they need to accomplish without getting stymied by minor obstacles.

Coaching Suggestions
1. Understand current road blocks to effectiveness
2. Work on live project or task
3. Use unsuccessful task as a case study

Training Suggestions
1. Have group articulate their current level of "cut through"
2. Look at common barriers to success
3. Work through tools to overcome procrastination and perfectionism

Challenge Level: 1 – Very Difficult
It is very challenging to have an accurate picture of our own levels of effectiveness in completion of relevant and value-adding tasks. Many leaders have significant "blind spots" when it comes to the relative importance and value of their own output.

A consistent approach to workflow management, task assignment, delegation and stakeholder management can dramatically increase any individual's ability to "make things happen" for themselves, their people, their managers and their organisation. However, this is no simple task as it often requires significant focus, energy, discipline and coaching to break non-productive work habits that may be ingrained through years of routine.

1.4.

PRODUCE RESULTS

Overview

People who consistently produce results have clear goals that are aligned with their organisation's objectives. Their plans, process and workflow all serve these goals, and their plans are effective because they always result in action. Their actions deliver predictable and positive results, despite challenges and hurdles. Unsurprisingly, people who are this productive, regardless of their level of busy-ness, are often more energised. Energy like this is infectious, and the people who surround a results-oriented person often find themselves more energised simply from working with them.

Setting the Scene

We've all dealt with that person who can't keep the bigger picture in mind: the bureaucratic underling who refuses to take a business founder's money because the address on the bank account didn't match the new office address; the co-worker who forces everyone else to work around their "process," impeding other people's work, and refusing to take on anything outside their written job description. These people have something important in common: they have lost track of their organisation's goals. They mistake loyalty to process for adding value, missing the point that the goal for all working people is to produce results. Without result orientation, these people might be able to keep their jobs (every company has someone in the ranks who can't see further than the Excel spreadsheet on their screen), but in most environments, it will be impossible for someone who thinks this way to move upward. Results-oriented employees don't just keep the bigger picture in mind: they also have clear milestones along the way to deliver meaningful results that serve that bigger picture. Because of this, they are consistently able to deliver results that serve the company's mission.

Development Instructions

1. Set realistic goals.

Are the manager's goals SMART? SMART goals are Specific, Measurable, Achievable, Relevant, and Time-Bound. Because goals should also be receptive to feedback and change, workflow experts now recommend making goals even SMARTER: Evaluated and Reviewed. Managers should always aim to set SMARTER goals, even if their job doesn't allow for specificity or measurable results. Even more importantly, set up a process that helps automate goal setting so that managers and teams are always working SMART, never just hard.

2. Demonstrate persistence and resilience.

The ability to produce results depends a great deal on emotional state and the ability to bounce back from adversity. Using tools to help manage emotional state and detach emotion from the task at hand, managers will be able to accomplish more with less stress. Help managers adjust their goals when the going gets tough, rather than simply trying to power through and wearing down their resolve before the task is accomplished.

3. Document plans and actions well.

All highly productive people have working, living plans that help them accomplish their goals. More than simply sitting and ruminating on goals and how they are going to achieve something that feels so big, they set up detailed, specific, action-oriented plans and schedules, as well as big picture, longer-term plans that help them keep perspective. Set up a system of 90 day, 30 day, and weekly planning.

Plans are extremely important, but they are only helpful if viewed as living documents. Making a work plan for the first time can be a bit like everyone's first attempt to make a budget: People spend a lot of time creating categories, allocating funds, and then matching those categories to actual spending. After all that work, it gets hard to sit down every month and do the input necessary to keep the budget up to date. Often, people let time lapse for so long, they have to start over completely the next time they decide to tackle their personal finances. Continuously updating and checking on plans is necessary for all the work that went into planning in the first place to be meaningful. Show managers how to maintain their plans as living documents, rather than artefacts of that one time when goals were set three years ago.

4. Display energy and drive.

What motivates people at a basic level? Does the manager work for the sense of accomplishment from doing a good job or for intellectual stimulation? Does an employee find a big pay/cheque motivating, or do they care less about the money they earn and more about the impact the work they do has on the world? There are as many strong motivators as there are productive people, and knowing what makes someone tick can help that person find the self-motivation they've been lacking. If it's mostly salary, employees should use that information to their advantage! Conversely, if there are specific working circumstances that managers find particularly demotivating, identifying those circumstances and minimising their impact is extremely important to productivity and energy maintenance.

5. Adopt a flexible approach.

"Hope for the best, plan for the worst" is a popular saying for a reason. Having alternative plans, as well as a variety of acceptable outcomes can help combat perfectionist tendencies while staying flexible in work approach. The journey can be as important as the end goal – but don't let process hamper results. Help managers shift away from a rigid mindset.

Negotiation skills are important in all areas of your work, but especially in terms of the ability to stay goal-oriented and productive. Without negotiation skills, managers can find themselves backed into a corner without the resources (including time, people, energy and money) necessary to complete the task at hand. Teach managers tested negotiation techniques using a flexible approach to find creative solutions.

6. Overcome obstacles.

Sometimes a project stalls, and the person in charge has no idea what the issue is. Did someone drop the ball, or were the goals set too high? No amount of planning can help managers overcome roadblocks they can't even identify. Help managers learn how to approach unforeseen roadblocks, avoid assumptions and get to the root of the problem quickly.

Process-oriented people often get in their own way by creating imaginary roadblocks that originated in their own minds. Sometimes, this comes out in the form of perfectionism: an unwillingness to accept work that is good enough. Sometimes, it's a lack of flexibility or a willingness to think creatively. If a team member is creating a roadblock and hampering their own success, a perceived problem can become very real for the people who have to work with that person. Managers need to be able to differentiate between perceived and real roadblocks (both coming from themselves or others), and how to help team members do the same.

Results-oriented people sometimes look like they can accomplish everything on their own, but in truth, there are very few accomplished, productive people who can do what they do without a support network. Learning when and how to ask for help, and doing so without shame, is necessary both for maintaining good relationships with others in the workplace and staying on top of tasks. Practice asking for help in appropriate, specific ways. Managers should draw on the energy they receive through the support of others.

7. Encourage others to buy in.

Getting buy-in from stakeholders is often the key difference between people who are known for getting things done and people who are known for "coasting." Influencing others' opinions doesn't mean manipulating them; on the contrary, the people with the most informal, non-hierarchical influence in a workplace are usually those who exhibit the most authenticity, or, the greatest congruence between their words and their actions. The best managers focus on finding opportunities for win-win solutions and negotiating in ways that focus on what the other person wants in order to get them on board with the project and the manager's needs.

Coaching Suggestions

1. Use goal setting as a starting point
2. Use previous project or task as case study
3. Review existing plans – do they align with stated goals?

Training Suggestions

1. Start "big picture" and work with organisational mission, vision and strategic goals
2. Encourage participants to consider how goals relate to their activities
3. Work on action plans that relate specifically to tangible results

Challenge Level: 1 – Very Difficult

Ultimately all organisations will succeed or fail based on the results they deliver. This makes it an absolute necessity for all leaders and employees within the organisation to have a strong results-focussed orientation.

However, it is all too easy for the work output of any one person to become misaligned with what's best for them, their team and, ultimately, their employer. Creating a clear understanding of what, when and why to do certain tasks is a key responsibility of all leaders, but a very daunting task across large and diverse teams.

The opportunity for misalignment is significant, and without a robust process and structure in place, good resources can be lost to inefficiencies, defects and poor morale.

1.5.

BE RESILIENT

Overview

For people who have resilience and grit, their ability to deal with stress resides not in their ability to slog through, but in how they see and respond to the slog. Resilient people search for the greater meaning in their difficulties, they ask for help when they need it, they focus on the positive, and they avoid getting trapped in narratives that take away whatever control they do have in an uncontrollable situation. They also take breaks when they need them. These are the people who make it look easy. They perform well under pressure and demonstrate a high level of emotional well-being even under adverse circumstances.

Setting the Scene

❝ The key to resilience is trying really hard, then stopping, recovering, and then trying again.
Shawn Achor and Michelle Gielan

Grit and resilience feel like military ideas, used to describe the soldier who can withstand hours of enemy interrogation and subhuman conditions. In fact, the way we approach resilience may be hampered by these very stereotypes: That resilience is about fighting through no matter what, or that grit is the same as being tough. In fact, resilience and grit are far more complicated than the ability to tough it out when things get hard.

It is not that resilient people never find anything difficult or have superhuman abilities to persist through difficulty. They use strategies, which can be learned, in order to help them remain calm and in a productive mental and emotional state during times of crisis, stress or pressure.

Development Instructions

1. Maintain optimism.

For people with high levels of resilience, planning is just that: planning, not worrying, or stressing or overthinking. Then they make a back-up plan, and then rely on that plan to help them if they need it. Managers can employ mindfulness strategies to help them focus on the positive while still maintaining a realistic outlook.

Resilient people keep their perspective on problems in proportion to the bigger picture. Something that seems like a major disaster may turn out to be a much smaller deal when seen within the bigger picture. On a trip to close a multi-million dollar business deal, the intern loses the rental car keys – now what? Worst case scenario, this problem can probably be solved with a taxi and paying a penalty at the rental car agency. Clearly, this isn't how a manager would have hoped their day would go, but in the grand scheme of the deal at hand, spending a few hundred dollars probably isn't the end of the world. Being able to keep this perspective under pressure is a skill that can be trained and nurtured. Managers should pursue strategies to help them learn their own triggers and manage their reactions in times of crisis.

2. Treat resilience building as personal attainment.

Like all new skills, resilience is learned in stages, and practice is key. Acknowledging progress and rewarding oneself, especially in an area that is deeply emotional, is key to continuing to make improvements. Teach managers methods for monitoring progress and innovative self-reward systems. Managers can learn to overcome obstacles by continuously developing creative workarounds. Just because someone needs support doesn't mean they are not resilient! There is always a new method to try, and the trying itself is excellent practice in this particular area.

3. Maintain self-control.

While emotional intelligence is a big part of every manager's success, making every issue an emotional one can be exhausting and counterproductive. Managers who can learn to take a step back from a problem and assess the emotional qualities of the issue without allowing their emotional investment to control their decision-making will be the most successful.

When does the manager feel calmest? Can they bring to mind a situation that makes them feel particularly positive and optimistic? What if we could translate these feelings to situations that do not make us feel this way at all? Explore strategies and techniques for improving mental state even in times of crisis.

We set up early warning systems in many areas of our work lives. Between calendar reminders so that we don't forget our appointments and accounting programs that won't save unverified or problematic data, we have plenty of stop gaps in case our humanness gets in our way. Why not with stress? Does the manager have an early warning system that lets them know when they are reaching their limit and need to take a break? Help managers notice when they have reached a point of diminishing returns before wellbeing and work output is negatively impacted.

4. Make helpful choices.

Thinking optimistically automatically puts us in a place where we can look for solutions instead of problems. Managers are expected to have creative ideas, but it's hard to be creative if they are thinking negatively. Managers can learn to reframe their thoughts during a crisis in a positive manner, and set themselves up for more creative, solution-oriented thinking.

Is the manager inadvertently jeopardising the success of their project by acting against their own self-interest? Sometimes, people engage in self-defeating behaviours out of fear or anxiety, and most of the time it's very hard to recognise, because the behaviours themselves makes the person feel better in the moment. Whether this is procrastinating before starting a difficult task, setting up false barriers or extra layers of unnecessary double checking, or any other counter-productive working behaviour, help managers identify the source of the behaviour and work to avoid that behaviour through practice and strategising.

Taking the time necessary to think isn't a luxury – it's a necessity. If a manager is constantly running from one task to another, chances are that they are working hard, but not necessarily smart. Taking the time to think and review can be simple and speedy, provided the manager can assess their situation systematically.

5. Maintain tenacity and effort.

Avoiding distractions seems like it should be relatively easy. Actually doing so often requires completely rethinking workflow. Distractions and derailers come in many forms, ranging from interrupting colleagues to personal thoughts and distractions. Managers should learn to design their workflow and space to work for them instead of against them, making it easier to maintain the kind of sustained concentration and positive feedback loops that make for the most resilient managers.

6. Build and maintain supporting relationships.

Our popular vision of resilient people are people who can handle everything on their own. This is a bit like looking at a workplace representation in a movie and thinking that this represents how things actually work in real life. The truth is far deeper and more complicated. The most resilient people set themselves up for success by surrounding themselves with people who can support them in specific ways. Who can the manager look to for support? Who are the key people to rely on in a crisis? Identify the kinds of qualities to look for in a supporter and help the manager increase their support network. Managers should look at their own strengths and the kind of support they are able to offer when someone else needs help, because giving support is often the best way to receive support.

7. Monitor progress and continually learn.

Like most skills, resilience is best learned through trial and error. Learning from setbacks and developing a method of tracking achievements can help. Create a tracking system and review timelines to help managers continue their learning.

Prevent stagnation by allowing managers to adapt as necessary. Just because one personal tracking system used to work doesn't mean it will keep working in every situation or for every manager. Letting people use the system that works best for them ensures that they are more likely to use the tracking system in the first place. Obviously, there is less leeway in situations where growth must be monitored company-wide, but for personal tracking, whatever system works well for the manager is the right one to adopt.

Coaching Suggestions

1. Review previous setbacks
2. Work through personal attainment milestones
3. Explore support network opportunities

Training Suggestions

1. Have group provide examples of how they experience resilience in others
2. Work through ideal "resilience" profile
3. Create plan that links specific behaviours to resilience building outcomes

Challenge Level: 1 – Very Difficult

Asking someone to "be more resilient" is akin to telling someone to "toughen up". It's easy enough to say but far more difficult to translate into specific actions and behaviours that can actually build resilience in an individual.

For leaders this is even more challenging as they will find their personal resilience tested in all directions while attempting to maintain resilience in their teams.

Resilience can most certainly be built up and improved with certain techniques. Before undertaking any training or mentoring on resilience, it's advisable to engage only the most experienced and competent of facilitators. The benefits of working towards building resilience are many, but working through the multiple potential roadblocks should not be attempted by someone inexperienced in dealing with multiple workplace challenges and personalities.

1.6.

DISPLAY EMOTIONAL INTELLIGENCE

Overview

Emotional intelligence consists of two major components: inward understanding and outward understanding. By understanding our own emotional state, how it impacts us and our actions, and the effect it may have on others, we are able to form healthy working relationships with others and problem-solve more quickly and effectively. Considering and understanding the emotional state of others gives us more insight into how to interact with them meaningfully and effectively. The components of emotional intelligence can be broken down further into five categories: self-perception (awareness of one's own emotions), self-expression (conveying emotional state to others), interpersonal (managing the emotional aspects of relationships), decision making (incorporating emotional knowledge into decisions) and stress management.

Setting the Scene

Astrophysicist and educator Neil deGrasse Tyson thinks we are missing out on a key skill through our schools' focus on "hard skills."

66

Humans aren't as good as we should be in our capacity to empathise with feelings and thoughts of others, be they humans or other animals on Earth. So maybe part of our formal education should be training in empathy. Imagine how different the world would be if, in fact, that were 'reading, writing, arithmetic, empathy.

While some of us were lucky enough to receive an education in emotional intelligence, either through socialisation, therapy or a really great mentor, many of us still struggle with understanding our own emotions, much less those of other people. Even worse, many of the qualities that should have been nurtured in order to increase emotional intelligence and empathy are heavily devalued within the business world. This often results in leaders who are extremely skilled at their work, but also deeply out of touch with their own feelings and those of their employees.

Emotional intelligence is the ability to use a real understanding of our emotions and the emotions of others to aid our daily functioning.

Development Instructions

1. Understand the difference between the inward and outward focus of emotional intelligence.

For some people, it's a lot easier to understand what others are feeling than it is to understand what is going on inside. Especially for many men, who may have been socialised to ignore the nuances of their emotions, anything beyond, "I feel bad," or "I feel angry" can be hard to recognise, name, understand or act on. For managers, learning to understand their emotional state and express that state to others effectively is the first step towards a deeper understanding of their own inner world. Can the manager name what they are feeling, right now? What other words can they use to describe the sensation, if the person they are talking to does not understand immediately? Consider business situations in which this knowledge may not just be useful, but essential.

At the same time, while some people may be able to recognise that someone else is upset, being able to empathise (understanding on a personal level) with them is a different skill. Empathy is a key skill for good leaders: Without it, other people can seem mysterious and irrational, when in fact, we all make decisions in similar, often emotionally-informed ways – and that's a good thing. Help managers understand both empathy and internal knowledge, and how to use both effectively in the work place to improve performance, rather than hinder it.

2. Identify, perceive and recognise emotions in others.

If a manager can't identify and manage their emotions, there is a good chance their emotions are managing them. Many employees and colleagues may be in the same position. Help managers recognise typical workplace behaviours, their emotional origins and how to interrupt negative patterns.

When someone starts yelling, does the manager freeze up? When someone starts crying, does the manager get angry or overly sympathetic? Understanding what a display of emotion means is one thing; knowing how to act on it effectively is a different skill entirely. Managers need to be able to handle different displays of emotions in others, which may mean improving how they manage emotion within themselves.

Dealing with emotional topics is necessary in the workplace, and acknowledging the emotions involved is key to handling those conversations thoughtfully and effectively. No one has ever calmed down because someone told them, "Calm down!" and very few people actually stopped taking something personally just because someone said "Don't take it personally." Managers need to develop better conversational strategies than the typical business language around emotions, which can often make matters much worse.

3. **Understand what certain emotions mean and have awareness of the spectrum of emotions.**
The potential drivers of emotion are not always obvious just because of the expression of the emotion. Sometimes, it's a "the straw that broke the camel's back" situation – a person has been on edge for a long time, and a final, minor thing is what made them emotional. Finally, some people have what appear to be inappropriate responses to emotional situations: laughing when everyone else is crying, or crying because they are angry. Often, these are a result of previous social conditioning, and are not a sign that the person's feelings are any less real or sincere.

Can the manager recognise a basic display of emotions when looking at a series of faces? People who are emotionally in tune can recognise a wide range of emotions just from looking at faces or hearing voices. Someone who is emotionally out of touch may have more trouble with this task, and will require more practice. Finally, consider that certain conditions, like certain autism spectrum disorders, may make it extremely difficult for people to recognise and respond appropriately to emotions in others. While these people still need to work to increase their level of emotional understanding, maintaining a level of empathy in these cases is always a good idea.

Taking responsibility (or staying "above the line") is usually a very good thing, but in some cases, highly emotionally sensitive people can go overboard and take responsibility for things that are not their fault. In these cases, it is important to recognise that there is only so much anyone can control in a given situation, and emotional responses are often not one of those things.

4. Develop strategies for using emotions effectively.

Most people would rather be trapped in an elevator with someone who is calm, centred and a good conversation partner, rather than with someone anxious, who panics easily and has a hard time being enclosed in small spaces. We know intuitively that emotions are contagious: We would much rather be stuck in an elevator with someone who stays calm and positive during difficult situations because the other person's emotions will affect how we feel too. Managers who can learn how to use their mood to their advantage can make an enormous difference in how the office functions. Moods can be a bit like the weather: leaders who bring a bad mood into the office are effectively raining on everyone else's parade. Even if the manager has a lot to do, it feels easier if the mood in the office is closer to sunshine and rainbows.

Many people continue to see showing emotion as weakness, but there is increasing research that shows our perception of people who demonstrate how they are actually feeling in an authentic and non-confrontational way increases their credibility and connection with others. Brené Brown's research on vulnerability demonstrates that leaning into discomfort and emotional elements of a conversation may be the best way to both internalise a sense of worthiness and confidence as a leader, and demonstrate these qualities to employees.

5. Display effective emotional management.

Obviously, emotional intelligence and authenticity is not an excuse to behave badly. Screaming at an employee is clearly outside the bounds of appropriate office behaviour. Create clear parameters for acceptable ranges of emotional display in the office, and learn how to show emotions effectively in order to solve problems rather than create more.

Emotionally abusive behaviour should never be tolerated. Make clear what constitutes emotional abuse in the workplace, from both a manager and an employee perspective. Managers need to learn how to handle these situations delicately and effectively, identify potentially abusive behaviour and put a stop to it.

There is a big difference between being able to sympathise or understand what someone is feeling on an intellectual level, and being able to understand what someone is feeling on an emotional level, or empathise with that person. Empathy is perhaps the most important emotional tool for a leader, which is the reason it's Tyson's missing soft skill: it is absolutely necessary if a manager wants their employees to trust them and problem solve with them. Like most other skills, empathy can be developed, even if some people have more talent for it than others. Practise using empathy with managers in specific work situations.

6. Adapt behaviour to work in different situations.

Not everyone manages their emotions the same way, and some people are more comfortable with displays of emotion than others. Being able to modulate approach for audience and read the room is an important skill, and can help managers become an office chameleon – able to connect with everyone at a level where they are comfortable, rather than forcing others to adapt to them. Show managers how to approach different situations, get better at reading emotional environments and adapt quickly if their approach is not working.

7. Use emotional intelligence to communicate effectively.

When public speaking experts talk about framing, they are talking about how to tell a story in order to make the most salient parts memorable and understandable for the audience. Emotional framing can be just as effective. Demonstrating the emotional content of the information through vocabulary, tone and body language can help people connect with the story more effectively, and understand the implications of what the manager is saying more quickly. Managers can practise emotional frames and methods of demonstrating emotional content effectively without overwhelming their audiences or coming across as overly dramatic.

Few people would deliver news they know to be controversial in the same tone of voice as universally good news. Being able to use this kind of emotional forecasting can help managers in all of their interactions. Anticipating how the other party might feel can help managers reframe what they are saying in a way that addresses concerns before the other party has a chance to react.

Work can be highly emotional, and sometimes, the stress can be a bit too much. Having a personal outlet or method for dealing with emotion is key for all managers, and great leaders also give their employees opportunities to deal with their emotions in a positive way. For some people, an after-work sports competition can help; for others, it's a walk around the block or a good book. Finding what works for the individual is key. Encourage managers to experiment with various outlets and strategise ways to give them the time and space they need in order to be at their best while at work.

Coaching Suggestions
1. Review a recent encounter and assess its effectiveness
2. Identify common workplace situations and create adaption strategies
3. Apply emotional intelligence principles to a group presentation

Training Suggestions
1. Ask the group to bring examples of emotion as it pertains to their workplace
2. Gain agreement and work through acceptable and unacceptable emotional behaviours
3. Create strategies for how to read and act upon differing emotional responses to typical workplace scenarios

Challenge Level: 2 – Difficult
Emotions exist for all people, and to gain the best effort from our teams in every situation we must be comfortable to recognise, acknowledge and deal with their emotional responses.

Some leaders are far more comfortable dealing with this awareness than others, but the good news is that developing strong emotional intelligence is possible for all who are willing to work at it.

If considering coaching or workshops which work through emotional responses, it's critical to ensure that the scene is properly set to allow honest sharing of ideas in a safe and caring environment.

1.7.

RAPIDLY DEVELOPS SELF

Overview

If loyalty and dependability are no longer key values at a majority of companies, how does someone with years of experience compete with younger colleagues in a rapidly changing field? The key is not to have all the knowledge, but to become excellent at acquiring the knowledge and skills as necessary. Becoming a great learner is an introspective task: first, leaders must figure out how they learn, so that they can tailor professional and personal development to their learning style. This will not only make the task of learning more pleasant, they will be able to acquire skills and knowledge more efficiently. In a way, the shift towards a workplace focus on performance over credentials helps level the playing field: if someone is good at learning, they can excel in this environment, regardless of their pedigree.

Setting the Scene

Many people enter the work force with dreams of stability. In their eyes, the perfect first position leads to a steady upward trajectory at the same company that lasts for an entire career, from graduation to retirement, with promotions based on seniority. They believe that loyalty and dependability should be enough to be considered a valuable asset within a company.

Though a few of these kinds of jobs may still exist, they are not the norm. Workers change jobs, on average, every 4.5 years: this rate of job change has already been true for decades. It has become more and more common to change careers entirely, even in middle age, and more companies are switching from credential-based assessments to performance-based assessments, especially at younger companies. All of this is happening in the context of a rapidly changing world: technologies and working environments are often updated annually, rather than once a decade.

Keeping up with constant change takes a willingness to learn and develop new skills, but this requirement usually isn't found in a job description. Therefore, each individual must take ownership of their own progress, because the necessity of doing so often goes unsaid. With low-cost, public access so many resources both on and offline, and the increasing business cultural uptake of professional and personal development, the opportunities are there.

Careers and learning: Old rules vs. new rules

Old rules	New rules
Employees are told what to learn by their managers or the career model	Employees decide what to learn based on their team's needs and individual career goals
Careers go "up or out"	Careers go in every direction
Managers direct careers for people	People find their career direction with help from leaders and others
Corporate L&D owns development and training	Corporate L&D curates development and creates a useful learning experience
People learn in the classroom and, sometimes, online	People learn all the time, in micro-learning, courses, classrooms and groups
The corporate university is a training centre	The corporate university is a "corporate commons," bringing leaders and cross-functional groups together
Learning technology focuses on compliance and course catalogue	Learning technology creates an always-on, collaborative, curated learning experience
Learning content is provided by L&D and experts	Learning content is provided by everyone in the organisation, and curated by employees as well as HR
Credentials are provided by universities and accredited institutions; skills are only certified through credentials	Credentials come in the form of "unbundled credentials," where people obtain certificates in many ways

Deloitte University Press

Development Instructions

1. Understand how learning happens.

What subjects did the manager like in school? Do they generally like learning, or do they resist it? According to recent studies, maintaining a growth mindset, in which someone believes that their abilities can change with education, can mean the difference between successfully tackling a difficult subject, and being unable to complete a lesson. At the same time, understanding, valuing and working to improve a manager's strongest suits can help them determine their most valuable professional development path.

2. Approach chosen skills and subjects thoughtfully.
Once the manager understands their learning style and mindset, it's time to take their life into account. How much time and energy does the manager have to devote to learning? What does their life look like at this particular moment? What mediums of instruction are they comfortable with? How motivated are they to learn a particular subject? How much experience do they already have with a particular subject, or related subjects? All of these questions should inform which professional development avenues a manager pursues.

3. Make a learning plan.
Track learning before it starts. What concrete steps does the manager need to take in order to ensure they meet those goals in a way that is meaningful and achievable? Having both clear and achievable goals and a plan for making them happen is key to succeeding in any learning project. Managers should plan to track what they have learned so that they can monitor their progress, track feedback and celebrate successes.

4. Identify learning gaps.
Sometimes, people find certain subjects or methods of learning much more difficult than others. It's obvious in the way we talk to each other: "I'm not a numbers person," or "I was never good thinking on my feet," or "Data makes sense to me, people are so confusing." Thinking of these as "learning gaps" rather than insurmountable challenges can help managers maintain a growth mindset, even when the going gets rough. Often, when someone attempts to learn something new, the first few experiences merely teach them exactly how much they don't know yet. Don't be discouraged: these first experiences are often crucial to fine-tuning a learning plan to fill any gaps, or expanding a learning plan based on this new knowledge.

5. Apply the right learning method to the gap.

Learning gaps are rarely as simple as "I'm bad at maths." "I'm bad at maths" could mean anything from, "Numbers get mixed up in my head" to "I can't remember what a parabola is" to "Working with formulas in Excel is hard for me." Knowing the nature of the gap and then learning to apply the right learning method to the gap can make the difference between someone feeling they are bad at maths and feeling like they can tackle this subject after all. For example, if someone has difficulty remembering the numbers they see, a geometry lesson will not help, but a specific memory technique might. No matter what the gaps are, knowing the method of inquiry that can help will change the manager's experience of learning for the better. The different learning methods and areas of inquiry include:

- **Behavioural:** learning by doing
  Example: learning the foxtrot with a dance partner in a class.
- **Cognitive:** learning from books, presentations or lectures
  Example: watching a TED video about quantum physics.
- **Inquiry:** learning through research and asking questions
  Example: writing a thesis in university by interviewing experts, and conducting research at the library or online.
- **Mental models:** understanding and changing how our brains process information and comprehend the world around us
  Example: using the Memory Palace method to remember random information as an interconnected map.
- **Collaborative:** learning through teamwork and discussion
  Example: discussing an engaging novel with a book club or creating a science project with a team for a school competition.
- **Virtual realities:** learning by using virtual environments as a replacement or supplement to in-person learning
  Example: taking an online class about anthropology or using a flight simulator to learn to fly a plane.
- **Holistic learning:** learning by engaging the entire human experience through the senses, emotions and mental abilities at the same time.
  Example: learning how to cook through a hands-on cooking class.

Many of the examples given fit into more than one category. Cooking in Grandma's kitchen is a holistic experience, but it also counts as behavioural learning.

6. Review, adjust and improve the learning plan.

What we start out to learn isn't always what we end up learning. Even if the manager has a great, workable plan from the outset, their goals can take more time or energy to achieve than predicted, or maybe the resources just aren't sufficient – and then life happens, people get busy and the plan is derailed. Knowing what steps to take when things don't go well can prevent discouraging setbacks.

7. Ask for help and accept feedback.

Contact experts and find mentors as necessary. Designate someone for the manager to lean on for support and encouragement when meeting goals becomes challenging. Involving others is often important, for both achieving the manager's learning goals and staying on track. Understanding who to ask is just as important as knowing what to ask: organisational structures, roles and responsibilities will all play a role in determining the appropriate point person for a particular question or need.

Coaching Suggestions

1. Start with their motivation and self-awareness to establish a foundation to build on
2. Brainstorm a learning plan template with key goals
3. Celebrate achievements along the way and look to erase potential roadblocks/issues

Training Suggestions

1. Start with a self-assessment, quiz or management assessment to establish a realistic starting point
2. Focus on mutual support such as teams and buddy learning
3. Have a practical learning plan as the key take-away

Challenge Level: 1 – Very Difficult

Self-development is often lost in the day-to-day activity of just "being busy".

Compounding the challenge is the fact that in many workplaces, no-one will actively follow up our self-development. It's for ourselves and often has to be driven by ourselves. It takes a very forward-thinking, organised and self-aware individual to maintain a consistent and strong path towards their self-education while balancing the day-to-day responsibilities of their work and home lives.

An experienced mentor or coach can often be critical to helping individuals commence and maintain the discipline required to create and benefit from a strong self-development pathway and mindset.

1.8.

MAINTAIN A POSITIVE ATTITUDE

Overview

A manager can be the most skilled, intelligent and experienced worker in their field and still get in the way of their own success. The biggest way people do this is by not preparing for success by working on their mindset and attitude, especially in moments of adversity. Successful people have a mindset that helps them achieve their goals: a positive outlook that lets them meet new challenges with grace and stay on track mentally even when everything around them is derailing. The experienced worker who is all complaints and no ideas? They are often passed up for promotions in favour of the less-skilled worker with a can-do attitude. The good news is, managers can make up for some gaps in their skillsets by simply having the ability to deal well with adversity, through grit, a positive attitude and resilience.

Setting the Scene

Let's say a manager is working on a major project and their boss "shifts the goalposts". The deadline has been moved up a full week, and that key element the boss was going to handle? The manager now has to do it themselves. Does the manager see rain clouds of doom, or are they able to power through?

We all need to take into account how we automatically react to change and uncertainty. Some people see the glass half full, while others continuously predict problems around every corner. Some people expect the best, and others constantly worry about the worst. While no one can be expected to stay upbeat under the worst of circumstances, remaining calm and confident and maintaining a good mental state is extremely important to future success.

Development Instructions

1. **Maintain a positive attitude even in the face of adversity.**

When we know ourselves better, this task gets easier. Understanding what makes us feel positive, especially in situations where others tend to turn to negative thinking can provide insights. What needs to happen in order for the manager to feel that they are genuinely capable of handling a problem? True attitude change can feel overwhelming, but the first step can be as simple as making a list of situations and actions that make the manager feel more positive than negative.

We've all worked with someone who complains all the time. Maybe it was a boss who never had anything nice to say about the work being done. Maybe it was the co-worker who was always convinced they were going to get fired that Friday. People who act like this are a drain on their colleagues' and employees' energy, and their negativity spreads like a virus. A manager's attitude not only affects their own work, it affects everyone else's work as well.

2. **Understand how to deal with negative influences.**

Help managers understand how typical negative influences that are likely present in their work lives can affect their work. Be careful, because negative influences can sneak in from personal lives as well. Keeping an eye on these influences, and simply recognising them is the first step to changing one's reaction to them.

Identifying a negative influence doesn't make it feel any more positive. How can a manager prevent that influence from impacting their attitude? Teach managers tips and tricks for "keeping calm and carrying on," because that is often much easier said than done.

There's a big difference between, "You created a problem," and "You are a problem." If the manager receives criticism, are they able to hear the difference between constructive guidance and pure negativity? If the manager needs to criticise someone, do they focus their language on personal attributes or on actions? Being able to understand the difference between negativity and constructive criticism is essential to success in the workplace. Focusing on constructive criticism only, whether the manager is the giver or receiver of that criticism, can help everyone involved maintain a positive attitude. Practice giving and receiving this kind of criticism.

3. Strong interaction between attitude and behaviour.

The physical act of smiling releases the endorphins that make people want to smile in the first place. A positive attitude is often a circular feedback loop like this: Even if someone doesn't feel positive, changing their behaviour as though they feel positive can help change their attitude. People can control their own attitudes to a certain extent through behaviour by exploiting cognitive dissonance. Fortunately, this means that as long as someone can bring the attitude to mind, and understand what they are feeling, they are able to change how they feel.

Just as behaviour can affect attitude, attitude can deeply affect behaviour in ways most of us don't even realize. Some of these effects can have far reaching, dangerous consequences if left unrecognised and unquestioned.

Plenty of studies have shown that sitting inside in a slouched position make it harder for people to come up with new and creative ideas than if they've just been for a brisk walk outside. Keeping in mind that everyone is different, some people's behavioural triggers may be unusual, and require some introspection to fully understand. Help managers find and understand their own triggers.

4. Focus on what can be influenced.

Some people have a very hard time staying positive when they feel out of control, or like they have no influence over what is happening. The key in these situations is recognising what we do have control over, and learning to let go of anxiety over the things we can't influence.

Sometimes, we actually can increase the amount of influence we have in a workplace situation through certain behaviours, or even just by changing attitudes and looking at the issue from a new angle. Being able to recognise where we have influence and where we do not have influence is the first step. The next step is learning to conserve emotional energy like the precious resource that it is. Help managers judge where output of emotional energy is most likely to bring results, and when it's a better use of energy to just take a step back.

5. Create a plan to be positive.

Take those first concrete steps towards improving attitude all around. Because it's so much easier to stay positive when working with positive people, practice small exercises to help spread positivity in the workplace. Discuss appropriate self-acknowledgement and rewards with managers: celebrating the small wins, and acknowledge the effort of the internal work required for a real attitude shift.

Managers should avoid planning to simply keep a smile on their faces no matter what the situation. Papering over negative emotions with falsely positive energy is a good strategy in small doses, but overdoing it can lead to serious psychological disconnects. The goal is not to soldier on no matter what, but to take the time and space necessary to maintain a generally positive outlook. Managers should plan breaks in which they are not required to be positive into their schedules, and make sure they are able to take those breaks away from the people over whom their attitude has the most influence.

6. Review and maintain a winning attitude.

Maintaining a positive attitude is like learning a new skill, and managers should treat it the same way they would manage their progress on any concrete skill: through trial, error and review. Implement methods for reviewing successes and failures and create a working template for a positive mindset. This will help managers see their gradual improvements in ability to use their new skill effectively in the workplace.

Practice makes perfect. Creating a positive mindset is generally dependent on consistency. Anyone who has spent time around kids knows that they love consistency and routines, and as adults, we aren't much different. The more consistent we are with ourselves and with our colleagues or employees, the easier it is to stay positive during challenging periods.

7. Avoid backsliding.

Once the manager finds their positive triggers, they must use them consistently, or risk backsliding. By creating positive habits that are so consistent they become as natural as making coffee in the morning, managers will be able to adopt a positive mindset fluidly into their daily lives. Making positivity a habit in easy times will make it far easier to access in difficult times.

Negativity can quickly become a spiral with no floor. Climbing out of a negative hole is far harder than avoiding creating the hole in the first place.

Whenever a manager notices themselves going into a negative spiral, it is important that they don't heap negativity on themselves for not staying positive. Instead, they should congratulate themselves for noticing that they were starting to spiral and stopping the spiral before it got out of control.

Coaching Suggestions
1. Create a positive self-belief in the coachee
2. Create a strong support network to maintain a positive attitude and mental state
3. Work on triggers to activate a positive attitude

Training Suggestions
1. Work through perceptions of different mindsets. Define "positive"
2. Group to articulate attitude v behaviour and their understanding of both
3. Create a workable plan related to workplace environment

Challenge Level: 3 – Neutral
In leadership roles maintaining a generally positive outlook is critical, as the manager's outlook will certainly inform the mindset and approach of their direct reports.

Of course some situations will test this positivity more than others. This is where the development of specific strategies to maintain a positive, outcomes-oriented approach is most helpful.

With the correct guidance, it's often the use of simple tools and techniques to change one's own perspective which can be the difference between maintaining a positive thought process and being caught in a self-defeating spiral of doubt.

1.9.

SET PERSONAL GOALS

Overview

While there are many areas in which people can set personal goals, the focus here is on goals that affect career and business life. These can still encompass a wide range of areas in which goals can be set, including family life, emotional well-being, education, financial and public service goals. Someone who is interested in public service but currently works in investment banking may need to reorient their career in order to meet that personal goal; someone who works for a non-profit may have a hard time meeting lofty financial goals without additional sources of income. Similarly, certain educational and family goals may or may not be attainable within an individual's current career trajectory. Finding the dissonance between career goals and goals in other areas of work life can help leaders decide which direction they want to pursue, in a way that looking purely at business or career on its own cannot.

Setting the Scene

Personal goals differ from business goals in several important ways. Business goals are usually tied to the success of an organisation or company, or the furthering of a career. Personal goals are about what someone wants their work life to look like while they pursue those goals. In some ways, for a career, business goals are about answering the question, "What do I want to do?" Personal goals are about answering the question, "How do I want to do it?"

What makes each person feel effective in the workplace and feel happy with themselves is different for everyone. For some, this may mean a focus on work-life balance, and keeping their personal time sacred. For others, this could mean focusing on their moral integrity and ethical stance in their career. Others may have goals meant to drive them to the top as quickly as possible, sacrificing everything that isn't necessary to personal well-being in pursuit of their goals. All of these are possible drivers for personal goals, and each may be important to the same person at different stages of their careers.

What Future Workplaces Want and Need

The Past	Our Future
My Paycheck	My Purpose
My Statisfaction	My Development
My Boss	My Coach
My Annual Review	My Ongoing Conversations
My Weaknesses	My Strengths
My Job	My Life

Re-Engineering Performance Management
Gallup 2017

Development Instructions

1. Create a personal vision.

Exploring aspirations in all areas of life are important on the way to goal setting. Many of us grew up with certain ideas about who or how we had to be; as adults, articulating personal vision is a good way to short-circuit an automated response to questions about career and family in particular. Have leaders create vision boards for different areas of their lives – these can consist of words, pictures, or even more abstract information on feelings. Then, look at how these boards align with each other. Does the emotional board have anything to do with the career board? If not, it could be a sign that some aspect of the leader's life isn't working properly, or their goals are not realistic.

Once managers have created a larger vision for themselves, distil that vision into one sentence. Start with sentences for each area of life, working towards a sentence that encompasses their personal vision entirely. What defines the manager's life goals? What is their primary source of motivation?

2. Link specific goals to personal vision.

Vision boards often cause certain words or ideas to stand out. Leaders can use these words to link their specific goals with their personal vision. Specific goals, unlike personal vision, are usually linked to action in some capacity. What words stand out to each leader will be individual and personalised, so it's important to give people the space and time to do this work thoughtfully.

Sometimes, specific goals come from outside the leader – when their job requires them to have certain goals, for example, or their family life comes with particular obligations. These are not necessarily out of line with personal vision. Managers should think about how they can incorporate goals that originated externally but are important to their success into their personal vision in a way that doesn't feel forced.

3. Create specific, measurable goals.
Personal goals, like business goals, should be SMART: specific, measurable, achievable, relevant and time-bound. Avoid setting personal goals that can't be reasonably achieved within a given period of time, are not measurably qualitatively or quantitatively, or are too broad or unrelated to the manager's everyday life to be integrated well.

Make a plan with managers to record how they are doing in their pursuit of personal goals. Many people find it incredibly hard to remember where they started when pursuing a goal that feels largely abstract to their everyday tasks: Recording their plan somewhere and creating a reporting template (which can be as simple as a checklist) will ensure that their goals are not forgotten about or ignored when achieved.

The recording plan should also have room to acknowledge achievements and milestones. For more abstract goals, what specific, concrete markers can managers designate to know when they have achieved their goal? Consider not only how to measure these milestones, but how to mark them and celebrate the win.

4. Balance work and home goals.
While work-life balance may look different for everyone, and different for the same person at various points in their careers, anyone who completely ignores balance will often find themselves falling behind in dangerous ways in either their careers or home lives, which will likely eventually affect the other part their life as well. For those with workaholic tendencies, building in mandatory self-care and breaks will be vital to their continued success at work. These people are often so good at pushing aside their personal

needs, they may not recognise serious health or emotional issues until they start to affect their work, and at that point, it may be too late to do anything about the problem without sacrificing their career track in the process. For people who value their home lives above all else, work can sometimes get lost in the shuffle, leaving them with careers they never intended, or worse, a CV so spotted with premature departures, they become nearly unhireable. Avoid any of these extremes by striving for the right kind of balance at the right point in the manager's career.

Career goals should always take into account the realities of a manager's home life and vice versa. If these goals are made mutually exclusive, either the career or the personal life of a manager will suffer. Ensure that career goals are achievable and reasonable given the manager's home situation, and ensure that home goals are manageable and relevant, considering the manager's career choices.

5. Demonstrate 90-day personal goal planning.

90 days may seem like an arbitrary time frame, but because so much of the business world works on a quarterly system, it's actually a great time frame to use for measuring personal goals. Create goals that are designed to be achieved within a 90-day time frame, and check in with managers at the end of that time frame to understand what was accomplished. Setting 90-day goals also breaks multi-year long-term plans into manageable units.

Goals documents should not gather dust in the metaphorical bottom drawers of a computer hard drive. All documents need to be kept live through continuous updates. Encourage managers to review their goals documents at least once quarterly, but preferably, anytime their work or personal lives change substantially, or they develop a new area of interest. Their goal planning should reflect their life as it is, not as it was a year ago.

90-day goal planning is the larger template. These goals can then be extracted to smaller to-do lists designed to be used on a monthly, weekly, or even daily basis. Breaking larger goals into smaller and smaller tasks will make the goals more achievable. A cake isn't consumed all at once – it is eaten bite by bite. Goals, similarly, can't be accomplished all at once – they need to be chipped away, little by little.

6. Use effective personal time management techniques.

If the squeakiest wheel always gets the oil in either our work or personal lives, it usually means time management and goal setting isn't where it should be. Managers need to be able to take a birds-eye view of their personal lives as well as their work lives, in order to see where the most important action items are, rather than just the most urgent. Understanding where personal time is being siphoned off for activities that don't advance the manager's personal goals is important if the manager wants to achieve their goals at all.

Keeping hours of the week marked for handling important but not urgent actions can help the leader make progress of major goals without letting go of their daily action items. People can do this in a variety of ways – the important thing is finding a method that works for the manager. To make time for important goals, managers should ensure they demarcate time in a clear way that will be respected by others. This can include measures such as avoiding technology, scheduling blocks of time on a publicly-viewable calendar, or just refusing to take meetings during the designated period. Protecting time isn't selfish – it allows leaders to do the work they need to do, rather than just the work that is most urgent.

7. Review actions regularly.

As with all plans, regular review is important to determining whether actions taken are appropriate to the goals set. It can be easy to get sidetracked – building regular review into the process ensures leaders will continuously align their tasks with their bigger goals.

Review of personal goals can happen at quarterly feedback rounds, but managers may want to create a review process for themselves that lets them see the kind of progress they are making before they go through a review with someone else. Depending on the goals and the manager's tasks, review could be as simple as looking through a checklist to see what is not yet checked off and what is, or as complicated as creating graphs and charts of goal progress. Help managers decide which review process works best for them.

Flexible goal setting is more likely to be effective goal setting. An all-or-nothing approach practically ensures failure for most big goals – things rarely go as planned, so an inflexible approach will leave managers frustrated and unlikely to follow up with their goals. Having the flexibility to revise goals as necessary will keep managers invested in their goals and in control of their action items.

Coaching Suggestions

1. Where is the coachee now? Where would they like to be?
2. Unpack previous experience with personal goal setting – success and/or failure
3. Check in regularly to keep actions "hot"

Training Suggestions

1. Always start with a personal vision
2. Participants to create words that articulate how and where they wish to be
3. Collate words into measurable goal statements

Challenge Level: 2 – Difficult

On the surface of it, setting personal goals is an intrinsically simple task. In reality however, the difficulty arises due to two factors. Firstly, the lack of willingness many people have to commit to a personal goal structure in writing. Secondly, the lack of discipline and organisational wherewithal to keep the goals "live" and constantly track one's own progress.

These two hurdles are best overcome by starting out with a goal setting plan. If the motivation for setting goals in the first place is strong and the plan is robust, goal setting can become a critical tool in maximising personal effectiveness.

The knowledge of how to set goals and create an effective but not onerous plan is the key to personal goal setting success.

1.10.

MANAGE YOUR BOSS

Overview

Healthy relationships with managers, even when that manager is a board of directors, are vital to everyone's work lives. While some bosses are quirkier or less forgiving than others, healthy and productive relationships should always be the goal for both employees and their supervisors. These relationships are vital for nearly everything that goes on in the work place, so a problematic relationship will likely stymie the efforts of both managers and employees to get their jobs done. While it's impossible to control another person's behaviour, especially when that person is in a superior position, employees have more power than they realise in fostering a good relationship with their manager and creating more upward influence for themselves.

Setting the Scene

Upward management gets a bad rap because many people associate it with being manipulative. However, the image of an underling who goads their unwitting boss into nefarious activities couldn't be further from the truth of upward management. In fact, an employee who does not use upward management is actually making their boss's job a lot harder.

In the same way that leaders must learn how to manage individual employees according to the employee's working style and personality traits, employees need to learn how to interact with their bosses according to the boss's needs, personality traits, working style, and position within the company. Bosses hate to lose employees who can do this well, because these employees make their lives infinitely easier. Someone who is highly effective at managing their boss likely knows a lot about how their boss works, including when their boss checks email throughout the day, what kind of information their boss wants or needs about a particular project, and what information their boss doesn't need to know. This helps the employee streamline communication and allows both the employee and the supervisor to be highly effective in their work without duplicating the other person's work or having to wade through reams of unwanted information. Furthermore, a relationship like this builds up a great deal of trust between the employee and the supervisor: The supervisor knows that the employee is paying attention, and can therefore allow the employee more independence than someone who hasn't demonstrated such attention.

Development Instructions

1. Demonstrate understanding and empathy.

Empathy is a basic skill that can aid all relationships in the workplace. For leaders, understanding their boss's specific personality type can provide a shortcut to understanding how the boss thinks and works. Personality instruments, such as the Myers-Briggs Type Indicator assessment, can help managers compare their working style to their boss'. If there's a major disconnect, these kinds of tools can help a manager figure out where the personality clash is happening, and how to work around it.

Beyond using tools, understanding how a boss works should really come from personal experience and observation. Does the boss get particularly worked up if the deadline is approaching and the manager hasn't started work on a project yet? Are there body language cues that might indicate certain moods or concerns, even if these are not explicitly stated? While it can be hard to adjust personal working style to fit someone else's preferences, even small adjustments towards common ground can improve relationships, especially if a supervisory relationship is filled with anxiety.

2. Understand "one-up" priorities.

Leaders aren't just responsible for knowing their own KPIs – they should also understand the KPIs of their teams AND their bosses. Understanding goals one level up will help managers align their strategies for achieving their own goals with those of their boss. This way, everyone can be working as a team, instead of struggling towards their own goals without regard for how this might impact others.

Avoid setting priorities that actively conflict with a manager's priorities. By keeping priorities in harmony, an implicit understanding about what is important can be reached by both managers and their bosses. This can become particularly important in moments when it feels like everything is important, or with bosses who have a hard time prioritising for their teams. In these cases, by aligning priorities with the boss' priorities, a manager will know what to tackle first, even if the boss can't or won't give direction.

3. Display proactivity.

Great employees are proactive, not reactive. Consider a classroom full of adults: often, people are nervous about speaking up and asking a stupid question, leading to a silent classroom. The teacher will continue lecturing, regardless of how easy or hard the material is for the participants, simply because the teacher has had no feedback. The student in the classroom who asks questions, even if they seem "stupid" is almost always doing everyone a favour. In this case the teacher can adjust their teaching to fit the level of the classroom, and answer questions that were likely on everyone's mind, but the teacher hadn't considered. A proactive employee-boss relationship should work the same way. Rather than simply waiting for direction, employees should ask their bosses for the direction and information they need. This helps the boss support their employees more effectively, and cuts down on support that is ineffective.

Once employees know their bosses well, using proactivity to take care of common issues will take their status from "hard worker" to "employee of the year." An employee who can anticipate and solve problems on their own, especially if they do so in a way that is in line with their boss's wants and needs, will quickly make themselves invaluable. This kind of relationship takes time to build, however. Start with small proactive measures, and gradually build on success to larger tasks.

Instead of bringing bad news to the boss and then waiting for help, great employees bring both negative news and their ideas for handling it to the boss. Someone who only presents problems without solutions quickly becomes annoying and useless to the larger team; someone who both calls attention to problems and comes up with a variety of reasonable solutions will gain a reputation for excellent problem-solving skills.

4. Communicate effectively.

Matching employee-boss communication styles can be the largest frustration for many working relationships. Different people like different methods, frequencies and styles of communication and finding a boss/

employee combo who have exactly the same preferences is exceedingly rare. Therefore, while the goal should be for everyone to meet in the middle, the reality is that employees usually have to take a step closer to their boss's communication style in order to communicate well.

Sometimes, if the boss' communication style is truly dysfunctional rather than just different, establishing communication protocol can help diffuse the tension. If it's necessary to send certain documents by email and a boss simply won't respond to emails, sending the email with a text message, and then asking the boss to respond via text when they have read it could provide a work-around solution. Setting clear time frames and expectations for communication can help employees and bosses reorient dysfunctional relationships and rebuild lost trust. Rules and boundaries that everyone can follow are more likely to help employees and bosses move back to a trusting relationship than setting unrealistic expectations oriented entirely towards one person's style or needs without taking the other person into account.

5. Create relevant consequences.

As with team members, employees can actually create consequences for their bosses if things are not going well. Exerting upward influence should be seen as helping their bosses become better managers, rather than attempting to manipulate them, so all consequences need to support this goal. For example, if a boss asks for something to be done one way, and then insists on last minute changes, employees can demonstrate how those changes will make the project worse because they were requested at the last minute by turning in both products.

Consequences should always aim to create more positive conditions in the future for both people. A boss whose time management skills are lacking will become a better boss if those time management skills improve, and their employees will be less stressed and less overworked. Consequences shouldn't damage the work or reputation of either party – rather, they should be implemented at moments when the work would have been damaged anyway by the boss's behaviour.

For truly egregious offenses, it is important for managers to feel that they can go over their boss's heads. If a boss harasses them, breaks the law or steals their work, it's time to go to upper management or HR, rather than implementing consequences. Consider when a problem warrants consequences, and when a problem requires outside mediation or legal action.

6. Offer/Ask for help.

Knowing when to ask for help from a boss and when to offer help to a boss is a key talent of a great employee. Needy employees who require constant attention prevent the boss from doing their job; employees who get lost in their own worlds often miss opportunities to add value to their teams and the boss's own work. Managers should strike a balance between these. If they find themselves with free time while waiting for responses on projects, this could be an ideal time to ask their boss if there's anything they can help with. A can-do attitude and willingness to take on small tasks, even if they are below the manager's pay grade, can pay off in the strength of the relationship later on.

Effective time managers do not offer help they cannot provide or ask for help they cannot use. Never use an ask or offer purely as a relationship builder: if there is no time or need, this can be seen as manipulative and backfire.

7. Provide feedback.

Formal upward feedback should be built into the reporting cycle, and bosses should not only welcome this type of feedback, they should make it easy for employees to provide informal upward feedback as well. Great bosses are always looking to improve. If the organisational culture or manager is not open to this kind of feedback, subtler feedback is still possible (and necessary). Managers should use "I" messages when delivering this kind of feedback, even when their boss is openly interested. This is because "I" messages frame the feedback in terms of the impact on the employee, rather than the behaviour of the boss.

Frequency of feedback largely depends on the boss-employee dynamic, but feedback should be given at least quarterly. Informal feedback on a weekly basis in a low-stakes environment is ideal in many office settings; other employee-boss relationships may require less frequent or more pointed feedback.

Receiving feedback with aplomb is all about listening. This doesn't mean that the boss shouldn't have a chance to respond; however the response should always acknowledge that the boss has heard the employee's feedback and taken it seriously, even if they are not going to act upon it. Employee feedback is always valuable, even if it is incorrect: it's a measure by which bosses and employees can track the strength of their relationship and readjust expectations accordingly.

Coaching Suggestions

1. Use live case study
2. Coachee to outline pros and cons of current relationship
3. Select one aspect and tailor assignments to suit, with relevant follow up

Training Suggestions

1. Understand bosses have bosses and use this to create understanding
2. Participants should not expect a carbon copy of themselves as a leader
3. Use differences among participants to generate greater empathy towards their leaders

Challenge Level: 1 – Very Difficult

For some individuals, the key influencing skills that are employed in effective employee/manager relationships never fully develop in an entire career. This leads to the employee feeling disempowered and totally at the mercy of the whims of their manager, for better or worse.

But like any other powerful workplace skill, the ability to "manage your boss" can definitely be learned by applying specific techniques and strategies.

This is an advanced skill best taught by a highly experienced practitioner, but well worth learning as it will lead to a working life filled with harmonious and productive relationships.

2

LEADERSHIP

INTRODUCTION

Promotion to a leadership role is a major milestone for an excellent employee. However, even if this transition is exactly what someone has been working for, it doesn't mean that the transition is always easy. To quote a wise comic book character: "With great power comes great responsibility."

It is those new responsibilities that can throw new leaders for a loop. It isn't that the people who are transitioning aren't prepared for the additional weight on their shoulders, or that they aren't meant to be leaders after all. Rather, many responsibilities require a leader to fully transition their approach to work from the bottom up. A new manager may find they have to delegate work that they had previously handled competently on their own, requiring them to trust other people more than they've ever needed to in the work place. Taking on their new responsibilities often means letting go of old ones; they may no longer be able to function as the team expert as they become the team leader and need to retrain focus on other people, rather than on developing their own skills. At the same time that new leaders are delegating responsibility to others, they are taking on responsibility for others: tracking progress, setting expectations and communicating clearly and with discretion. Managing this shift in focus well can elude even the best new leaders and their bosses. Navigating these leadership transitions thoughtfully and successfully fosters success not only for new leaders – everyone around them, from their bosses to their employees to the organisation as a whole, will feel the benefits of a leader who is well prepared for their role.

Red Flags to Look For

Indicators that a new leader might be struggling:

- **"Stressed-out" is their normal.** This could be a sign that they are not delegating effectively (2.9) or that they are having issues handling the shift into leadership (Handle Change, 2.7). As new leaders, stellar employees often find themselves having to let go of tasks they owned before and learn new skills to manage their new responsibilities.

- **Their employees seem to be redoing each other's work often.** This could be a delegation problem (Delegate Effectively, 2.9), but it could also be a sign that employees aren't receiving clear communication from their leader (Solve Problems Effectively, 2.1) or that they are encouraged to compete rather than collaborate, when collaboration would be more effective (Display Win-Win Team Approach, 2.8).

- **Making a decision seems to take longer than average.** Great decision-makers aren't born, they are trained. If making choices stresses out a new leader, it's time to step in (Make Good Decisions, 2.2).

- **They are constantly running late.** Sure, some people run about 10 minutes behind on average, but otherwise, they complete projects when they are supposed to. If the lateness is new, or the leader is delivering work product dangerously late, it might be a sign that they need better time management skills (Plan Effectively and Manage Time, 2.4)

- **Their employees seem underutilis ed or don't seem to know what their goals are.** Motivation issues can strike even the most competent teams if effective performance appraisals (2.11) aren't implemented. If motivation is still an issue when performance appraisals are done regularly, it could be that the team hasn't adequately connected their tasks to the greater goals of their work (Motivate Others, 2.3)

- **Change makes the leader extremely nervous.** Change is rarely an easy process, even if it's necessary. However, if a leader resists even small or necessary changes because "the old way is easier," or the quality of their work diminishes immediately if the project throws them a curve ball, it could be a sign of a deeper issue (Handle Change 2.7)

- **Everything is always fine when you ask...until suddenly, it's not.** All leaders want to prove to their bosses that they are doing a good job. Sometimes, this can mean that they hide problems with their team or their work until the problems become too big to handle. If a team member keeps saying things are fine, but you're pretty sure something isn't right, it might be time for additional training. Check Handle Confrontational Situations (2.5), Influence Others (2.6) and Proactively Mentor (2.10) for ideas.

Preparation

When you start developing talent, it is important to assess where everyone is starting from. What problems and challenges do key leaders exhibit? What skills do they have that can be better utilised? The questions below can help you assess where an employee may experience problems as they move into leadership roles.

Negative attitude	Extremely	Very	Moderately	Slightly	Not At All
1. Is paralysed when confronted with a problem.					
2. Avoids including others.					
3. Handles conflict poorly.					
4. Doesn't communicate.					
5. Low risk tolerance.					
6. Doesn't trust others.					
7. Decisions are questionable, or require more time than expected.					

Motivating Drivers

Everyone is motivated differently and understanding yourself is the first step towards understanding others. When a leader knows their own motivations, they are then able to explore the individual motivational drivers for each person on the team. This knowledge can completely change how team leaders interact with their teams and drive team success, so this is where we start.

Each motivational driver comes with its own set of "triggers" – concrete ways to jump-start motivation for someone with that driver. Below, we discuss the four main drivers.

Developing Others: People who are motivated by developing others find satisfaction in bringing out the best in those around them. They help others reach their full potential through the means available to them. This could include mentoring, managing, coaching or even advice giving, depending on their role, personality and the connection they have with co-workers and employees. Whether they are providing constructive criticism or just a listening ear, people with this driver enjoy their work most when they are helping others succeed.

Fun: People motivated by fun are quick with jokes and smiles. They bring a sense of levity and humour to everything they do, and their best work days are spent in the company of others, leading people through their indomitable optimism. They see no point in keeping things serious when work can be joyful. They do best when they know they have set everyone else at ease and positively contributed to the atmosphere in the workplace.

Ownership: People motivated by ownership feel most satisfied and accomplished when a project is theirs from start to finish. They appreciate being in control, not only of their own work, but also through their ability to influence others and bring them into the fold as they lead. They generally have few problems making decisions and experience an enormous sense of accountability for their work – they generally own their mistakes as much as their successes.

Decision Maker: People motivated by decision making see themselves as having sound judgment and the wisdom to use it well. They feel they have contributed the most when they are able to make decisions that affect organisational direction or move things forward quickly and efficiently. They are comfortable with ambiguity and uncertainty. They constantly look for opportunities to use their wisdom and good judgment for the good of their work. Individuals with this motivation often seek input from others and experience the pressure involved in big decisions as fun and interesting.

2.1.

SOLVE PROBLEMS EFFECTIVELY

Overview

It is hard for employees to be effective leaders if they are not effective problem-solvers. The leader of a team is expected to help their team overcome obstacles and find work-arounds for issues that arise along the way to meeting their goal. We have all been on teams led by people who are not strong problem-solvers. Maybe it was the boss who couldn't make decisions quickly. Maybe it was a teacher who couldn't adapt to a curriculum change. Maybe it was the coach who suggested solutions that worked in the moment, but created more problems in the long-run. Whatever the case, learning to effectively problem-solve can make a world of difference in both a leader's work and their team's experience.

> **"**
> A leader must never view a problem as a distraction, but rather as a strategic enabler for continuous improvement and opportunities previously unseen.
> Glenn Llopis

Setting the Scene

The leader's plan was perfect. They had an excellent team and the right resources. Then the perfect plan went sideways, and their excellent team is waiting for their direction. What happens next?

If this situation makes the leader of a team look like a deer in headlights, it's time to examine their problem-solving strategies. Dealing with problems is a matter of "when" not "if." No matter how well a leader plans, how many great people they have working for them and how many resources they have at their disposal, it is impossible to avoid problems entirely. The key is to have a clear strategy for solving problems effectively when they do come up. This competency will help leaders learn to plan for and handle contingencies so that they can still achieve a desired outcome.

Development Instructions

1. Recognise problems quickly.

Determine the depth and importance of the problem, because if a leader doesn't know what's wrong, they can't fix it. When the going gets tough can they tell what is wrong? Or does the leader take a long time to figure out what the problem is, and whether it's a small fix or a big issue? The first step is to identify and assess problems quickly.

2. Gather relevant data needed to understand and solve the problem. Sometimes, even if a leader understands the problem, they may be missing the key information they need to solve it. To solve a problem well, leaders need to be able to determine the kind of data they need to resolve a major issue, and how to use that data effectively.

3. Develop a clear communication strategy.

Who needs to be told? Getting out in front of major issues can be tremendously important for the continued success of a project. Whether this means telling the boss when a team won't deliver on deadline or creating a press strategy for a major corporate issue, a communication strategy should be a key part of the plan. Be sure to communicate missteps and issues clearly and respectfully, without tanking morale, to get the best response possible from stakeholders.

4. Develop and apply a clear relevant problem-solving model.

Personnel issues can't be solved using the same methods a leader would use to resolve budget issues. The more experienced the leader is, the more easily they will gain insight into how certain archetypal problems can be resolved quickly and easily. Great leaders learn to to solve standard problems with repeatable methods so that they don't need to reinvent the wheel each time a problem arises.

5. Develop a clear, prioritised list of criteria that the solution needs to meet.

With big problems, it is impossible to tackle every angle at the same time. What is most important? Is there a specific person who needs to participate in solving one aspect of the problem? Are some parts of the problem causing more issues than others? Manage the solution strategically by solving the high priority issues first and creating a realistic timeline.

6. Evaluate potential solutions strategically

There are almost always more possible solutions than there are problems, so how do leaders know which solution is the best option? To overcome this, create a strategy for evaluating potential solutions, looking into possible future pitfalls, and revising solutions to work best for all stakeholders.

7. Implement solutions as soon as reasonably possible.

When a leader has made a mistake, it can be tempting to avoid making a choice – maybe the mistake was embarrassing, and part of the solution involves acknowledging they created the issue. Maybe the solution is far more time and labour intensive than the original method. Whatever the reason, a great problem-solver is able to move past these roadblocks and start implementing a solution as soon as possible, so that the team can move on from past mistakes. Strategising how to manage roadblocks and inertia is key when moving towards a solution, especially when it feels too big to tackle.

Highly effective leaders are able to do all of these things and evaluate when a simple or a complex problem-solving model will be most effective. The goal is to find a balance between speed and quality, and to move forward confidently.

Coaching Suggestions

1. Coachee to bring specific problems to discussion
2. Test understanding of issue
3. Have coachee develop relevant model for solution

Training Suggestions

1. Live examples in classroom – debrief effectiveness
2. Build theory base including specific models
3. Test with scenarios and debrief

Challenge Level: 1 – Very Difficult

Problem solving at leadership level is difficult by definition. The issues that are easily resolved rarely need leadership input. Compounding the difficulty is that while the problems leaders confront will invariably be high in complexity and potential consequence, the leader themselves may be lacking in the tools and experience to deal with the issue at hand.

Matching an advanced problem with an ill-equipped leader can have potentially significant negative impact for the profitability, safety or brand of any organisation.

Organisations who recognise this potential risk wisely invest in learning programs to ensure leaders at every level have the confidence and competence to handle this incredibly challenging and ever-present component of their role.

2.2.

MAKE GOOD DECISIONS

Overview

An effective leader must be an excellent decision maker. However, there are many different ways to make decisions, and the process can look very different depending on the context of the decision and the personal style of the decision maker. The key is to have a reliable process for decision making that uses experience, wisdom, analytics and judgment.

Decision fatigue (feeling overloaded to the point of not caring much about the outcome of their choices) can affect even the best decision makers. Applying a reliable, automatic and consistent method to decision-making can help fight the urge to make the easiest choice out of exhaustion.

_____

66
I am not a product of my circumstances. I am a product of my decisions.
Stephen Covey

Setting the Scene

A group of friends is organising a picnic. The people involved are all adults, and they seem competent: they have jobs and families and they pay their rent on time. But despite days of emails, they still don't know where to meet, or what time or who is bringing the salad.

One friend steps up. Suddenly, with this person in charge, things feel easier. They get the input they need from the group and choose the location and time. They assign tasks to other people. They decide where to get the supplies the group needs. They organise transportation.

A person like this is indispensable to every group, whether social or professional. Unfortunately, not all professional decisions are a "picnic" to make. Being able to make decisions that are smart, timely, ethical and benefit both the whole group and the individuals within it is an invaluable skill for all leaders. Learning how to make good decisions will teach team members how to become this kind of leader.

Development Instructions

1. Clearly define the issue.

No one can make a choice until they know what their options are. If the decision at hand feels too big or difficult, chances are that the decision-maker doesn't have enough information, and that they haven't clearly defined their task. In addition to knowing what decision must be made, it is important to know why a decision is necessary and the possible consequences of each choice. Let's say they are organising their company's annual conference, instead of a picnic: what choices will need to be made? Clearly defining the issue makes it easier to choose well and choose quickly.

2. Encourage input and debate where relevant

Is there more easily accessible information that could help the leader make an informed decision? Ask for it! If other people know more about the subject than they do, it can be helpful to have their input, or even to encourage debate when a team hasn't studied the topic closely. Who organised the annual conference before the person who is in charge now? What can the new team learn from the old team's experiences? Do certain stakeholders have important ideas about what needs to be different this time? Hone judgment skills to determine how much input is useful, and to avoid an echo chamber effect in which teams only hear their own opinions repeated back to them.

3. Move towards action.

Don't get bogged down in the quest for perfect information. A leader who waits until all of their ducks are in a row will not be able to take action in a timely manner. Ducks will wander off and go for a swim – but the leader still has a deadline. For the annual conference, the leader might not be able to make a perfect choice regarding transportation for everyone because all flights have yet to be booked; perhaps group transportation from the airport needs to be booked now to avoid having to pay late-booking fees. The best decisions can often be made with 80% of the required information and sometimes it's more important for the decision to be made on time than for it to be the perfect choice. If it all feels like too much, making choices in chunks and setting realistic timeframes can help keep a a task or project on track.

4. Apply ethics in decision making process.

Too often, it can be easier to make choices based on "hard" data like budget numbers and billable hours. However, decision-making should always take factors other than the bottom line into account. Making sure all choices are in line with the organisation's ethics guidelines is a good place to start, but generally, leaders need to make choices that they would personally support on a moral level. Ethical violations are rarely simple cases: there are almost always mitigating factors that made the decision seem reasonable to the person at the time. However, just because everyone else seems to bend the rules, or a leader doesn't have the time to do it the right way doesn't mean it is an ethical choice.

5. Communicate.

Once a decision is made, tell people! If a leader needs others to act on their decision, the choice must be communicated immediately. The catering company needs to know when the event planner has decided on the menu for the annual conference; don't leave people hanging until they ask for important information if that information is already known.

6. Evaluate impact

A good decision-maker evaluates the impact of their choices even after the decision has been made and acted upon. The most important question to ask is: did the decision produce an expected or an unexpected outcome? Making a choice and moving on deprives leaders of the opportunity to tweak a decision and obtain valuable information for the next decision they need to make…because there is always another decision. What went well at last year's conference? What could be done better this year?

7.Record and retain

Hindsight is 20/20, and bad decisions can still be useful if we can learn from them. Recording choices and impact for future reference can be essential to improving leaders' decision-making in the future. If a similar circumstance arises, leaders will want to remember what they did the last time...even if it turned out that it wasn't the best option. This can also help leaders get to know themselves better as decision-makers: do they always go for the biggest reward or the safest bet? Do they need to change their process?

Coaching Suggestions
1. Consider current decision-making process used by coachee
2. Coachee to explore organisational knowledge base to see if it assists
3. Risk vs reward analysis to be conducted pre and post decision

Training Suggestions
1. History of previous decisions and impact
2. Role play discussion and debate in classroom
3. Overlay with organisational values and standards

Challenge Level: 2 – Difficult
Another very challenging component of leadership. Put bluntly, making decisions is easy; making good ones, less so. Making decisions hastily without due process or consideration can have potential costly impact to any organisation. Conversely, excessive hesitancy will cause backlog and loss of confidence in the leader's ability to handle their role.

Quality decision making is like any other skill. It can be learned with the correct application of the right tools and techniques via a considered learning and mentoring program.

2.3.

MOTIVATE OTHERS

Overview

Leaders have more impact on the motivation of their team members than they may realise. The behaviour of the person at the top can inspire and encourage, or discourage and demotivate. Ensuring leaders' expectations and behaviour towards their team are congruent with the tasks team members are expected to perform is critical to keeping a team motivated: team members are constantly looking to their leaders to model behaviour.

Good leaders often lead by showing instead of telling: their behaviour, relationships and working style set a positive tone in the working environment. A great leader backs this up by aligning their goals with those of their team members and the business by providing high-quality, actionable feedback and by gaining a deep understanding of each of the members of their team.

" Motivation will almost always beat mere talent.
Norman Ralph Augustine

Setting the Scene

Motivation varies a great deal from person to person, even in the same professional setting. What sparks a feeling of excitement to start a work day is different for everyone, but it is something that must be explored if a leader wants to motivate others.

Some of us find a big pay/cheque highly motivating, but not everyone feels most appreciated through a monetary reward – public acknowledgment, or even the feeling of having done a good job might be more important.

Perhaps more tellingly, what makes someone NOT want to go to work in the morning? Too much on their plate, or they don't find any of their tasks interesting? A feeling that their work is not impactful or appreciated? Problems with people at the office? A stressful work environment?

If it affects the leader, it's probably affecting their team members too. The good news is that small changes can have a big impact on a team's morale. Learn how to create an environment that positively impacts team members' engagement, quality of work, productivity and behaviour.

Development Instructions

1. Understand own level of motivation.

If asked, could they define what motivates them? Are they feeling burnt out, or are they excited about their next project? Do they think their team members can tell? How might their level of motivation impact them in their work? Learn to do the introspective work necessary, and use emotional analysis to improve work, rather than hinder it.

2. Identify what motivates team members at work.

As discussed above, different people are motivated by different things. Does the team leader know what makes each of their team members "tick"? Everything from cultural differences to family circumstances can make a difference in incentives and the kind of environment that will draw out their team's greatest potential. Furthermore, a leader's behaviour can have an important impact. Leaders need to assess whether their method of leadership is positively or negatively affecting their team members.

3. Determine motivation level of team members.

That one team member who never looks like they have had enough coffee? There might be something else going on that can help motivate them. Learn to uncover how team members really feel, without putting them on the spot or making them feel obligated to give certain answers.

4. Empower others and make team members feel appreciated and valued.

Are team members empowered to act or do they need leadership's approval for everything? Is there a system in place for recognising good work? How does the leader show their team members their work is valued? These kinds of soft skills can be essential for ensuring a team is not only motivated, but self-motivating – and that leaders aren't pulling team members along every step of the way.

5. Encourage feedback and act on feedback.
Feedback shouldn't just be top-down; leaders' teams can also help them. Is there a process that allows for upward feedback? Is that feedback actionable and directed, or does it tend to be vague or otherwise questionable? Leaders' responses to feedback can deeply impact their team's motivation, so explore how to respond with genuinely good intentions.

6. Connect business goals with team member motivation.
This connects the team more deeply to the business at hand and helps them understand their goals more clearly. By aligning personal and business values, everyone can be better understood and appreciated.

7. Effective use of reward and recognition.
Many bosses avoid recognition and rewards because they would rather focus their energy on progressing the work at hand. However, learning how to use recognition and rewards to their advantage can actually help a leader's team work more efficiently and produce better quality work product. Learn what rewards and recognition are effective and why, as well as how to apply these motivators consistently.

Coaching Suggestions
1. Review what motivates team members and how they apply that in the workplace
2. Create an action plan for demotivated team members
3. Create and implement a reward and recognition initiative

Training Suggestions
1. Role model and debrief a team building exercise for motivational effectiveness
2. Baseline current team motivation and set aspirational goal
3. Allow differing points of view to surface – no motivator is universal

Challenge Level: 3 – Neutral
Leaders, when questioned, would universally agree that they'd rather a motivated team than an unmotivated one. Working in their favour is that their team also wants to be motivated!

However where many leaders come unstuck is in assuming the job role itself contains intrinsic motivation for their people, or confusing "motivation" for making inspirational speeches at the weekly sales meeting. It's rare that either of these factors have significant impact on the day to day motivation of teams.

Motivating a team is not necessarily difficult, but it does take an investment of time, effort and interest in learning the correct methods and techniques for tapping into key motivators for each team member.

2.4.

PLAN EFFECTIVELY AND MANAGE TIME

Overview

In a world where many business processes can happen instantly, keeping tabs on time has never been more important. For some people, this means becoming more efficient. For others, it means protecting scheduled time to complete the day's highest priorities. Leaders who can plan in advance and handle the normal peaks and troughs of workflow with grace are able to better maintain their own physical and mental wellbeing, avoiding the burnout that comes from a constant state of overwhelm.

66
Lack of direction, not lack of time, is the problem. We all have 24 hour days.
Zig Ziglar

Setting the Scene

Time management seems simple: write down major goals for the next month, the next year or the next week. Create a daily schedule and stick to it. But even people who do these things may find themselves running minutes, hours or days behind. They hit deadlines, and because the task has not yet been completed perfectly, they turn in work product late. How can strong leaders avoid these pitfalls?

Everyone has worked with poor time managers. Perhaps it was a boss who assigned urgent tasks at 4pm on a Friday. Maybe it was a colleague who was always late to meetings, or the meeting moderator who can't stick to the agenda. Or maybe it was the company head who couldn't prioritise, so every task took on equal urgency and importance.

Excellent time management doesn't mean completing all tasks perfectly – the colleague who runs late and the boss with the Friday assignments probably both produced excellent work product. Instead, learning to effectively manage time allows leaders to achieve goals on time using their available resources to their full potential.

Development Instructions

1. Develop effective daily plans.

When an effective leader leaves work, they already have a plan for what they will accomplish tomorrow. Planning effectively is the first step towards better time management. Ensuring the day is planned before it starts also allows leaders to proactively tackle the most important things on their agenda, rather than reacting to whatever shows up on their desk. The key is to learn how to find the balance between planning comprehensively while still leaving room for the unexpected.

2. Prioritise tasks for maximum results output.

Remember that company head who couldn't prioritise? Assigning tasks with designations like "urgent" and "important" can help leaders see what needs to be done today and what can be put off until tomorrow. Often, we do things out of habit, and keep tasks on the agenda just because they were important at one point, but aren't anymore. Developing a model which will allow leaders to completely eliminate some unnecessary tasks can help with this.

3. Maintain focus on highest priorities.

Is the leader's workspace a veritable playground of distractions? Are there days when they check their email, glance at their phone, get a coffee, watch a cat video online, talk to a colleague about their vacation, and then come back half an hour later to find they have accomplished nothing? Staying on task mentally is crucial to building towards better time management. Designing a workspace with minimal distractions and teaching concrete strategies for staying on task can help leaders deal with interruptions without getting distracted.

4. Complete tasks within deadlines.

Working on a deadline can be incredibly motivating for some people, but if they have perfectionist tendencies, it can sometimes be hellish. Deal with deadlines effectively by creating a work process that is efficient, regulated, and time-conscious – getting the job done, rather than doing it perfectly, is the goal.

5. Allocate resources within budget.

Time is a scarce resource, so managing it as a resource is key. Leaders need to focus on negotiating for more time and protecting their own time so that they can minimise the cost of setbacks. Use concrete measures for improving time allocation, including backwards calendars, agendas, timers and other planning tools.

6. Apply a proactive approach to complex and challenging tasks.

It can be hard for some people just to get started, so the most important step is to just start somewhere. If there is a task that feels extremely difficult or stressful, even if it is important, it is easy to procrastinate until just before the deadline. Teach team members how to take that first step, and how to effectively prioritise tasks within a project.

7. Manage contingencies via effective communication.

Factoring in time for mistakes and problems from the beginning can help leaders avoid setting unmeetable deadlines. Create plans for the best case and worst-case scenarios. Allow extra time in case things don't go exactly as planned. Finally, if a leader is running behind, who needs to know? Is there a clear communication plan? Ensure leaders and teams are prepared to handle time-consuming problems if they should arise.

Coaching Suggestions

1. Understand what the current planning process looks like. Is there one?
2. Have coachee self-prioritise current tasks
3. Follow up small milestones and reward

Training Suggestions

1. Have groups consider all tasks in current job role
2. Work as a team to find solutions to common prioritisation, resource and time management issues
3. Have each participant walk away with tailor-made planning template

Challenge Level: 4 – Easy

Although many leaders suffer from time management issues, the solutions to this are not at all difficult to put into place. All it takes is the acknowledgment that work methods could benefit from modification and the courage to try things differently.

A proactive approach to work, dealing with "time suckers", prioritising tasks and avoiding distraction are all skills that can be learned easily with the correct support and guidance.

2.5.

HANDLE CONFRONTATIONAL SITUATIONS

Overview

Proactively managing conflict can create stronger, more resilient teams. Like change, the key to dealing with conflict effectively can be seeing the opportunities where others only see problems. Conflict and negative emotions can sometimes expose larger problems within an organisation, or create larger problems when left unchecked. Learning how to master conflict resolution and management is an important skill for every leader. The question is never if there will be a conflict within a team or organisation: the question is only when.

_____

66 Success is never final. Failure is never fatal. It is courage that counts.
Winston Churchill

Definition

Confrontational situations affect everyone emotionally, though that emotion can express itself in different ways. Some people feel their heartrate rise, and their palms begin to sweat. Some people shake physically with anger or anxiety. Often, the incident that sets off a major conflict can seem small: an email from a co-worker who seems to be taking credit for a team member's work; a colleague suggesting the team try an approach that was exhausted months ago; a team member who simply won't take direction. The straw that broke the camel's back? In the office, a more accurate conflict metaphor might be the email that broke that internet. The ensuing chaos can leave everyone wondering, "But how did something so small balloon so quickly?"

The truth is that if a conflict has already escalated to the breaking point, leaders have missed an opportunity to manage a confrontational situation well. Conflict is an unavoidable part of working with other people: the question is merely, how can leaders manage conflict most productively? And if a conflict has already led to feelings of anger, anxiety and frustration, how can leaders slow things down, engage and come to a resolution, even under immense pressure?

Development Instructions

1. Identify common causes of confrontation

"Don't take it personally" is a mantra we hear day-in and day-out in the workplace – but sometimes conflict can feel awfully personal. Once emotions are running high, it can be hard to identify the original problem. Sometimes that problem is deeply personal: the source is a clash of personalities and working styles, or an old issue that started outside of the workplace. Correctly identifying the source of the conflict is necessary if leaders want to have a chance at resolving it. Leaders should learn to identify common causes of conflict and how to troubleshoot these common issues through role play practice.

2. Understand the impact of constructive and destructive behaviours.

Is a leader's conflict resolution method making things worse? When they are upset, do they shut down and stonewall, start yelling or rolling their eyes, or allow the conflict to spread to other areas instead of dealing with the problem at hand? Is the leader interested in the resolution, or in placing blame? Are they openly confrontational, or do they engage in passive-aggressive note wars? Do they criticise or do they complain? Identify constructive behaviours as well as destructive behaviours that can make or break leaders' ability to manage a confrontation effectively and work to replace the destructive behaviours with constructive ones.

3. Know why confrontation escalates and identify strategies for defusing.

Is the leader constantly surprised by how quickly conflicts can escalate? Understanding why confrontation escalates and identifying methods for defusing conflicts when emotions are running high is key to finding a productive resolution. Deciding when to engage and when to walk away and cool off is hard for anyone, even people who are not directly affected by the emotional nature of the conflict at hand. A good leader can redirect anger and other emotional responses effectively at the right moment and encourage a détente when the situation has become too volatile. Practice strategies for easing escalation and defusing conflicts.

4. Understand the role that assumptions play.

Different people handle change and confrontation differently. Understanding those differences can be key to managing leaders' own assumptions. Maybe a leader comes from a background where "healthy conflict" was encouraged: if they are managing a problem with a team member whose previous work culture discouraged all types of open conflict, the leader will need to adjust their expectations. Different types of conflict and behaviours can create stress for different types of people: for example, some people find raised voices to be extremely stressful, while others would much rather yell than deal with someone who is being passive-aggressive. Understanding where everyone is coming from and managing conflict in a way that reduces stress increases the likelihood of a successful resolution.

5. Gather appropriate information.

Start with defining the problem, clearing up all facts needed and ensuring everything is explained in detail, even if it seems obvious, can change the tone of the conversation entirely. Encourage all team members to question their own basic assumptions, and learn strategies to ensure no assumption slips through the cracks and creates unnecessary stress or confrontation due to asymmetrical information among the participants.

6. Reframe words for congruence with objectives.

Language matters. When someone is angry or frustrated, it can be especially difficult to use conciliatory language instead of inflammatory words and statements that further stoke the fire. What words will help to resolve the issue? What words will make it worse? Helping leaders become more conscious of the language they use, say things in the simplest terms possible, and encouraging all participants to speak in language that avoids blame and stereotypes can help teams reach an easier, clearer resolution. Define what language works and what doesn't, and how to use words expertly to avoid common pitfalls in conflict resolution.

7. Understand and practice the framework for preparation and discussion.
Conflict resolution is a skill that requires practice to make perfect. A standard process for dealing with conflict can take some of the guesswork out of conflict resolution and reduce the emotional intensity of an argument by giving all participants a clear framework to work within. Having boundaries and clear expectations will give everyone the best possible chance to succeed. Leaders need to define this process, practice using the process in various scenarios, and use the language that is most likely to reconcile rather than inflame the conflict further.

8. Create a conflict management plan for specific scenarios.
Does a team have ongoing conflicts, either personal or professional, that simply can't be resolved? Managing conflict is as important a skill as resolving conflict. When a problem is unsolvable, developing a specific plan for managing the conflict over time is essential to a team's continued functionality. Create work-arounds that allow everyone to do their best work and avoid clashing over issues that just won't change.

Coaching Suggestions
1. Do a joint self-assessment of conflict management skills
2. Role play a previous confrontation situation
3. Help prepare for a potential upcoming confrontation situation

Training Suggestions
1. Beware of the environment this workshop is conducted in – sensitivity to current situation and relationships is paramount
2. An experienced facilitator is essential
3. Assessment tools and role plays are very useful learning devices

Challenge Level: 1 – Very Difficult
The truth is most people seek to actively avoid confrontational situations in all aspects of their lives. Confrontation often makes us feel very uncomfortable and can even provoke unpleasant physiological reactions such as elevated heart rate and sweating. It's no surprise then that even experienced leaders often find handling confrontation one of the most difficult skills to master.

The bad news is that a very large part of any leader's role is to effectively deal with confrontation, sometimes even initiate it, whether they are comfortable with it or not. The good news is that there are specific methods that if applied well and consistently make the process of handling confrontation for positive outcomes considerably easier.

Becoming highly skilled in this area is something that takes a good deal of practice and is best learned with the guidance of a highly capable mentor experienced in dealing with confrontation in real-world situations.

2.6.

INFLUENCE OTHERS

Overview

It isn't enough to have a vision: a great leader is truly an influencer who can take that vision and generate excitement in others. Getting people on board is often no easy task, even when there is supposed to be a full team helping with the job; some people are not predisposed to cooperate just because a task is within their job description. Achieving goals often requires buy-in from peers, superiors and external parties. Getting that buy-in is a skill all effective leaders must cultivate.

> 66 Sometimes, if you want to change a man's mind, you have to change the mind of the man next to him first.
>
> Megan Whalen Turner

Setting the Scene

Great negotiators don't just ask for what they want: they find solutions that help others see that giving the negotiator what they want is also in the other party's best interest. Consistently influencing others' choices is not an outcome that can be achieved simply through formulating the right job description, signing contracts or relying on hierarchical power.

Let's look at the possibilities just within a typical team leader's network. An unwilling team member might technically do their job, but the job will remain mediocre if the employee's attitude towards the work remains purely contractual. A stakeholder in a giant project might not take deadlines seriously, even though the deadlines are written in the contract. There is always some sort of mitigating circumstance, but the truth is the stakeholder just isn't prioritising the work. A boss might have ideas for the project that the team leader doesn't agree with and even after the team leader has voiced their concerns, their boss is going ahead anyway. Now what?

What if the team leader could make these people see things differently? How much easier would it be to achieve their goals?

Development Instructions

1. **Understand the importance of influencing in the workplace.**
People who are less skilled influencers often avoid using their influence or learning to negotiate well because it makes them feel as though they are playing games. For them, "playing organisational politics" can feel as though they are trying to succeed on something other than merit. The fact is, refusing to engage with the politics of the organisation can actual hamper their chances of succeeding based on merit, because they may be viewed as obtuse, inexperienced, or worse, incompetent. This doesn't mean that they should become manipulative or always be indirect, but understanding how to navigate a sensitive situation with aplomb is a skill that all managers need to have to succeed.

2. **Identify key principles involved in influencing others.**
The last time a team leader needed others to cooperate with them, did that leader know exactly what each person needed or wanted? Knowing what others need, what is important to them, and what they hope to get out of a situation can help a leader understand how to negotiate for their own goals. Include identifying others' needs and wants as part of project strategy.

3. **Different cultures operate in different ways.**
A savvy leader adapts their strategy to fit the culture of the company.

4. **Demonstrate rapport and authenticity.**
If someone hates "playing politics", it's probably because they feel inauthentic doing so. Building rapport and learning how to use honesty to an advantage in difficult situations can help fight that fake feeling. Understand how to demonstrate congruence and consistency in interactions while still negotiating strongly.

5. **Build and maintain relationships with a diverse range of people.**
Knowing who needs to be influenced is just as important as knowing how to influence. Making use of informal networks as well as formal networks

can mean the difference between a project that succeeds and a project that fails due to lack of excitement and buy-in. Sometimes, a well-connected employee with significant influence may be below the leader in the company hierarchy, because of the reach of their informal network of friends or the scarcity of their skills or knowledge base. Show the team how to identify people whose influence could be valuable and leverage personal networks in ways that make sense for the situation at hand.

6. Engage easily with a range of interpersonal and group situations.
Employees who are easily bored at meetings, or find after-work socialising unnecessary, are often overlooking a valuable opportunity. Leaders need to learn to strategize based on the most likely scenarios and politics within an organisation and adapt their personal styles to the group they are attempting to influence: a kind of expert-level "reading the room" that takes into account everything from the context of the gathering, the physical environment, the time of day and the people present.

7. Find strategies that work at an individual level.
The direct, no-nonsense attitude that works for one team leader might come across as angry or abrasive when used by another. Troubleshoot interpersonal approaches with individual team members in order to give better feedback and maximise their ability to make a good first impression.

8. Demonstrate approachability and empathy.
People want to help people who help them. "Paying it forward" and vulnerability can be valuable tools in forming mutually-beneficial relationships. Look at appropriate ways to manage social debts and maintain strong relationships through strategies to help leaders forge those relationships in the first place.

Coaching Suggestions
1. Focus on understanding the points of view of others
2. Work on improving a recent negative interaction
3. Build an ongoing development plan

Training Suggestions

1. An excellent team building exercise during times of change or stress
2. Prepare for sensitive or personal issues that can derail the attitude of participants
3. Ensure there is a thorough follow-up strategy to keep up the momentum from the workshop

Challenge Level: 2 – Difficult

The reality is that influencing is a difficult skill to master. Even a leader who has formal authority over a direct report may not get the best out of that individual if their ability to influence is poor.

In addition, for leaders to achieve maximum effectiveness they need to influence outcomes with peers, superiors and other stakeholders, some external to their organisation. A leader with poor influencing skills will find people work with them because they feel compelled to, not because they want to.

Influencing skills, when taught well, enable leaders to perform at maximum effectiveness by ethically leveraging the discretionary effort of all those around them.

2.7.

HANDLE CHANGE

Overview

A flexible, adaptable, "rolls with the punches" team leader is hard to find. Often, people who are naturally great planners have trouble adapting when plans go awry, and people who would rather just wing it are doing so because they expect things to turn out a certain way more easily. Change is hard for everyone; the difference is that some people find change exciting and interesting and see opportunities where others can only see challenges. These are the kinds of people who everyone comes to for advice amid uncertainty, who seem rock solid when everyone else is being tossed around by metaphorical rough waters. On the other hand, a team leader who is truly change averse may panic when they receive bad news and would rather continue to do things the same way because familiar feels easier, even if the new way would make things easier in the long run.

These leaders struggle to adapt because their first impulse when a new idea is presented is to think of all the reasons why it won't work. These team leaders and their teams generally find their jobs exceptionally stressful. Therefore, it is critical to learn both how to manage our own expectations for change, and lead others who might be resistant through periods of uncertainty.

_____

" When we least expect it, life sets us a challenge to test our courage and willingness to change; at such a moment, there is no point in pretending that nothing has happened or in saying that we are not yet ready. The challenge will not wait. Life does not look back.
Paul Coelho

Setting the Scene

Ironically, change is an unavoidable constant. Though we tell our friends who are struggling that "this too shall pass," we often have a hard time applying the same logic to positive periods – inevitably, something will change and we will need to adjust to new circumstances. It seems that the minute we get comfortable with the order of things, something shifts and we have to manage a major transition all over again.

Change is a combination of chaos and opportunity. Being able to see the opportunity in the chaos is a skill that can be nurtured and developed. This can be especially difficult when change arrives just as things are going well – it can feel nearly impossible to see the positive in a situation that feels as though it could threaten everything they have worked for. As a leader, they are not just responsible for handling their own reactions to change; they have to help their team members navigate uncertainty and manage their own expectations. Embracing change and finding the adventure in uncertainty can help them put aside worries and fears and spot the opportunities in the chaos.

Development Instructions

1. Assess ability to navigate change.
How have team members handled change in the past? Are they ok with small changes, but big changes make them nervous? Encouraging team members to study their own responses to change can help them identify strategies for managing it better in the future. It is useful to analyse our histories with change so that we can improve our relationships with uncertainty.

2. Identify practical strategies for managing common reactions to change.
Practice makes perfect, and waiting until a major change happens to deal with fear can only make the experience more frightening. Instead practice managing change before the stakes are high through role plays of past, present or expected scenarios.

3. Understand the change cycle and employ effective actions at each stage

Seasons are predictable, and there is also some predictability within the chaos of organisational shifts. In the same way that people know they need to buy a jacket before the first cold snap of winter, employees can prepare for their own reactions to the cycles of change within business.

4. Identify and apply important skills critical to effective change leadership.

Understand the difference between a proactive and reactive approach to change. The logic of change management is self-fulfilling: If a person believes they can influence how change affects them, that person will actually have more influence over how change affects them. By learning to think proactively, team leaders can guide their teams more effectively through a crisis.

5. Identifying opportunities.

Our culture has so many sayings for the opportunities that come out of unexpected change, and none of them are particularly popular with the people who hear them. People dealing with change are told, "When a door closes a window opens," that it might be a "blessing in disguise," or that they just have to "see the silver lining." When people are tired, angry or anxious, it can be next to impossible to see a change as any of these things. However, learning to do so can mean the difference between taking advantage of a hidden opportunity or letting it pass accidentally. Team leaders can practice this skill in several ways: for example, by choosing a more productive response deliberately, or asking good questions to mitigate uncertainty.

6. Develop an action plan to adapt to change effectively.

What does the team leader need? What does their team need as a whole? How is each individual on the team affected by the change? It is important to tailor the plan to fit the situation, the needs of individuals and the needs of the team as a whole.

7. Allow time to process emotions.

Change is stressful, even when done well, and allowing adequate time and space for team members and leaders to process that stress can be the difference between successful implementation and failure.

Coaching Suggestions

1. Assess the strength of strategies used to lead change
2. Identify gaps in change leadership skills
3. Create an action plan

Training Suggestions

1. This training is appropriate at any time in the change cycle
2. Works well with people from all divisions
3. Preparation of comprehensive role plays is recommended for this training

Challenge Level: 3 – Neutral

Change management is inevitable in the life of all leaders. Not only do they need to have the ability to cope personally with variability in the internal and external environment, but they are expected to guide others through it too.

An understanding of the inevitability of change and having the tools and strategies to deal with it productively is essential. Although "change is constant", leaders must ask themselves are they constantly dealing with it in a best practice manner?

A good mentor can be a huge benefit to ensure leaders regularly self-check their ability to handle change and provide positive guidance to their teams.

2.8.

DISPLAY WIN-WIN TEAM APPROACH

Overview

Teamwork is such an important skill, it is now routinely included on CVs and in job descriptions: Assigning each individual a single task with no team coordination necessary is nearly impossible. Furthermore, attempting tasks without collaboration can mean a slower, less efficient department, and more problems down the line due to lack of coordination or in-fighting. However, a win-win approach doesn't necessarily mean that everyone is collaborating all the time; sometimes, it's more efficient to have everyone do their parts individually and collaborate at the very end. In these cases, what is important is managing team member expectations; they won't win if their fellow team member loses. The ability to design an environment in which a win-win solution is not just encouraged but essential to every individual's success is increasingly critical to leaders' success within modern organisations.

> 66 There is little success where there is little laughter.
> Andrew Carnegie

Setting the Scene

In game theory, a variation on the classic prisoner's dilemma game can be used to describe the benefits of a win-win approach to teamwork. Two prisoners have been arrested on suspicion of committing a crime: the police tell each prisoner that if they 'rat out' their partner in crime, their partner in crime will go to prison for life, while they will be released. However, if neither snitches, the police only have enough evidence to convict the prisoner for a crime with a light sentence (only a year of jail time). If both snitch, the police can send both to prison for life.

What would they do? The best solution for both prisoners is clearly to collaborate, refuse to snitch, and accept the year in prison. However, choosing to do this requires a great deal of trust from each prisoner: They must believe that the other person will also act in the collective self-interest instead of aiming for the all-win-all-lose snitching option. In a work environment, team members who are rewarded when they collaborate and do not find themselves pitted against each other in prisoner's-dilemma-type scenarios are far more likely to be open to collaboration in the future. They are also more likely to work towards the common interest, rather than acting selfishly and, for example, taking credit for work that was done by a colleague, or sabotaging a colleague's efforts on a project for their own gain. As in the prisoner's dilemma, trust among members of team is extremely important to finding a right win-win approach that best serves everyone and meets organisational goals.

Development Instructions

1. Know when to engage others in a win-win effort.

Understanding when collaboration will make for a better end result is just as important as knowing when competition will inspire the best work. Which projects have been more successful with a team-based approach in the past? Which have had great results when infused with some healthy competition? Not all projects can be win-win, but maximising the ratio of win-win projects to competitive projects within a team will foster stronger morale within their team. Know the appropriate times to encourage a win-win approach, and when healthy competition may be best.

2. Recognise potential barriers and apply actions to overcome these issues.

Is there one team member who has a hard time working with the others? Does recognition matter more to one team member than to the others? Do certain members of a team seem to avoid taking responsibility for problems at all costs? These could be signs of possible barriers to a win-win approach within their team. Identify common roadblocks and practice strategies to overcome and manage dynamics within teams or work environments that are less conducive to a win-win approach.

3. Use key principles to lead and demonstrate strong collaborative skills.
If a leader finds teamwork difficult, they may inadvertently be demonstrating counterproductive behaviours to their team. To foster a positive team environment, include a focus on the climate, personality types, individual skillsets and boundary setting, and how to implement these things in each person's own work, including the leader.

4. Apply influencing skills where necessary.
Using the key principles addressed in influencing, consider how team leaders can move towards accepting a win-win solution over a win-lose scenario, even if they have a couple of hypercompetitive members on board. What kinds of influencing behaviours might be helpful in this context? Synthesise knowledge from other competencies and build skills through competency sessions to practice influencing team members in a positive, authentic manner.

5. Address conflict when it arises.
If a team member feels they have worked hard on a project and someone else has contributed minimally, it can be hard to accept a "team win" over an individual win. While the hope is that all team members feel appropriately valued for their contributions, sometimes, conflicts will arise, and the ability to handle those conflicts is key. Draw on other competencies to learn how to manage conflicts that arise from a win-win approach without damaging the team dynamic.

6. Create an action plan for a win-win collaborative opportunity.
What does a work environment that promotes collaboration look like? Is it possible to design an environment like this within a company with a strong competitive ethic? What concrete actions can leaders take in order to make a win-win approach a reality instead of just a talking point? Develop a proactive plan for implementing more win-win opportunities, even within work structures that foster competition.

7. Build trust among co-workers.
Some workplace cultures establish personal trust through games and socialising; others allow people the time to get to know each other's work

within the working environment. However, creating opportunities for trust-building almost always means creating opportunities for short-term low-level vulnerability. If team members can see that they can be vulnerable without a colleague taking advantage of them, the groundwork for trust has been laid.

Coaching Suggestions
1. Review a previous cross-functional work effort
2. Create a plan for a future win-win scenario
3. Consider and create ways to overcome future barriers to success

Training Suggestions
1. This workshop works very well across different divisions
2. Prior to an upcoming cross-divisional project is a perfect time to run this workshop
3. Preparation should include a case study from a previous collaboration

Challenge Level: 4 – Easy

A smart leader will always be keen to explore win-win opportunities. Competition is a reality of business life, but when that competition is minimised internally, it allows an organisation to be so much more competitive externally.

All team members want to be on the winning side. There are specific strategies that leaders can be taught which will allow their team members to see that they can all win together. An advanced extension to this concept is to teach leaders to recognise their peers as their team, and work collaboratively to ensure a win-win approach across business functions.

With the right teaching program in place, there is great potential for any organisation to benefit from this seemingly logical but rarely practiced approach to teamwork and win-win outcomes.

2.9.

DELEGATE EFFECTIVELY

Overview

There is a reason people work in teams – we simply can't get everything done by ourselves. However, many people move into a manager role because they were able to take on more responsibility than the average worker, not because they were effective delegators. These people often have a hard time letting go of aspects of their projects and may be at risk of micromanaging their employees, distributing tasks but never responsibility. Effective delegation isn't just about letting go, though. Great bosses know how to distribute work based on a complex matrix of the individual strengths and job titles of their employees, upcoming deadlines, the needs of the organisation and their own capabilities. They provide work with the supervision necessary to complete it, but without trying to oversee every aspect of the project, or snatching it back the minute something goes wrong.

Setting the Scene

The first rule of management is "Delegate, delegate, delegate" for a reason. No manager can possibly do everything themselves with all the responsibilities, tasks and time-consuming travel and meetings that routinely come with the job. Learning to do so effectively not only shows employees that a manager trusts them, it keeps the manager sane and ensures work product is delivered on time. All employees want to feel indispensable, but the truth is, no one should be indispensable for the good of the organisation. If something happened to a team leader tomorrow and they were suddenly unable to work, who would take over? Is the team set up to manage unexpected absences? Indispensability isn't based on who the organisation would fall apart without – it's about who adds the most value by being there. When a great manager delegates, it isn't just another task to manage someone else – they are passing a torch to a particular person, who is now entrusted to complete the task. Offloading responsibility doesn't mean offloading worth – in fact, by valuing the work of other people, leaders can make themselves more valuable to the organisation.

_____

66 Your most important task as a leader is to teach people how to think and ask the right questions so that the world doesn't go to hell if you take a day off.
Jeffrey Pfeffer

Development Instructions

1. Recognise the warning signs.

Does a team leader seem overwhelmed and overworked, while their staff seems under engaged, unenthusiastic? Does the leader's staff work extremely regular hours while the leader stays late most days? Are team members constantly asking if they can help with something? All of these could be signs that a team leader is hoarding work and responsibility, delegating only closely supervised tasks and refusing to trust their team.

2. Notice opportunities to delegate.

Does a team leader avoid delegating because "it's just easier" to do a task themselves? This is likely a teaching moment that could have a huge pay-off in the future if the responsibility is one that repeats regularly. Keeping a visual reminder of team goals and tasks can help leaders identify new opportunities to delegate.

3. Avoid personal bias.

Many leaders like their work best because they understand it the best, but that doesn't mean that someone else's work is inferior – in fact, quite the opposite might be true if the leader has gotten too used to their own way of doing things. Delegating can be a learning opportunity for leaders as well as team members. Implementing review techniques that the whole team can use on work product can help keep managers' personal biases in check.

4. Choose the right people.

If delegating has worked out poorly for a team leader in the past, there is a good chance it's because the person they delegated to was the wrong person for the job. Allow team leaders to surround themselves with team members they trust and help them learn to push responsibilities and tasks as far down the hierarchy as possible.

5. Delegate fully.

Assigning tasks is time consuming and can be confusing for both managers and employees. Great leaders rarely assign tasks: they assign responsibility. If a team member is fully responsible for a project, that team member will be better able to anticipate the needs of the project, ask the right questions and will be more motivated to accomplish their tasks in a timely fashion. Assigning discrete, decontextualized tasks often results in a disjointed work environment for team members – they handle one thing they don't understand, followed by a different, disconnected thing they don't understand. In this scenario, the only motivation team members can work for is their boss' approval. By giving team members increased responsibility, managers can ensure buy-in and project cohesion.

6. Give team members a voice.

If a leader has a hard time delegating, creating a system that holds the leader accountable can be key to getting a project done. Team members can do this if they are allowed to call out a team leader who is hoarding work. Upward feedback about delegation can help leaders see their weaknesses in delegation and give them the information they need to do better.

7. Delegate, assess, delegate, assess.

Once a task or responsibility has been delegated, leaders need to keep track of how well the delegation went. Sometimes, this can be done through performance appraisals, but there are other methods for tracking progress on tasks without micromanaging employees. Leaders who can strike this balance are able to delegate more effectively in the future and avoid giving too much or too little guidance when doing so.

Coaching Suggestions

1. Examine current state on urgent v important matrix
2. Identify delegation-ready tasks
3. Work through process with individual examples

Training Suggestions

1. Understand current barriers to delegation
2. Use four quadrant delegation model
3. Have group assign tasks based on urgent v important matrix

Challenge Level: 2 – Difficult

Delegation often seems easy from the outsider's perspective. But there's far more to it than just offloading work. Experience tells us that many leaders find delegation exceptionally difficult to implement effectively. It's one of the most underutilised time management tools, but has the potential for the greatest morale boosting impact amongst teams.

A workplace where leaders are reluctant to delegate is often identifiable through poor morale, lack of understanding of organisational goals, high turnover and poor succession planning.

Like all leadership disciplines, applying a consistent method to delegation, combined with a thorough knowledge of one's team, can be taught and applied with immediate and powerful, positive impact.

2.10.

PROACTIVELY MENTOR

Overview

Great mentoring not only helps the mentee; it can have a reverberating effect throughout the entire organisation. Mentoring can nurture a junior talent into a skilled powerhouse, allowing them to fulfil their career aspirations. At an organisational level, the mentee often feels a great bond with the organisation where they received excellent mentoring, even if the mentee eventually moves on, with many mentees maintaining long and mutually beneficial relationships with the organisation where they began their careers. This respect has an impact on all employees. For leaders of influence, mentoring not only helps the organisation: It allows leaders to directly impact someone else's life for the better.

Setting the Scene

Everyone goes through transition periods throughout their careers. For some, at certain times, these transitions are quick and clear; for others, a transition can be protracted and painful. Often, the difference between a manageable transition and a make-or-break moment doesn't come from the nature of the transition itself or someone's personality. The difference is having a mentor who can support, guide and advise them during a period of instability. Great leaders usually have someone they looked up to when they first started their careers. How did this person help them reach their goals? How did this mentor shape them into the manager/leader/employee they are today?

Mentors model success for their mentees and help them achieve it by providing excellent guidance and advice. They have a higher, longer-term perspective, thanks to their leadership experience, and their vantage point as a senior member within their organisation. Any experienced leader can become a mentor. Do they see potential in a more junior member of their team? Who can they help boost to the next level of their career, in the same way mentor(s) have helped them?

> **"**
> If your actions create a legacy that inspires others to dream more, learn more, do more and become more, then, you are an excellent leader.
> Dolly Parton

Development Instructions

1. Know the difference between mentoring and coaching

A coach is important, and coaching can be part of a mentoring relationship, but it is far from the only part or the most important part. A mentor provides connections and a real-world example of how to move through the organisation. Mentorship signifies a deep relationship that goes beyond simple advice-giving.

2. Understand and use the benefits of mentoring to motivate and recruit talent.

A reputation for excellent mentoring not only helps recruit talented employees, it can help an organisation retain them for longer than average for the industry. Conveying the benefits of mentoring, not only to the mentee, but to the mentor and organisation, can encourage leaders to choose to become mentors, and to mentor effectively.

3. Know the current level of each leader's mentoring capability.

The traditional model of a single mentor guiding a mentee through all career challenges is now outdated. Most people have several mentors throughout their careers, often providing advice, guidance and assistance in different areas of their work. Understanding what they bring to the table is essential for any leadership position.

4. Understand the mentor's role.

Mentors provide advice, guidance, networks and occasionally even friendship. In modern mentoring relationships some of these benefits can flow in both directions. Create a working relationship that fosters the success of both parties, establishes appropriate boundaries and is supportive without coddling.

5. Apply a mentoring process.

Some mentorships fail simply because the logistics don't work for the parties involved. Being open to a structure and relationship that works for both the mentee and mentor is key to long-term success. If a regular in-person meeting time doesn't work well because of conflicting work schedules, solutions may be to schedule phone calls, or have meetings on an ad-hoc, as-needed basis. Create a process that works for the parties involved, and don't put too much pressure on the relationship to function exactly the same way at all times.

6. Demonstrate effective mentoring skills.

As a mentor, leaders may find themselves in unfamiliar territory. There is often a big gap between being able to do something and being able to teach it. Similarly, success in business and mentoring ability often don't go hand in hand – in fact, some of the most successful people may have a harder time understanding what makes a strong mentor, because success came more easily to them. Practice basic mentoring skills and create a strong mentorship model that can help guide leaders in their relationships with mentees.

7. Apply a mentoring discussion structure.

Like teaching, mentoring encompasses a variety of tasks, which, when done well, can produce excellent results. Leaders should practice active listening skills, refresh their industry knowledge, and beef up on their own networking abilities in preparation for taking on a mentee. Regardless of whether the mentor meets very regularly with the mentee in person, or they conduct their relationship on an ad-hoc basis, there should be regular check-in points when the mentor gauges the various ways in which the mentee needs support, and the progress the mentee has made.

8. Identify potential pitfalls.

There are some situations in which mentorship might not work, or this kind of relationship simply isn't appropriate for the needs of the mentee or organisation. Identifying these situations can prevent them from wasting time trying to establish an ineffective or inappropriate mentorship that may ultimately do more harm than good.

Coaching Suggestions

1. Review a mentoring session
2. Review and improve a mentoring plan
3. Seek and use mentee feedback

Training Suggestions

1. Needs top management buy-in and ongoing support
2. Preparation should include practical and relevant role plays
3. Output from the training should relate directly to the next mentee sessions

Challenge Level: 1 – Very Difficult

Proactively mentoring at a highly effective level is indeed challenging. Leaders are faced with the following questions: Am I qualified encugh? Whom to mentor? How to mentor? Do I have time? What's in this for me? What if my advice and guidance is not valued? How to identify mentoring opportunities? What are the boundaries of my mentoring relationship?

An advanced and highly experienced teacher is recommended to ensure mentoring is undertaken in a positive and beneficial way, and not merely an organisational "tick and flick" exercise.

2.11.

PROACTIVELY CONDUCT APPRAISALS

Overview

Many leaders and team members approach performance appraisals with trepidation. Some worry that if they point out something negative, it could damage their relationship with their team. Others are concerned that their team members will not be able to act on feedback well, so they avoid giving any at all in order to avoid disappointment. Finally, some team members worry that they will receive an onslaught of criticism with no suggestions for how to improve. Provided that the feedback process happens regularly and is implemented consistently, and both downward and upward feedback is actionable and well-delivered, there is no reason for either side to be nervous.

66

Performance management goes a long way in developing better individuals, fostering teamwork that directly leads us to achieve our organisational objectives.

Asha Poluru

Setting the Scene

Giving and receiving regular feedback is deeply important to a functional team. Without it, team members will have a hard time understanding how they are performing or making any changes in their behaviour in order to better meet expectations.

Sometimes, feedback that is done well can be truly revolutionary across multiple fields. Consider the check-list system pioneered by pilots during World War II and adopted recently by many hospitals to reduce human error: by soliciting feedback from surgeons, nurses, hospital staff, patients, and then comparing the qualitative data against medical records, hospitals were able to understand that a large number of errors were a result of stressed but highly competent people forgetting the easiest steps in the process. A checklist solves the problem, and allows those highly competent people to continue to function at their best.

This doesn't mean the feedback was easy to hear: many surgeons were extremely resistant because the idea that they could do their jobs better with something as simple as a checklist, and that this checklist may be best implemented by members of staff with lower training (i.e. nurses) grated deeply. It can be difficult to strike the right balance, so we aim to give feedback in a way that acknowledges both a skilled professional's abilities and the areas where improvement is possible or even necessary. Stress the importance of consistent, regular feedback processes based on pre-established criteria, as well as how to give good feedback, and how to follow up.

Development Instructions

1. Identify what is involved in an appraisal.
Creating a consistent process for all team members can help avoid many common pitfalls of performance appraisals. Do some team members only receive negative feedback? Do some leaders manage the process differently with certain employees because of those employees' jobs or personalities? Maintaining consistency creates the best possible working environment for all team members, who may find it impossible to resist comparing how their performance reviews went. Identify the components of a good performance appraisal and present the tools leaders need to consistently and regularly conduct appraisals for everyone under their supervision.

2. Use the key principles of performance management.
Great performance management in every industry has distinct commonalities. No matter whether managers are working at a school or a Fortune 500 company, their feedback should meet these expectations. Key components to address first are meaningful feedback, employee recognition and the correct frequency of discussion. Next, help leaders support employees in reaching new goals, either through personal support from professional development or a form of mentoring.

3. Avoid common performance appraisal mistakes.

A good performance appraisal leaves everyone feeling secure in their knowledge of what is working and what isn't. Even if a leader does all of the above correctly, using the right language and format within the performance appraisal can be tricky. Help leaders avoid giving a performance appraisal that mistakenly backfires, either because the content or the language were not ideal.

4. Identify constructive versus destructive criticism.

People tend to remember the best teachers they've ever had, not because that teacher never criticised them, but because the teacher helped them learn from mistakes. Feedback should always be clear and actionable. Similarly, people often remember the worst job review they have ever received, often because the review was actually an attack on their character, filled with criticism about things they couldn't change or had no control over. Teach leaders to identify constructive and destructive criticism methods, and focus on remodelling their language to fit constructive models for feedback.

5. Set goals.

Once feedback has been received, what is the team supposed to do with it? A great feedback round gives everyone a new goal to work towards, whether the project is going well or could use some improvement. Show leaders how to develop an action-oriented model for ending a feedback round, so that their team knows what to do based on appraisals.

6. Apply techniques for managing difficult conversations.

Sometimes, no matter how well a leader uses constructive criticism, how gently they speak, or how strong their feedback process is, the news is just difficult to hear. Team leaders should develop methods for handling hard discussions and managing emotional moments during feedback rounds.

7. Create relevant timeframes.

Consistent feedback is key, but no one has time for monthly formal performance reviews. Instead, define a feedback schedule that incorporates regular informal feedback, formal performance appraisals, upward feedback to managers, and allows employees to ask for additional feedback as necessary. Formal performance appraisals should not be the first time employees receive feedback on their work – hopefully, if feedback is done consistently, informally and clearly throughout the year, nothing in the formal performance appraisal will be a surprise.

Coaching Suggestions

1. Observe an actual appraisal
2. Review appraisal output
3. Work on likely difficult situations and how to handle them

Training Suggestions

1. An excellent workshop planned for at least two months prior to annual appraisals
2. Pre-work should address the assessment framework criteria
3. Well-constructed role plays are a very useful learning device

Challenge Level: 2 – Difficult

Performance appraisals have the potential to highly motivate or completely demotivate team members. Smart leaders recognise this and can often be overwhelmed with the responsibility this knowledge implies. This can often leave leaders dreading performance review time, with visible consequences being late, inaccurate or simply ignored reviews.

When the correct method to conduct performance appraisals is learned, they are fast, efficient, helpful and an interaction that both leader and team member can actually look forward to, no matter what the outcome of the conversation.

3

COLLABORATION

INTRODUCTION

Whether at work or in your personal life, it can be next to impossible to get things done without collaboration. People are inherently social beings – the idea that any of us is capable of functioning fully on our own is a myth that makes for great movies, but unfulfilled lives and careers. In good collaboration, each person is able to use their skills, talents and knowledge to work towards a goal that would be difficult or impossible for any individual to achieve alone. This doesn't mean, of course, that working with others is always easy. Teamwork takes skill and patience, but both of these things can be learned, and it is possible to produce great things even in a team that got off to a rocky start, or includes people who have historically struggled to work well with others. When that friction is removed, however, collaborating can be a rewarding experience for everyone. When relationships include values like mutual openness, idea sharing, reciprocity, mutual accountability and commitment, value can be added, no matter the level of personal connection. While some managers can feel it's just easier to do everything on their own, the real value in collaboration is in the efficient use of time and resources.

Red Flags to Look For

Any of the following could indicate that a new manager might be struggling with this skillset:

- They struggle to keep important stakeholders in the loop, or to meet their needs.
- They often do things by themselves, rather than involving others, because "it's easier" and they only trust themselves to do it "correctly."
- No one seems to want to buy into their big ideas.
- They can't easily explain a project they are working on to an outsider within a few sentences.
- People seem to avoid them, especially if it isn't clear why.
- They have limited contacts outside the organisation.
- They take credit for the work of others, in full or in part.
- Their team isn't working much, but they are at the office late every evening.

- Their team is doing important work but no one seems to know about it, or why it's important.
- Their work is strong, but it feels out of touch with the organisation's larger goals.
- They prioritise consensus over timeliness.

Preparation

When you start developing talent, it is important to assess where everyone is starting from. What problems and challenges do key leaders exhibit? What skills do they have that can be better utilised? The questions below can help you assess where an employee may experience problems as they move into leadership roles.

Negative attitude	Extremely	Very	Moderately	Slightly	Not At All
1. Communicates in convoluted or inefficient ways.					
2. Believes that if they are responsible for the success of a project, they should get all the credit too.					
3. Avoids working with others whenever possible.					
4. Is competitive with colleagues.					
5. Is too formal with colleagues.					
6. Overshares or oversteps regularly.					
7. Tries to do everything alone first.					
8. Believes in their own competence more than they believe in anyone else's ability to get most jobs done.					

Motivating Drivers

Everyone is motivated differently and understanding yourself is the first step towards understanding others. When a manager knows their own motivations, they are then able to explore the individual motivational drivers for each person on the team. This knowledge can completely change how team leaders interact with their teams and drive team success, so this is where we start.

Each motivational driver comes with its own set of "triggers" – concrete ways to jump-start motivation for someone with that driver and many people can be equally motivated by multiple drivers. Below, we discuss the four main drivers within the skillset of collaboration.

Empathy: People with deep empathy feel most useful when they are able to help others resolve issues by using excellent listening skills and a birds-eye life perspective. Empathetic people tend to be great at comforting others and resolving conflicts because they are able to see a situation from multiple perspectives. They often enjoy the emotional work of managing relationships, in part because they are good at it, but it can leave them exhausted to be so tuned into others' emotions all the time. They feel deeply rewarded when they help someone feel more "understood."

Relationships: People motivated by relationships find meaningful, long-term connections to be the most important form of collaboration. They tend to prioritise work-life balance, since their relationships outside of work are essential to their sense of well-being. At work, relationship people tend to view collaboration as an opportunity to deepen their relationships with co-workers and other stakeholders, and to build trust and security within those relationships. They feel most rewarded when they have great rapport with and affection for the people working around them.

Teamwork: People who love working in teams often believe on a basic level that the best work is produced by collaboration – they believe strongly in the ethos of collaboration itself. They tend to deeply enjoy the process of helping a group bond and complement each other, as well as the processes of teamwork, even when things aren't working at the highest level. True team players tend to get annoyed when anyone on the team tries to steal the spotlight or take credit for others' work – it goes against their deepest beliefs about the purpose of work itself. Team players avoid letting their teammates down at all costs – their reliability and respect for their team members can often become more important for them than the outcome of a project.

Belonging: People motivated by belonging feel most themselves when they are part of a group – like team players, they like to find the place where they can contribute, and they deeply believe in the power of collaboration to get work done. However, unlike the team-oriented people, belonging oriented people tend to be focused inward, rather than outward – they prefer managing where they fit into a group, rather than the dynamic of the group itself. As such, they can be excellent cheerleaders and deeply positive forces within a larger group dynamic, because they feel most rewarded when they are part of something bigger than themselves. While they are often deeply conflict averse, belonging people tend to be extremely social, and will often be found organising afterwork activities and facilitating group cohesion. The more cohesive the group, the happier a belonging-oriented person is to be part of it.

3.1.

MANAGE STAKEHOLDERS

Overview

When planning a project, the easiest place to start is usually with a to-do list – set meetings, send emails, assign tasks, create deadlines and meet those deadlines. What's implicit in that list is stakeholder management. A stakeholder is any individual or group that could potentially be impacted by the team's business activities. All those meetings, emails and assigned tasks? There's a person on the other end, and they probably have goals and preferences that differ in substantial ways from the team's goals and preferences. Stakeholder management is a method of ensuring that you are engaging in thoughtful and productive ways with the people involved with a project as part of an overall work process. Doing this well allows managers to keep control of their projects and outcomes by involving the necessary people in ways that works well for everyone.

Setting the Scene

Imagine an Australian multi-national with offices all over the world is running a major project with a field office in Senegal. The main office in Australia relies heavily on email to communicate – the team likes to have a record of decisions that were made for reporting purposes, and most of them hate unplanned interruptions, so even for small things, people usually write an email rather than phone or stop by for an informal in-person meeting. However the situation in the Senegal office is very different. Written communication is seen as too formal, and it's hard for everyone to communicate quickly and professionally in writing when using their second, third, or fourth language. Additionally, many people are out and about all day long, and can walk and talk, but can't walk and read. The Senegal office does almost all business by phone, and rarely sets formal meetings, partly because nothing runs on time at that office anyway, and people are frequently held up by activities in the field. Employees at the

Australian office keep sending emails to the Senegal office, and are upset when they aren't answered in a timely manner or at all. The employees at the Senegal office will often call during business hours without warning, and are upset when the Australian employees don't want to speak with them, or reply by email. How could stakeholder management help this organisation manage project stakeholders more effectively?

Development Instructions

1. Understand how stakeholder management is currently undertaken. Very few organisations employ an active policy for stakeholder management. Is the process thoroughly thought through or ad-hoc? In the example above, this process is clearly well planned within each office, but not throughout the whole organisation.

Identifying stakeholders is the first step to understanding how to manage those stakeholders. Try building an "existing stakeholder map" for one manager's projects that defines who the stakeholders are, what their "stakes" are (how they are invested in the project or organisation), and the stakeholder management policy (or lack thereof) they subscribe to.

Does the process for stakeholder management match the map? Are there people who have been left out, because of an oversight, the structure of the process or a lack of engagement with the rest of the team?

2. Define different levels of engagement appropriate for different stakeholder types.
A stakeholder map should show that not everyone needs to be engaged at the same level. In the example above, the people in charge of the project at both the Australian and Senegalese offices need to be more deeply involved than the people on the periphery who are only responsible for one or two tasks. Involving everyone at the same level is a waste of both time and resources. Effective stakeholder management does not mean telling everyone everything, but rather, determining the appropriate level of engagement for different stakeholders.

When does communication become "too much"? What type of communication is appropriate, given stakeholder engagement and preferences? Assess both the appropriate level and type of communication based on stakeholder needs and preferences.

3. Identify challenges present in stakeholder management.

For the office in Senegal, written communication is not the cultural norm and is difficult for many employees to do well. Roadblocks that go unaddressed can lead to reluctantly communicative stakeholders. When this happens, some managers can find that it feels easier just to do things on their own and ignore the need for engagement at all. If the Senegalese employees don't answer emails, and the Australian employees don't pick up their phones, how can the organsiation manage communication effectively? This is an opportunity for both sides to reassess how they manage stakeholders who are not part of their local office cultures. Neither side is correct, but sometimes stakeholders have constraints that make it easier for one side to compromise than the other. This could be an opportunity to find a new avenue that works for everyone, and ease communication on all sides – could the Australians employees call when they have time, and the Senegalese employees send a text message before they call? Therefore, it is key to identify specific challenges to create opportunities for better communication all around.

There are many ways to effectively manage stakeholders, but, as is clear from the Australia/Senegal example, one size does not fit all, especially when working across national or cultural boundaries. Forcing a stakeholder to engage in a way that they find uncomfortable will often produce reluctance and lower the quality of their work in unnecessary ways. Even if everyone is using online communication, if one team mostly uses a specific online tool to manage conversations, it may be difficult to engage with a second team that prefers a more "old school" method like email. Finding a communication method that works well for everyone does not mean forcing everyone to use new tech or sending everyone back to less effective old tech. Make room for nuance in stakeholder management, in order to engage with all stakeholders in a way that aligns with their needs or preferences.

4. Build stakeholder management into a project.

Actively identifying communication as a project need can make it easier to quickly change course when things aren't working, and help team members talk about their needs before communication becomes a problem. Set communication milestones, and schedule stakeholder management into project timelines.

5. Analyse what may be important to various stakeholders.
Consider the goals and investments of various stakeholders. Often, stakeholders may have vastly different goals for a project depending on their role in the organisation, their past experience, or even the ways this project interacts with other projects. Analyse the primary drivers for the most common types of stakeholders, and discuss the possible stakeholder drivers for each person on the stakeholder map.

6. Identify and manage conflicting priorities and objectives.
Just because everyone is working on a project together doesn't mean that everyone has the same goals. The financial team probably has very different end goals from the R&D team; HR may be interested in a project for reasons that conflict with the marketing team's ideas. Managing those negotiations deftly is crucial to project success. Because it is so important to find resolutions that work for everyone, successful managers develop methods for working with uncooperative or uncompromising stakeholders, including when and how to escalate and de-escalate during project negotiations.

7. Identify and plan differing levels of communication intensity.
As discussed above, agreement around communication is key. Frequency and method of communication should be agreed upon formally by as many stakeholders as possible, with the flexibility to reassess during the course of the project. Create a communication plan that allows for readjustments, and identify where the gaps in communication exist before they become a problem.

Coaching Suggestions
1. Identify current stakeholders with coachee
2. Where has stakeholder management failed in the past?
3. Use a current challenge as a live case study

Training Suggestions
1. Group exercise – map out stakeholder relationships
2. Build communication plan for live project
3. Encourage stories of success and areas for improvement

Challenge Level: 1 – Very Difficult

Successful stakeholder management requires a strong overview of multiple project elements, combined with an understanding of, and empathy for, the position and perspectives of the relevant stakeholders.

It's frequently done poorly, and in many organisations results in low morale, brand damage and financial cost.

With a structured approach guided by an experienced professional, there's potential for significant upside in building, maintaining and leveraging stakeholder relationships at most organisations.

3.2.

GAIN SUPPORT OF OTHERS

Overview

People like to follow people who are sure of themselves. The ability to convince others to put their trust, time and resources towards priorities is part of what makes a leader strong: others must believe in them in order for the leader to be able to do their job. But how can a manager create that support in the first place? Ironically, it is often by specifically doing actions that are not designed to gain the attention and admiration of others that managers are able to create the kind of following and support they need to do their jobs well.

Setting the Scene

In movies, the typical "hero's journey" plotline often includes a deeply average character who has the mantle of leadership thrust upon their shoulders. While it works well on the big screen, our social desire to see leaders who are just like us, not seekers of admiration, often translates to real life as well – it's why politicians emphasise their "down home" roots and giant corporations focus on their humble garage-based origin stories. In some ways, the humble leadership model works: someone who focuses on their work, who is able to ask for advice early and often, and who demonstrates genuine care for their employees is able to get more people on board with their project. However, if a manager takes this too far, they can become hard to follow, because a leader also needs self-confidence, an ability to sell their project and a clear vision that they can communicate well to others. Often a project will fail due to a lack of support from key influencers in the business. Winning and maintaining support is vital to ensure planning and implementation goes smoothly and roadblocks are minimised.

Development Instructions

1. Develop a strong, clear vision.

All managers should have an "elevator speech" prepared in the early stages of a project. What's an elevator speech? Imagine a manager gets in an elevator and a potential stakeholder is already inside. The stakeholder asks the manager "What are you working on?" An elevator speech is an easy way for the manager to answer this question clearly and effectively in the time it takes for the two to ride the elevator together. All projects can be distilled into elevator-ride-length speeches, and doing so can help managers clarify their vision. When trying to woo potential stakeholders, the same speech won't work every time: when speaking to the CEO of the company, the speech with likely be much different than when trying to talk to a fellow manager in a more technical division. Therefore, it is impossible to create a perfectly-scripted elevator speech that works for every situation: the key component of an elevator speech is that it is adaptable depending on the audience.

What elements are necessary for a strong, clear vision? Just because the elevator speech changes doesn't mean the vision does. Create a clear list of priorities and goals. Once the manager has developed this list, edited it, and finalised it with the team, the vision doesn't change: all that changes is how the vision is presented.

2. Explain the "why".

"What" is usually pretty easy to explain. For example, a jet company builds airplanes. An IT company provides computer services. "Why" is often a lot harder (why is this plane so much better than the previous models? Why is this IT service necessary?). Therefore, managers should focus their goals and elevator speech on explaining the "why" of their project.

While the internal "why" should never change, the way in which it is presented to various stakeholders might. This doesn't mean that managers need to have different stories ready for different people; rather, they should be aware that different parts of the story will be more interesting to certain people, and some story elements may have more salience in a specific audience. Avoid telling different stories, but keep in mind that different stakeholders care about different things.

3. Build high-quality connections.

What is a high-quality connection? If a manager wants to ask for help, who do they turn to? Who would they turn to for advice, or simply for buy-in? The deeper the connection, the more that connection is worth. A connection with someone the manager can reliably ask for help is far more valuable than an online connection with nothing behind it. The worth of a network isn't measured in size but in depth.

Building deep networks takes time and persistence, and unfortunately, there are no shortcuts. Just as friendships take time, nuance and patience to develop, strong professional relationships require the same finesse. Networking workshops, introductions and mentoring can help, but at the end of the day, building deep networks simply won't happen overnight. In the meantime, managers should focus on building their confidence, honing their people skills and managing their expectations about how quickly relationships can develop.

4. Develop relevant knowledge.

Credibility and authenticity are the bedrocks on which all managers must base their reputations. Attempting to get buy-in without these qualities is a bit like trying to build a house without a foundation: It's possible to get the walls to stand up for a while, but in all likelihood, the whole thing will fall apart the minute a strong wind comes along. Authenticity is the easier of the two to build: being genuine with people and acting with integrity can help managers build a reputation for authenticity over time.

Credibility, on the other hand, can be harder to build quickly. Managers should think about what makes someone in their profession or setting more credible: is it reliability, a close relationship with people in power, the right credentials or long-term experience? Credibility will likely be built differently depending on the situation, so there is no one-size-fits-all approach. Instead, creating values maps for both people leadership and the company itself can help uncover which areas are required to produce credibility in specific settings.

5. Deliver value at every stage.

What is the value added for stakeholders? If the manager can't define it, chances are that the stakeholder won't be able to either. Playing on peoples' self-interest often works better than asking for help out of sympathy or pity. If there is added value to be found on both sides, make it obvious.

Studies have shown that people feel obligated to return gifts when they receive them. Gifts can come in the form of time, professional contacts or other favours, and they are not just social niceties: gifts are one of the most important ways in which we build relationships. Therefore, doing something nice for someone may just be in the self-interest of a manager seeking the support of others.

6. Plan a strategy to win necessary support.
Everyone has had the experience of telling a long story over the phone to customer service, only to hear that the person on the other end of the line can't help, and someone else will need to hear the story all over again. The easiest way to avoid similar time wasting in the business world is to strategise before attempting to win support. Who are the most important stakeholders? Who has the power to influence? What is the best way to reach those people, without wasting energy gaining support from people who are not able to add value to the project?

Setting key communication milestones can help with organising a support-gaining strategy. In the same way that teams plan out project milestones, communication milestones can be set to show who needs to be told what when. Plan to mark milestones in communication, and reward communication within the team in the same way that the project would mark other kinds of accomplishments.

7. Ensure messaging is clear and positive.
Hitting the "Goldilocks Zone" of messaging can be hard to get exactly right: Almost always, teams end up with too much or too little communication. Furthermore, outlook matters: ensure that messages, especially to upper management, are presented positively. This doesn't mean the message itself has to be positive: sometimes, it's necessary to be honest (and authentic) about the problems a team is facing. However, positive messaging on a negative topic gives the impression that the manager and team are ready to work on the problem, even if they need help; a negative message indicates that they've already given up.

Different people need different types of messages, depending on their role, involvement in the project, expertise and interests. When developing messages, always keep in mind who the audience is, and ensure that the majority of the audience, when presenting to a group, will be engaged by the message.

8. Allow others to take credit and be rewarded.
Part of gaining support from others, as discussed above, includes supporting others. People generally don't jump to work with someone who is known as a credit hog, and it can be hard to work with anyone who doesn't allow a team to relish their wins. Stepping back and allowing others to take credit, especially when credit is due, can be the easiest way of building a credible, strong reputation within a company. A manager who allows employees to take adequate credit develops a reputation for fairness, and is more likely to have support when they decide to take a risk.

Coaching Suggestions
1. Coachee to identify key targets for support
2. Identify strategies already implemented
3. Build an influencing plan

Training Suggestions
1. Identify key gatekeepers organisationally
2. Participants to consider their own paths to support or lack thereof
3. Examples of what's worked well and what hasn't in the past

Challenge Level: 2 – Difficult
Gaining the support of others is a critical first step in establishing almost any large project. This skill comes more naturally to some people, while others find it quite elusive.

Many endeavours in the business world fall at early hurdles due to key players in the process not having fully committed to their success. This can manifest itself in lack of political, financial or resource-based support.

Consistently gaining others' support requires the simultaneous use of multiple advanced skill sets, applied consistently.

3.3.

COMMUNICATE EFFECTIVELY

Overview

We live in an age of infinitely accessible information, and yet somehow, communicating well has become harder rather than easier. Perhaps it's the number of mediums: do you email, text, call, schedule a meeting, use an app, leave a post-it note? Or maybe it's the speed: we now expect replies in seconds, rather than in minutes or hours. It has never been more important to communicate clearly and succinctly. All communication should, in theory, be clearly understood by the recipient, and be complete and direct in any requests so that the recipient can act on that information accordingly. In reality, most communication in the workplace rarely lives up to that standard.

Setting the Scene

We communicate in so many ways in the workplace, and while there will always be people who seem to never answer emails, or that one employee who only seems to want to text rather than speak on the phone, the real barrier to communication is skill, not the methods for conveying a message. Writing clearly and eloquently is often a topic covered in school, but a 5-paragraph essay format rarely translates directly to the workplace. Furthermore, most people never formally learnt how to organise their thoughts when they communicate verbally, or how to listen actively.

Many people believe that being "good with words" is at the core of strong communication, but the reality is that the best communicators are often better at skills that don't require using words at all. The primary skill that makes for truly top communication? Listening. Great communicators not only listen and understand well, they are adept at engaging with their conversation partners in a way that shows how well they have understood what was said. Active listening is a skill that can be developed and learned, and is essential for all managers, especially in high-pressure situations. Sure, being "good with words" helps, but what good are the words if they are addressing the wrong issue?

Development Instructions

1. Identify and use the key components of communication.

What elements are encompassed by "communication"? This can include everything from language learning activities like vocabulary and grammar, to non-verbal body language, to the logistics of conveying and receiving a message. Not all communication is verbal or written, so it is important for managers to have a clear idea of what is meant by "communication" before beginning to assess where the problem is.

Those skills everyone learned in school? It's time to brush them off and reapply them to the workplace. Anyone who has taken a language, literature, theatre, art, film or public speaking course has a formal education in communication – what can managers translate from a formal class to the workplace? For example, while it is unlikely that anyone in the office will be interested in your ability to memorise Lady Macbeth's monologue, understanding where to put the emphasis in order to make Shakespearean English understood can help someone trained in drama learn how to make their own instructions clearer for their colleagues.

2. Display effective listening skills.

The way we talk about it, "communication" as a subject area can begin to sound like a solo activity. The reality is that it's anything but. Communication must always include at least one other person, and often many more. Great communication is not something one person does; it is something several people create together.

A good communicator both knows their audience and is able to adapt and respond to that audience. This means that what happens when the communicator is not talking or writing is just as important, if not more so, than what they say. Learning to be an effective listener takes just as much practice as learning to speak well. Using techniques designed to encourage active listening and memory making, managers can learn this skill.

An active listener can use various techniques to ensure their conversation partner knows they understand, and that they remember and respond to what was said. One particularly simple technique is repeating and asking for additional information or clarification. This not only helps the listener understand, it allows the person who just spoke to hear how well their message was understood.

3. Communicate effectively across all media.

Different media calls for different communication styles. We don't start emails with, "Can I speak to Leslie?" and we don't end phone calls with, "Best wishes, Morgan". Managers often need to learn different communication styles for different media, especially if a certain type of medium is new to them. For example, when people are new to text messages, they often try to write them in the same way as emails at first. Similarly, someone who is used to texting for all of their needs may need to learn new skills in order to have a strong conversation over the phone.

Each organisation has different communication protocols. Setting up clear best practices for various types of communication allows managers to handle most minor communication issues in one fell swoop. If some colleagues are too formal in emails, while others are sloppily informal, the overall impression of the team is diminished, and the impact can be lost. Prevent these sorts of problems by establishing clear guidelines for style, medium usage and response time.

4. Change tenor and tone of message with recipient in mind.

One guideline managers should never set? An inflexible one that forces all employees to use the same tone and style in all communication. Active listening principles tell us that communication must be adapted to the audience – the simplest way to adapt is to change the tone and style, rather than the message. An email to colleague in an extremely formal style can feel distant and almost aggressive, but the same style may be completely appropriate when addressing a high-level official for the first time. Adapt communication to the situation and the recipient for the best results.

While style and tone can change, the key messages should not. Recipients should always take away the message a manager intends from a given communication. An easy way to check for this is to simply ask what was understood for the manager's own learning goals, which is often best done in person or over the phone, as doing so by email can feel to the recipient like the manager doesn't trust them to be able to understand basic information.

5. Understand the role communication plays in influencing.

So much influence is created through good communication, it can sometimes be hard to define exactly where one skill ends and the other begins. Good communication lays the groundwork for good relationships, but again, it doesn't always have to be verbal. Paying attention to body language and developing good listening skills is usually the more important part of communicating in building relationships. As with influence, great communication is exceedingly authentic: few of us are good enough liars to avoid the backlash of disingenuous talk.

One area where verbal skill can have a major impact on a leader's ability to influence is when that skill is used superfluously. Overcommunication can be just as damaging to relationships as too little communication. All managers need to navigate not only the landmines of inappropriate topics and oversharing, they must do so without dominating the conversation so often that people lose interest in what they have to say.

6. Identify and avoid inappropriate communication styles.

The caricature of the older man trying to talk like a teenager is a comedy staple for a reason: This guy is so out of touch with his own presentation, he thinks he can relate to younger people by using a few of their own words, but on him, the words sound ridiculous, almost like he is making fun of the teenagers rather than trying to relate to them. Know thyself and thy position should be the mantra of leaders, especially those in positions of power. It is often necessary to speak with less formality, but managers need to do so in a way that is both respectful of their audiences and their unique relationship with their audiences.

7. Use communication to defuse challenging situations.

When a professional situation gets tense, many people react with either 1) avoidance or 2) aggression. Great communication comes out of neither action. Instead, using strong communication to defuse a situation usually involves a great deal of quiet listening, repeating what was said and a perpetual focus on a positive outcome. Managers can learn to do this through workshops that mimic the tension of a real confrontation. Workshopping a confrontation allows managers not only to practise communication techniques, but also their ability to manage their emotions under pressure.

Coaching Suggestions

1. Baseline existing communication skills
2. Roleplay challenging communication scenarios
3. Coachee to bring live examples to sessions to work on

Training Suggestions

1. Work through common media in groups
2. Use examples of strong and poor communication
3. Look for common pitfalls to avoid

Challenge Level: 3 – Neutral

All of us communicate every day, in every workplace, to ensure we are able to achieve our goals with the help of others. We also are constantly in communication in social settings outside of the workplace.

Those who we observe that we would consider to be "good communicators" are simply applying (often subconsciously) a set of skills and techniques that allow their messages to cut through, which in turn enables them to be effective in achieving their personal goals.

With enough practice it is possible for even the weakest communicator to significantly increase the efficacy of their messages, in any medium.

3.4.

DISPLAY INTERPERSONAL SKILLS

Overview

It's pretty easy to tell when someone has a problem with interpersonal skills from the outside. People seem uncomfortable around them, or avoid them unless necessary. A socially inept person often makes basic social mistakes that people around them overlooked or allowed for when they were young, or has failed to adapt well to changing social norms or culture. Or, perhaps they make cultural faux pas that are easily explained by their newness to a particular company, but are extremely awkward and problematic. For some people, this may be a mild issue caused by inattention, and is easily corrected with some introspection and practice. In other cases, there may be a deeper reason why a manager or team member lacks interpersonal skills, medical or otherwise. In all cases, despite what many people have been brought up to believe, interpersonal skills, like all skills, can be taught and practised. Many of the best techniques for developing this skillset come from outside the business world – theatre, behavioural sciences and psychology have all contributed techniques for managing interpersonal relationships with more aplomb. Even though the techniques can be learned, most people think about strong interpersonal skills only in terms of their manifestations: "respect", "charisma" and "like ability".

Setting the Scene

Interpersonal skills might be categorised as "soft" but they can be extremely challenging to learn in a business context. Many people who struggle with this area are actually quite social and friendly; however, their professional and personal histories may have produced a dearth of opportunities to practise these skills in a business context, or they have developed coping mechanisms due to past trauma that are hurting their ability to effectively relate to people. Humans generally work in groups, however, so "people skills," or the ability to work effectively with others, are often a requirement for success, even in professions that appear deeply "unsocial."

Development Instructions

1. Display verbal and non-verbal communication proficiency.

Keeping vocabulary in line with cultural and workplace norms can be difficult for some people. Even where there seem to be clear lines that should never be crossed, like sexual harassment, it can be hard for some to tell why what they said is problematic. Establishing a feedback loop for someone who has exhibited problematic behaviour in the past can be a lifesaver. For example, if an employee is simply awkward, and seems to be offending people, it can be helpful to have a point person they can turn to in order to discover why something they said was offensive, or their joke fell flat or someone is avoiding them. Additional techniques for managing problematic speech need to be equally tailored – a senior level manager who makes inappropriate comments needs to be handled differently from a new manager who speaks with weird formality towards their team. As with all communication issues, the key will be learning to listen more thoughtfully, which will help the person with the communication problem improve their own use of words through observing good examples.

We've all been at parties with "close-talkers". However, most body language problems aren't so simple. Someone may be giving off an aggressive vibe from their physical stance, or chronically misreading situations so that a behaviour that isn't problematic in itself becomes an issue because of the context in which it was used. As with speech, managers can learn to "listen" to body language – sometimes, the easiest way to determine appropriate body language is to mirror the conversation partner. However, improving body language issues must be tailored to the exact problem, and establishing a feedback loop that allows for self-correction is essential.

2. Demonstrate awareness of cultural sensitivities and norms.

Collaborating internationally creates opportunities for both great successes and epic failures. Norms very greatly from country to country – in some countries, it is customary for opposite gender colleagues to kiss on both cheeks when greeting each other, but in others, touching a colleague of the opposite gender can be considered deeply offensive, if not outright harassment. Furthermore, adapting to those norms as an outsider can be incredibly difficult, because when something is normal, it is essentially invisible to the insiders. This is especially true for smaller or less obvious cultural characteristics. For example, the way a culture treats hierarchy, or appropriate workplace conversation topics, may not be as easily explained. Managers can learn these things through practice and observation skills.

Even within the same country, different industries can have vastly different cultural norms. An investment banker probably doesn't go to work wearing the same clothes as a teacher, though they may keep similar hours. Similarly, even if industry culture appears the same from the outside, it's unlikely anyone will fully understand the culture of another industry unless they've worked within it. Culture can include everything from behavioural norms to values, which can make cross-industry collaboration a bit fraught, especially when for-profit business collaborates with non-profit or government organisations.

Finally, within industries, each company has its own culture. That list of acronyms every organisation has? They might not be the same at every company. Allowing people to make mistakes, ask questions and take longer to do certain tasks in the beginning can help get new managers on track, especially if they are coming in from outside the organisation. Furthermore, just because a process works in a particular way at one company doesn't mean it is the best way or the only way. Allow managers to stay open and flexible to new ideas, but keep in mind that it is the manager's job to adapt to the organisational culture, not the other way around.

3. Use effective questioning techniques.

Asking questions is the easiest way to manage interpersonal relationships well, because doing so well requires active listening. There are three basic types of questions: open, leading and closed. Most great conversationalists asking a lot of open questions, with a few leading and closed questions sprinkled in. Open questions, which allow the other person to answer in many different ways, and usually at length, help the conversation to flow naturally. Leading and closed questions help the conversation partners maintain clarity and verify understanding.

At the same time, acting like a reporter or a police interrogator rarely makes anyone friends in an office environment. Asking too many questions, or coming across as either disingenuous or aggressive can ruin whatever progress good open questions might have created. Practising conversation skills in a workshop setting can be extremely helpful for someone who is nervous or has a hard time listening well.

4. Demonstrate social awareness.

In school, some people had an easy time socially and others experienced extreme ostracism at the hands of their peers. Those same people grow up to be adults in a workplace, which can sometimes feel like a strange microcosm of the schoolyard – albeit one that someone can leave if it's truly awful. While most adults are able to relate to people more effectively than when they were teenagers, plenty of people bring their teenage insecurities or ideas about social life with them into the workplace. Where some become social climbers, others can find themselves consistently excluded, or purposefully distance themselves from the office politics that make them so uncomfortable. Unfortunately, none of these responses is a particularly good one for a manager. Understanding the office as a microcosm of the larger social world can help managers learn to navigate their social work life without reverting to old habits.

"It isn't personal" is a workplace mantra, but the fact is, if you're dealing with people, everything is personal. Refusing to take others' needs and feelings into account just because the environment is business-oriented not only shows a lack of empathy, it demonstrates a lack of workplace competence. Good managers know that many decisions and actions are emotional, even in the workplace, and even when people are trying to remain objective. Helping managers acknowledge and take into account the emotional lives of their teams and collaborators will allow them to function at a higher level both in and out of the workplace.

5. Display self-discipline.

For some people, social anxiety can be so intense that it overrides other good instincts for how to behave. Some people can't stop talking when they get anxious; others clam up completely or become aggressive. Help managers figure out what makes them anxious or uncomfortable in a social setting, and devise a plan to encourage self-discipline in the face of counterproductive behaviour. Observing managers, providing feedback and developing new behaviours to replace problematic, anxiety-driven ones can help managers deal with these issues.

6. Know when to take responsibility.

No one can control anyone else's actions or ideas, no matter how well they negotiate or how socially adept they are. Instead, it is important for managers to focus entirely on their own behaviour and on what they can control. For example, it may be that a manager has a specific emotional response to a certain type of interaction. The manager may not be able to control that interaction, or even how they feel about it – however, with practise, it is possible for managers to control how they react, despite their feelings.

Sharing credit can be confusing for new managers, especially if they have risen through the ranks to this point of leadership specifically by looking out for themselves. If sharing credit is an issue, help managers to understand their success differently – for example, rather than worrying about their contributions, a manager can focus on the way in which the team's success reflects well on their work in supporting the team.

7. Listen before acting.

Nearly everyone has something that causes a visceral and unpleasant reaction. For some people, it's the sound of fingernails on chalkboard; for others, it might be the smell of rotting fruit. These triggers can create involuntary physical and emotional reactions – our shoulders tense up, we wrinkle our noses, we feel our stomachs turn. Usually, however, if we take a moment to relax, breathe, and wait before responding, we are able to calm the reaction, even if the stimulus hasn't stopped. The same is true for people who react badly in specific work situations. After recognising the problematic behaviour, the next step is taking the time required to calm down and respond with thought and empathy, rather than to immediately react. Managers should learn techniques for keeping their heads in the game even in a crisis, which can range from mindfulness techniques to step-by-step programmed responses to slow down problematic situations and make decision making easier.

Coaching Suggestions

1. Coachee to rate current proficiency through use of examples
2. Work through morally challenging scenarios
3. Set task to discover cultural norms and discuss in session

Training Suggestions

1. Use examples of individuals with strong interpersonal skills
2. Define each concept clearly for group
3. Use the group to create fun, scenario-based skills practice sessions

Challenge Level: 2 – Difficult

So much of what we view as "interpersonal skills" is based upon values, attitudes and behaviours we have all learned in our formative years. As an adult when apply these skills to our work environment, we find that some of these learned behaviours work for us more effectively than others.

Given that the way we interact with people is a key determinant of success in the modern workplace, it's worth investing in improving our facility in interpersonal interaction by understanding our current behaviours and what triggers them.

A skilled and experienced facilitator or mentor is essential in providing the "arms-length" feedback and guidance needed to improve in this regard.

3.5.

NETWORK EFFECTIVELY

Overview

The impact of "hub" people has been dramatised extensively on TV – whether it's in the context of an international heist or a soapy relationship drama, high value networkers often provide the centrepiece of a plotline. In the real world of business, these people are also highly important to the "plotline" of their workplace. They have the ability to turn a casual contact into a long-term and mutually beneficial relationship. While some people mistake networking for manipulation or disingenuously competing in a popularity contest, the reality of great networkers is far from that image. Instead, they focus on building meaningful relationships in whatever time they have with someone – they immediately see nearly everyone they meet as of value and worth getting to know. Networkers see contacts where others may only see a colleague, a supplier, or, worse, an obstacle. Furthermore, great managers know that they will add value to their contacts' business lives in the same way that those contacts add value to theirs – through introductions to people within the manager's extensive network.

Setting the Scene

Great networkers build webs of contacts around themselves, connecting them to other people, both inside and outside of their organisations and fields. These contacts are not just business cards or email addresses – each one is a meaningful and mutually beneficial relationship, waiting to be deployed. Therefore, highly effective use of networking not only helps managers in their careers, it can allow a business to operate more efficiently. Networking can attract new customers, retain existing ones, result in more efficient solutions to bureaucratic and logistical problems, and help a team navigate complex internal and external organisational structures.

Development Instructions

1. Strategically plan networking.

Managers should take a look at their current networks to understand both strengths and gaps. Sometimes, it may become obvious that while a manager is great at relating to someone at their level, people who work below or above them are less represented. Often, networks tend to be heavily weighted towards people who work in the same profession as the manager, even though outside contacts would be extremely useful. Evaluate both the strengths and weaknesses of a manager's existing network mindfully.

Who does the manager need to meet? If there are certain people who would clearly help a manager achieve their long-term goals, the first step is to identify those people. Next, come up with a strategic plan to leverage the manager's network and make that introduction possible.

2. Understand personal style and use to advantage.

If the manager is an introvert, that doesn't mean networking can't be effective, just that they need to use a different style than the party-happy extroverts at the organisation. Identify the social interactions in which this person excels in order to set them up for success. Are dinner parties harder than coffee? Do they do better in casual situations in low-key environments, or is the preparation required for formal networking events helpful to them?

Nerves are part of social interaction for many people, and networking can be particularly nerve-wracking, even for people who are usually the life of the party. Try different techniques to help with networking weaknesses, including reframing, power posing and introducing situations that result in poor outcomes or are anxiety-provoking in tandem with easier situations where success is more guaranteed.

In all networking situations, it's important to remember that networking should always be mutually beneficial. Therefore, managers should always approach new contacts as though they have a great deal of value to offer, even if they aren't sure exactly what will be valuable to the contact just yet. Practise these approaches so that the managers comes across as confident and flexible, rather than rigid and arrogant.

3. Build and grow important relationships.

Initial contact is great, but the key to building relationships is to allow them to develop over time. That means pursuing contact over time, rather than letting a relationship lie dormant after a business card exchange and two emails. Once contact is made, plan to meet or speak regularly to keep the relationship alive. These meetings don't have to be formal or time consuming – sometimes, a quick email update, a phone call or grabbing coffee is enough to keep a strong business relationship solid.

Sometimes, the benefits of maintaining a contact aren't immediately apparent. This doesn't mean the contact isn't of value – on the contrary, the contact may be providing added value in areas the manager didn't even realise were weak. Keep in mind, however, that compensation is often appropriate for work done through contacts, and don't take value added for granted.

4. Know when and how to engage others.

The saying "all it takes is chemistry and timing" is normally used to apply to romantic relationships, but timing and appropriate engagement is really the key to all human connection. Approaching someone when they are already surrounded by others or extremely busy with an unrelated project probably won't work as well as waiting until the right moment. Instead, hep managers identify the times, places and circumstances when they would want to be approached. If it wouldn't work for them, it probably won't work for someone else.

5. Effectively self-promote without boasting.

A promotional opportunity is any chance a manager has to relay important messages about themselves or their organisation. Unfortunately, many people shift to one extreme or the other on the self-promotion scale: either, they boast, brag or create awkward situations in pursuit of self-promotion, or they have trouble talking about themselves, their work or their organisation at all for fear of alienating people. Help managers find the right balance between reasonable and useful self-promotion, and problematic behaviours through individual coaching and litmus tests. Eventually, a manager should be able to do a 'gut check' to figure out when self-promotion is called for, and when to hold back.

There are plenty of ways to create more promotional opportunities – events, presentations, even casual coffee chats and informational interviews can provide these. The key is to always be upfront when scheduling something specifically for self-promotion, and to use a light touch, rather than trying to manipulate people into listening.

6. Articulate value added.

An elevator speech is an incredibly important tool that can help managers distil and express the basics of their projects. An elevator pitch is like an elevator speech 2.0: not only does it explain what they do and why, it sells their project and their abilities to the other person in the elevator.

A unique selling proposition (USP) is the thing that makes a project or a person unique in its work. Why should someone choose one organisation over another, or one manager over another. To discover USPs, managers can brainstorm their strengths and connections to various projects alone, with family and friends, and their colleagues and boss.

Most of the time, scripting can work against a less experienced manager in anything but a highly formal setting. Therefore, rather than trying to script every conversation, managers should instead outline the basics of what they want to talk about, including key words and phrases. Scripting works best in formal settings when managers have a great deal of preparation time for a very formal talk.

7. Demonstrate advanced social networking techniques.

Managers who are already gifted at developing networks can still use the practise to add nuance and efficiency to their networking development. Role playing scenarios, including efficient exits and management strategies for awkward situations, can help managers, who are already skilled, foster their talents.

While it's important to value everyone as a potential contact, connecting with the wrong group can have serious consequences for unwitting managers. If a manager realises that association with a group or organisation could create more problems than the connection is worth, they should have a clear exit strategy and a method for managing that exit without offending the group in question. Identifying these problematic associations early, whether it's a conflict of interest issue or something more personal, allows for the cleanest exits, but it is also possible to move away from an association gracefully even if deeper contact has been established.

Nerves can be useful: just ask any performing artist how they feel before a show. Most will say that a certain level of "butterflies in the stomach" actually improves their performance because that feeling raises the stakes. Fear, on the other hand, is rarely a productive emotion. Help managers learn to recognise the difference between productive "butterflies" and unproductive fear, and analyse what aspects of networking create that unproductive fear. Learning to mitigate triggers for fear can mean the difference between making a contact and letting an opportunity pass.

Coaching Suggestions
1. Gain understanding of coachee's current business network
2. Look for expansion opportunities
3. Develop networking strategy

Training Suggestions
1. Group skills practice for social networking opporutnities
2. Spend time on informal networking scenarios
3. Have participants build strategic personal networking plan

Challenge Level: 4 – Easy
Networking and the ability to improve skill at building networks is significantly easier than it first appears. The reality is that the vast majority of people are already participating in certain networks and have the ability to expand and leverage these, without even realising it.

The key to improvement here is to apply structure and technique to already existing skill sets. With a modicum of guidance, it's easy to build effective business networks, regardless of the personality of the networker.

3.6.

PLAN COLLABORATION EFFECTIVELY

Overview

Collaboration doesn't come naturally to everyone, even though it is the foundation on which all organisations are built. Some organisations start out based on collaboration, but as they grow larger, their employees or managers can lose sight of the benefits of a collaborative approach, mistaking hierarchy for an effective substitute. A manager who is an effective collaborator is able to leverage the skills, talents and resources of the people around them in order to achieve their goals more efficiently, with higher quality, or with greater efficacy. An effective collaborator has the ability to leverage the skills, talents and resources of the people around them to achieve greatly increased output. A manager who resists collaborative approaches will often find themselves outpaced in the modern work environment which privileges people who can work together effectively.

Setting the Scene

The "open office" floor plan has become extremely popular in recent years, especially among companies looking to project a younger, 'hipper', more agile image. While there is a sizeable proportion of the population who would prefer walls and doors, the selling point of open offices is almost always their ability to facilitate collaboration. Certainly, for human resources workers and others who spend a great deal of time either on the phone and otherwise creating noise, or dealing with confidential information, open office is a burden at best and a disaster for productivity at worst. For people who would otherwise spend their entire days silently staring at their computer screens, or sending emails to their colleagues when speaking in person would likely be more efficient, open office formats can create the kind of environment where collaboration becomes the easy option – and that can be a great thing. Organisations run on collaboration: if there was no point in working together with other people to achieve a common outcome, why work in a group at all?

Development Instructions

1. Know what method of collaboration suits each circumstance.

Like the open office floor plan, certain types of collaboration are suitable for certain groups at certain times. If recruiters, who are constantly on the phone, have to work in an open floor plan next to the engineers who need to talk to each other regularly about their joint projects, both groups will likely annoy each other so much within a couple of days, any future effective collaboration will be stunted. The same is true of collaboration methods that do not involve the arrangement of office space. Managers should consider what kinds of collaboration are likely to increase efficiency, and which are likely to add unnecessary complication without much added value.

The most effective partners may not be obvious. Often, managers are inclined to look upwards to find collaborators, but often, the most eager and helpful collaborations are formed with people working for them or at their level. Managers should look for people who are not only great stakeholders or contacts but people who can add value to the project through their interest and commitment ability, regardless of their level.

The approach matters. When a manager takes it upon themselves to start a collaboration, it is important to keep in mind that the way the project is presented could define the tone of the collaboration throughout the process. Therefore, managers should prepare for how they will present the collaboration based on their intended audience, and think critically about what they are looking for before approaching an intended collaborator haphazardly.

2. Recognise and overcome roadblocks to effective collaboration.

If collaboration has been an issue for a manager in the past, it's important to analyse the reasons collaborations have failed before. Was the problem structural (i.e. not enough organisational buy-in, lack of funding, re-organisation before the project could be completed)? If so, managers should design strategies that help mitigate these issues before attempting another collaboration. If the collaborations seemed to fall apart for more personal reasons, help a manager master the issues that are currently challenges.

Finally, choosing the right collaborators is key. A collaboration in which the interests of individuals (either business or personal) are not aligned is likely to fail before it gets off the ground. Identifying the right collaborators and managing expectations well from the outset (3.1) can help prevent "doomed to fail" personality and business interest clashes.

3. Understand and navigate the organisational network.

Building a collaboration within an organisation requires effective knowledge not only of the organisation's structure (including funding, resource and human resources approvals) but also of its internal politics. Ignoring these elements will limit the effectiveness of a collaboration immensely, even if a manager makes an effort to learn these things later on. If a collaboration has already started and there is an insurmountable organisational roadblock to the current design, it will be much harder to backtrack and start over than if that roadblock had been identified in the first place. That pause in momentum and subsequent inertia can kill great ideas.

If a manager is interested in working collaboratively, but does not necessarily have the bandwidth to start a collaboration themselves, a good option can be to self-promote as a potential collaborator. The best ways to do this generally depend on the industry and the specific organisation, but if a manager is keen on collaborating, they need to find ways to make this known within the organisation. Managers can seek out "collaboration mentors," people within the organisation who always seem to be leading interdepartmental projects or starting new initiatives. Associating themselves with people who are already doing it, a manager can make it known that they are interested in collaborative projects while learning how to make them work from highly effective collaborators.

4. Know who and who not to involve collaboratively.

When planning an event, the maxim is always to start with the guest list and then find a space that works for everyone who needs to be there. When planning a collaboration, managers should instead think about the goal of the collaboration first: What are they hoping to get from the project? This should define both who they involve and what resources they request.

The value-add for the collaboration does not have to be entirely business oriented, but at least some aspect of the collaboration must serve core business goals. However, managers should keep in mind that some of the value-add from a collaboration can be things like skill-learning, the encouragement of self-analysis or introduction to outside perspectives. All of these are valuable additions to a manager's work life.

What level of collaboration is necessary? Sometimes, a quick brainstorming session is more useful than a formalised committee, and in some cases, collaboration may actually make a process less efficient or less productive. Knowing how far to take the collaboration without immediately jumping into a full-blown team with consensus-based voting will help managers create the best opportunities for good outcomes.

5. Use influence to free up resources.

Selling the importance of a proposed collaboration, both to superiors and potential collaborators, can help ensure the collaboration is taken up seriously. Sharing work can leave everyone involved more time to work on other things. For example, if multiple departments spend time updating the same documents, is it possible to share those documents online and take turns updating so that no work is being duplicated? Consider ways in which the collaboration could free up time and resources instead of requiring more commitments from those involved.

When working with superiors, managers need to keep in mind that they likely won't be able to force the project to move forward if the superior is resistant. Therefore, taking the time to fully convince superiors of the merits of the collaboration and establish reasonable and timely benchmarks without being pushed can have big payoffs for the end project. A strong collaboration produces results – managers should make a plan to describe and quantify those results on a regular basis.

6. Set guidelines for effective collaboration.

Even in an informal collaboration, people can become frustrated if their roles or jobs are not clearly defined. For example, if someone asks for feedback, but is not clear about what part of the work they are concerned about, the feedback process can become fraught, with the feedback receiver feeling over-criticised and the feedback giver feeling undervalued. Managers should be clear about what they expect from their collaborators and negotiate those agreements in good faith.

How will the collaborators communicate and within what timeframe is communication expected? Scheduling regular check-in periods is key; whether managers are working with office mates or collaborators in a different time zone. Check-ins can happen through a variety of methods, but managers should establish ahead of time what topics need to be covered, how the check-in will happen and when it will happen.

7. Apply conflict resolution strategies if necessary.

Working with people is hard, and conflicts large and small can arise even within the best collaborations. Starting off on the right foot, with clear roles and jobs, as well as enough buy-in from the correct people and organisations, can help minimise the possibility of challenging conflicts. However, things rarely progress exactly as planned, and everyone handles stress differently. Learning to manage personal conflicts, as well as business-based conflicts of interest is a necessary skill when leading a collaboration. Beyond structural solutions, managers can mitigate personal conflicts through acknowledging the importance of the problem to the people involved and remaining calm throughout the process while working towards a mutually acceptable solution.

Coaching Suggestions

1. Review current collaborative project
2. Have coachee define existing networks and how they're used
3. Work on collaboration plan

Training Suggestions

1. Works well intra and inter-team
2. Have participants build network map
3. Build collaboration plan for specific project as a template

Challenge Level: 5 – Very Easy

Planning and working through a successful collaboration can be a relatively simple task, due to the face that almost all organisations encourage and are set up to facilitate collaboration. In fact, many businesses include the word "collaboration" as an overt organisational value.

The above said, the planning process is important, and if undertaken well will greatly enhance the chance of a collaboration delivering the expected outcomes.

3.7.

PROMOTE THE VISION

Overview

All organisations need a strong purpose and vision in order to clearly guide their work. Without a clearly-articulated and widely-understood vision statement, organisations often find themselves floundering under the weight of many unconnected projects, with managers moving in opposite and competing directions without clear goals. This can result in an organisation that resembles a cobweb full of delicate, disconnected lines with no central brain. A healthy organisation is more like an octopus, where all the limbs are working together in concert with a highly intelligent command centre. Organisational vision defines purpose not only for the company as a whole, but for the managers and teams who work to support that vision. Furthermore, a manager who can promote both the organisational vision, and articulate how their vision for their team aligns with that organisational vision has the best chance to success within an organisation that is working well, and help team members not only achieve greater productivity but job satisfaction in the process.

Setting the Scene

Managers have a great deal of power over the more abstract elements of their teams' day-to-day lives. They define the tone of the environment in which their team works. They oversee their team's day-to-day tasks, and in some cases they define what those tasks are. Perhaps most importantly, their vision of the team's work can guide the way the team interacts with customers, colleagues and the organisation as a whole. Many managers, however, were promoted to the role without any idea how to communicate that vision properly. They were promoted because of their ability to see the big picture, their work ethic or the value they added to their teams. Often, they have a clear idea of what changes would make their team more functional, or even a bird's-eye perspective of deeper organisational workings and how their team fits into the whole. If they can't share this vision, however, the team may be operating in the dark, and therefore not doing the best work possible. Finally, if the manager's vision for the team is not aligned with the organisational vision, teams will find their work at odds with the purposes of the larger organisation, which can lead to feelings of burnout and helplessness. Managers therefore need to be able to define and communicate organisational goals and align those goals clearly to their vision for the team.

Development Instructions

1. Understand the vision.

If their organisation already has a working vision statement, this is where managers should start. Compare this vision statement with other organisations' vision statements, especially if they are in the same industry. Which vision statement feels strongest? How could the vision statement be strengthened by the manager's work on a smaller scale? How well do their team's goals and processes align with the organisational vision?

Vision statements are designed to be overarching and all-encompassing: they do not describe the day-to-day or even the yearly activities of an organisation, but rather, its aspirational goals. Because vision statements can be so abstract, it is often helpful to break a vision statement down into component parts, in order to understand how the vision might apply in more practical ways.

2. Explain the vision.

Now that the vision statement has been broken down into component parts, it is time to define what that statement might mean for departments, teams and individuals. Map the vision statement onto KPIs and other deliverable actions. How do the actions of the team and the individual support the vision statement? How can the vision statement support a manager and their team?

Not every element of an organisation's business can be expressed in a vision statement, and nor should it be. However, vision statements can define tone and direction for an organisation which may help describe how certain work should be approached. For example, a shoe company may have a vision statement that highlights great customer service. This company would operate in a very different way from a company whose primary goal is to take over the shoe market. Consider how team actions can conform to the tone of the vision statement, and which actions may be implicitly condoned, while others are implicitly condemned.

3. Lead by example.

Before the manager has communicated the vision verbally, their actions need to align with the vision. Employees find it nearly impossible to follow and respect someone who expects their staff to behave one way while they ignore their own advice. In advance of communicating the vision to the team, the manager should analyse their own actions and make necessary changes so that they can lead by example.

4. Correct others where appropriate.

Many times, a realignment with the vision statement will result in a realignment of not only priorities but also behaviour that was previously acceptable and is now considered inappropriate. For example, at the shoe store whose vision includes great customer service, it might have been ok previously for employees to have limited knowledge about the stock or the way the shoe wears. Now, that behaviour may no longer be acceptable, because the goal is to help customers find the right shoes. Rather than getting angry with employees who exhibit problematic behaviours or exacting punitive measures, managers should keep in mind that the change is new, and focus on encouraging employees to think about the situation differently, rather than merely changing behaviour. It will be a lot easier for employees to change their behaviour if they understand why the change is necessary and why it's worth the extra work.

5. Connect vision with strategic goals.

The goals and KPIs of both individuals and teams should not only align with the company vision, but support the achievement of that vision. Managers can start this process by referencing the vision statement and any developments at the company level when setting KPIs with individual team members. For themselves, it may not be as easy: often, it can be easier for managers to see how another person's work should align with a vision statement than to see the changes they themselves need to make. A mentor or adviser can be key here. Having an outside perspective point out the ways in which their strategic goals are not supporting the vision can help managers do the same work for themselves that they do for their teams.

The strategic alignment process works best if it is instigated at the top levels of the company. Therefore, it is extremely important that top managers communicate the way in which major strategic goals align with the vision. Often, vision statements are abstract and broad to the point of vagueness. If interpretation is left up to individual managers, the company may not receive the support for the core vision it was expecting.

6. Incorporate vision in long and short-term planning.

Visions need to be broadcast widely, but casting a vision in stone will result in inflexibility and an out-of-touch attitude in the long term. Therefore, managers need to strike a balance between short-term and long-term planning in relation to the vision, and keep in mind that the vision will likely evolve over time. Leaving room in the plan for changes will allow the manager to increase their agility and move with the organisation, instead of resisting change. To start planning, managers should first consider the short-term goals that are clearly related to the vision and work outwards towards the long-term. If the vision is unusually specific, there may also be a specific long-term goal that will define the team's work (i.e. "Become the first profitable flying car company by 2035"), but most visions are sufficiently abstract to allow for a variety of possible futures.

7. Understand how day-to-day activities align with vision.

Some employees find that their KPIs are often completely irrelevant to their day-to-day activities. If this is the case, the first thing the manager needs to do is figure out why. Often, the source of the problem is that the employee's KPIs are aligned with the vision, but their daily activities never changed – they are still doing the same things and checking the correct boxes. While there are certainly some employees who are happy to show up to their job every day without a goal in mind, most often, this kind of situation leads to employees feeling that their jobs are pointless, it doesn't matter if they show up to work, and that this position is really just for the pay check. Realigning daily activities so that they actively support the organisational vision is not only good for managers who want to lead productive teams, it allows employees to contribute to the organisation in ways that they find meaningful.

Even if a role is menial, having an understanding of what it contributes to the larger picture of an organisation can keep employees from feeling like their job is pointless or even just dull. All employees should know how they fit into the organisation and why their role is necessary. A manager should be able to map every role to a necessary function for the organisation, and employees should always be able to articulate why their job is necessary.

Coaching Suggestions
1. Work with/create vision statement
2. Break down and define parts
3. Apply to strategic plan

Training Suggestions
1. Works well with peers at same level
2. Align vision with documents such as 90 day plans
3. Identify incongruences with the team and rectify or resolve

Challenge Level: 2 – Difficult
The ability to create, understand, communicate and enact a vision is a key component of leadership at both organisational and personal level.

There are specific methods and skills for creating and distilling a meaningful vision that will create huge motivation and relevance for all those in an organisation. Unfortunately these skills and methods are rarely taught and little understood. The right guidance here can make a significant impact on any organisation.

3.8.

DELIVER EFFECTIVE FEEDBACK

Overview

A manager who struggles to give feedback often thinks about feedback as a formal process that should happen when someone has done something wrong, or only in the context of a regularly scheduled review. If this is how all feedback is delivered, it's no wonder than giving feedback is terrifying. The best way to give feedback is consistently, regularly and informally, in addition to acting promptly when something is wrong and scheduling formal reviews for all employees. As long as a manager is acting on the assumption that everyone comes to work ready to "do their best" every single day, and everyone wants to succeed in their jobs and work well with others, the feedback is likely to come from a genuine place of kindness. If someone falls short, a major part of the manager's job is to ensure they are aware of the ways in which they have fallen short and provide the resources or help necessary for them to grow and improve.

Setting the Scene

According to management coach Erika Anderson, managers often find giving feedback even more difficult than firing people. Why is the feedback process so terrifying for so many people? This is probably because most people see feedback as an inherently negative process and are scared of living with the consequences if they get it wrong. In fact, the goal of feedback should always be to reinforce good behaviour and outcomes and helping someone avoid poor outcomes and problematic behaviour in the future. The net effect of both giving and receiving feedback should always be positive because it allows both the giver and receiver to move forward towards the future on more secure footing.

_____

66 We all need people who will give us feedback. That's how we improve.
Bill Gates

More than half of employees receive minimal feedback from their manager

How often do you receive feedback from your manager

Daily	7%
A few times a week	19%
A few times a month	27%
A few times a year	28%
Once a year or less	19%

Re-Engineering Performance Management
Gallup 2017

Development Instructions

1. Establish protocols for regular feedback.

If the organisation already has a framework for feedback, managers should both follow the framework and add opportunities for feedback as necessary. For example, the annual review might be an organisational requirement, and there may already be protocols in place for handling problematic behaviour. However, in this case, it is up to the manager's discretion how often they deliver casual feedback outside of these guidelines. Managers should make plans to fill gaps in the organisational protocols so that their employees receive sufficient feedback.

Team meetings are a great opportunity to give feedback. Team meetings can be ideal situations in which to give general feedback to a group, or to recognise outstanding contributions, either by an individual or a team. Meetings are not the place to deliver negative feedback to one person, or to deliver bad news that only affects a few people in the room.

One-on-one feedback can vary from formal sit-down performance reviews to quick emails or in-person chats to discuss an action and what went right or wrong. Using one-on-one sessions can be extremely helpful for detailed planning and sensitive feedback, but if a person did something that should be recognised, make sure that happens in front of the group if at all possible. Sometimes, a political situation makes it important to recognise someone's work in private, but more often than not, acknowledgement in front of the team is the better venue.

2. **Know what type of feedback is appropriate in what situation.**
If a manager needs to give feedback, they need to do it sooner rather than later. The more time a manager lets pass between an incident, positive or negative, and the criticism, the less impactful (and potentially more damaging) that criticism can be. No one wants to know they offended someone six months later. If a manager is looking for the right time to give feedback and it never seems to arrive, the time is now.

At the same time, blurting out criticism without considering the emotional consequences or situation can backfire badly. Use interpersonal skills to determine a time when everyone is calm and the recipient of the feedback can be approached in private.

If a manager needs to deliver negative feedback, they should be clear about that. Giving unclear or fuzzy messages can leave team members in the dark about what went wrong or even thinking that nothing is wrong and the feedback was positive if the tone and content isn't clear. Managers should aim not be the stereotypical Hollywood producer who tells an emerging talent "We'll be in touch" with no intention to follow through.

3. **Understand appropriate environment for messaging.**
Casual feedback can happen in a variety of environments. Short words of praise or a quick correction can happen immediately, as the job is being done in many cases. However, for delivering feedback that requires more than five words, and especially negative or emotional feedback, managers should ensure that there's a private space to speak where there will be no interruptions.

If serious feedback needs to be given, the environment probably shouldn't be a casual coffee outing. Similarly, if the feedback is positive, delivering it in a closed conference room with no one else present undermines the celebratory message. Match the environment to the message.

4. **Display ability to structure feedback appropriately.**
Managers should prepare for delicate conversations with the same attention that they would use to prepare for presentations. As with presentations, feedback conversations must take the potential emotional impacts on the audience into account. Unlike presentations, however, feedback conversations work best when managers allow for significant flexibility.

Managers should resist the urge to overexplain. If someone is receiving negative feedback, a clear, consistent and kind message works best.

Keeping wordiness to a minimum makes it more likely that the recipient will be able to hear what is being said. The more words used, the harder emotional information can be to process.

5. Undertake constructive feedback process.

Constructive feedback gives the recipient hints as to how they can fix the problem. It doesn't criticise the person: rather, it criticises the action. For example, "Your presentation last week wasn't focused and lacked enthusiasm" is constructive; "You are a bad presenter" is not.

Feedback should be taken with grace and respect. Debate and argument only distracts from feedback, which is why many groups decide to institute rules about who can talk when and about what during feedback sessions. While it can sometimes be hard to hear, feedback givers significantly minimise the chance for argument if they present their points with evidence, keep feedback specific rather than general and criticise the action, not the person.

6. Deal with reactions to feedback.

Reactions to feedback can be varied and occasionally unpredictable. Remembering that feedback is often emotional can help managers better understand various reactions. Even if the feedback is business related, team members will sometimes feel that their egos are on the line, so it is important to reassure them that it is the action being criticised, and not the person. Rehearse various scenarios in order to plan responses, even if things don't go as well as planned.

How can a manager plan for reactions? Through empathy, it becomes easier to understand what the other person might be experiencing. Even if the manager has never experienced this particular issue, it's possible for the manager to predict how a recipient might be feeling. Work with managers to encourage empathetic and active listening and body language while giving feedback, to ensure the best possible chance that the feedback is heard, understood and followed.

7. Display ability to deliver 360 degree feedback.

Feedback shouldn't just come from managers to subordinates. Managers also need to be able to accept upward feedback from the people who report to them, and from superiors who monitor their work. Accepting feedback relies on the same skills as giving feedback, and again, it doesn't always need to be a formalised discussion to be effective.

However, it is important to recognised the differences between giving feedback to subordinates and giving feedback to anyone else. In a boss-employee relationship, the hierarchy is clear and well delineated, giving the boss some leeway to jump in with direct feedback and get to the point quickly. Upward and sideways feedback can be a bit trickier. A great way to determine if someone would be open to feedback, or is in a position to hear that feedback, is to ask the person directly if it's a good time for some feedback. The tone also must be different between a manager and a superior or a colleague, and a manager and a subordinate. When giving feedback to someone who does not work for them, the manager must become more friendly and less teacherly, if they want feedback to be received well. Practising various ways to delivering feedback depending on the audience can help managers define how they give feedback and when.

Coaching Suggestions
1. Role play scenarios – use live situations as examples
2. Work on most difficult conversations
3. Watch for mixed messaging

Training Suggestions
1. Skills practise opporutnity
2. Have pariticpants create scenarios based upon experience
3. Weight training time to more difficult challenges

Challenge Level: 1 – Very Difficult
Many workplace human resources challenges emanate from feedback that has been given inappropriately or is poorly understood. Even more people issues arise from the simple avoidance of giving feedback at all for fear of offending the recipient.

Managers in all industries find this type of conversation among the most challenging.

The key to giving excellent feedback is to create a strong structure and gift managers with excellent skills to remove the fear factor from giving and receiving constructive feedback.

3.9.

BUILD PERSONAL BRAND

Overview

Personal branding has become increasingly important in modern workplaces as more interaction takes place online and reputation becomes important in professions where it previously was not a concern, simply because of how many options there are out there. Creating a strong personal brand can benefit managers in any profession, but especially those whose roles are more forward-facing: where interaction with clients, the ability to recruit new clients, or the ability to represent the team or the organisation is key to achieving their goals. Knowing how to brand oneself will allow a manager to move within the business world with more ease, regardless of the exact requirements of their role.

> **"** All of us need to understand the importance of branding. We are CEOs of our own companies: Me Inc. To be in business today, our most important job is to be head marketer for the brand called You.
>
> Tom Peters in Fast Company

Setting the Scene

What do people think of when they hear a brand name? Usually, the idea sparked by a name isn't very complicated. Some brands exude "cool" or "high tech." Others inspire visions of "dependability" and "tradition". Regardless of the brand, well-known labels can often be summed up in only a couple of key words. Usually, the people working for that company or who know the company more deeply see more than those key words, but generally, the brand represents something very specific if it is so recognisable. Personal brand works the same way. Personal brand is the image a manager portrays within their work environment, and how they are perceived by collaborators and stakeholders in a business context.

Development Instructions

1. Create personal vision.

Personal branding can feel complicated because people are complicated. We can't distil a person down to a few key words the way we can a brand. Therefore, instead of trying to create a personal brand that encompasses all of who they are, managers should look at what they want to be known for. What qualities do they wish to project in their business life?

A personal vision is the first stepping stone to a personal brand. Managers can create a vision of who they are in the business world, summed up with a few sentences. These sentences could include their aspirations, their personality, their skills or even a description of their job. How does who they are now potentially serve their future ideal self? From there, it can be helpful to look at the personal visions of others. What do they want to draw on? What would they rather leave behind?

2. Articulate personal brand goals.

What does the manager hope to achieve through personal branding? Will it make their work life easier? Are they hoping to bump themselves to the next level? Do they want to make more connections outside of their industry? Depending on their goals, the manager may want to highlight certain aspects of their personality or work life over others in their personal branding mission.

Starting with a vague goal is fine, but once managers begin to invest either time or money in personal branding, their goals need to become more specific and concrete. Work with managers to make their goals measurable and achievable. Goals can include everything from timelines to the number of contacts to increased digital presence as measured by followers.

3. Create personal brand actions.

The next step towards better personal branding is to create an action plan. Managers need to know what steps they will take to achieve their goals. Without an action plan, a goal like, "Gain a following of 1000 or more on LinkedIn" becomes unactionable. A good plan will start with smaller actions the manager can take in order to achieve those goals, with evidence-based research to back up their choices.

Depending on the manager's institution, goals and industry, different types of branding may be necessary. A publicly visible person (like someone in PR) needs to consider their clothes, whereas someone like a journalist who expresses themselves exclusively through writing will need to focus more on written branding opportunities. Define the parameters within which branding will take place, and focus within those lines, to avoid getting distracted.

4. Align personal brand to organisational brand.

A manager on a personal branding mission always needs to consider the ways their organisation must influence their brand. At the top levels of major corporations (as well as well-known government agencies), personal brands must be deeply aligned with the organisational brand in order for the manager to be able to do their job well. Lower level employees and people working for smaller companies may have more leeway in this area. However, considering organisational brand when fostering a personal brand is always important, because an employee's workplace defines so much of their work life.

Plan to map out all the ways in which a manager's brand intersects with their organisation's brand. In addition to industry alignment, why is the manager a good fit for this particular organisation? Managers may find that they are better equipped to handle their jobs after a personal branding endeavour, because they can more clearly see the ways in which they work well with their organisation, and what they bring to the table.

5. Consistently display valued behaviours.

Anyone who wants to successfully brand themselves must align their behaviour with their brand. For example, someone who wants to be known for their interest in environmentalism, driving a gas-guzzling car probably isn't the best look. Any behaviour that directly contradicts the brand should be avoided, but it's hard to stay "on brand" at all times. Plan to prioritise behavioural goals based on impact, rather than trying to be perfect.

Prioritise brand-based behaviour changes based on visibility. While it would be great if we could all be our best selves at all time, and hypocritical behaviour is never desirable, managers should focus on changing the most obvious contradictions first to improve their appearance of authenticity and cohesiveness. Someone who is a great leader but a poor public speaker should focus on their public speaking skills before altering their clothing.

6. Articulate brand voice.

Voice is the unique way in which individuals express themselves. Voice can be what we produce with our vocal cords, but it can also encompass everything from our writing to our art to the way we physically carry ourselves. Help managers consider which parts of their voice are currently working for their intended brand, and which parts need better brand alignment. Sometimes, a person's writing and speaking voices can seem extremely different – work to bring all voices together under one brand, even if there's a little variation in tone and texture.

7. Manage social media effectively.

Not all managers need great social media management to improve their personal branding, but our world is now so deeply plugged in to digital presence, it's hard to do personal branding without some attention to social media. Start big and then move progressively smaller. What comes up in a Google search? What platforms does the manager currently use? What platforms should they use more? Finally, consider any ways in which they should pull back social media involvement. For example, a manager who works for a government agency that is supposed to stay politically neutral probably shouldn't have any web presence denoting political affiliation.

When looking more deeply at social media profiles, analyse what parts of the brand are already visible and which are absent. Often, people have been online for so long that there can be a lot of extra noise for someone who has been quite active, and the goal is to pare down profiles and posts to match current branding goals. Other times, people have signed up for platforms, used them for a few months, and then all but forgotten about them. Update the basics first, like profile pictures and summaries, and then consider the other ways in which social media presence can support personal brand, using the same voice used for other business writing.

Coaching Suggestions

1. Start with "big picture"
2. Ensure coachee can articulate what they want their brand to look like
3. Have coachee develop specific actions relevant to brand goals

Training Suggestions

1. Start with well-known identities as examples
2. Ensure personal brand goals are aligned with organisational values
3. If comfortable, analyse a participant's social media presence

Challenge Level: 2 – Difficult

We all have a personal brand, but few of us actually know what it is. How we are perceived is influenced by how we present ourselves in the world, but is ultimately determined by others.

Work on improving and/or maintaining one's own reputation in and outside of the workplace should be constant and outcomes-driven, but can be very challenging to do without the "one-removed" perspective of a trusted consultant or mentor.

3.10.

ALIGN GOALS

Overview

Goal-setting and alignment is not just an activity for top-level management. Without clear alignment and goal-setting on a team level, it can be difficult to motivate a team well: either their work doesn't support the organisational vision, or it is not being done in the most efficient way, costing team members time and energy. Therefore, team members need to be just as invested and included in goal alignment as their managers. Because goal-setting can alter daily tasks and processes, it is also necessary to involve stakeholders who may be impacted on all sides. This can include those people who are laterally affected within the organisation, as well as outside stakeholders who will need to know the ways in which basic work strategy is going to change. Therefore, communication to achieve buy-in is essential, not only within the team and upper management, but with anyone impacted at the organisation.

Setting the Scene

As we've noted before, a well-aligned organisation works like an octopus, all limbs operating in concert to serve a central purpose. But perhaps the better metaphor for the ways in which goals can be aligned in the first place isn't from the animal kingdom, but from the construction world. When building a house, "alignment" literally means the ways in which things fit together and support one another. A wall that is off-kilter won't support a roof properly; a window that isn't installed properly will let the elements in, which can damage the house long-term. Sure, the structure might stay standing for a while, but it isn't built to last forever. For some businesses, a short fast burn is ok, but most companies want to stick around as long as possible. If each department's or team's goals aren't aligned, the walls of the house are stressed by the wait and will eventually collapse; the floor will eventually rot from the damp let in by the poorly-done windows. Aligning goals not only keeps an organisation healthy for longer, it allows the entire business to function at a higher level. Align goals both within the organisation, as well as with outside stakeholders for the best chance of success.

---

66 When in doubt, check if your actions are aligned with your purpose.
Azim Jamal & Brian Tracy, *What You Seek Is Seeking You*

Development Instructions

1. Understand organisational vision.
To effectively align goals, it's important to have a deeper understanding of those goals at the top level. Organisational vision, while often more abstract than the everyday goals managers handle, informs how all of the parts of the organisation work together. Therefore, managers need to align their team's goals with the organisational vision before attempting any sort of collaboration with outside stakeholders. It is vital to the success of a project that it fits within the organisational vision, because if not, the manager will essentially find themselves fighting against their own organisation. Furthermore, having to stop a project before it even gets off the ground can damage personal brand.

2. Collaboratively workshop strategic goals.
Aligning goals, at its core, is about collaboration. Keeping in mind that all participants are individuals with their own ideas, experiences and skillsets, it's important for managers to take the ideas of their subordinates into account when aligning goals. The subordinates may actually have a better idea of how work runs on a daily basis than the manager does, which makes them better candidates to help align small picture tasks with larger goals.

After initial discussions, give managers the opportunity to check in regularly to ensure goals and tasks are still aligned. It can be easy for team members to slip back into familiar patterns because it is easier in the short term. Making the "lazy option" the correct option can help everyone stay aligned and on task.

3. Create specific, measurable goals.

A common reason why goals aren't achieved is that there was never any clarity around what goal achievement actually looked like. Create measurable (either qualitative or quantitative) benchmarks to ensure that goals are actually achievable, and to help with the process of developing a plan for achieving goals.

When developing a plan for achieving goals, managers can guide their teams through step-by-step outlines, or simply create outlines for benchmarks that must be achieved on the way to meeting the major goal. Either approach can work in the right circumstances, but confused teams may benefit more from a fully-planned-out approach that lets them know what they have to do when, and why.

4. Deal with multiple inputs.

A key way to encourage team member buy-in is to take team members' perspectives, experiences, and opinions into account during the goal setting and alignment process. Team members often have great value to contribute, and while incorporating their ideas takes time, it can also generate more commitment to the goals once established.

If one person is contributing many ideas, it can be hard for multiple people to chime in. Encourage everyone to contribute at least one idea, and if someone has been so vocal that it suppresses other voices, ask them to take a step back in order to encourage teamwork and give the others a chance who might be slower to come up with ideas.

There is such a thing as too much of a good thing, and opinions can become overwhelming if not managed properly. Managers can try to divide opinions and ideas into more general categories that everyone can agree on. Rather than looking for consensus, managers should aim for a give-and-take between the various parties. If one person isn't a fan of a certain goal, make sure there is at least one goal they do like.

5. Obtain buy-in.

Once goals have been established, they should be written down, along with the ways in which they align with the vision of the organisation, and turned into a professional-looking document that can be circulated among relevant stakeholders. What this document looks like will depend on the team, organisation and industry, as well as the intent of the goal-setting process. However, the most important part of any document is clarity. Anyone who reads these goals should understand what they mean.

If necessary, enlist help in communicating goals to necessary stakeholders. If clients need to know, the communication help required will likely be very different from the communication assistance needed to inform upper management appropriately. Again, all communication should keep the audience in mind, and avoid overcommunicating and diluting the message.

6. Understand lateral impacts.

If the goal setting and alignment process is likely to impact additional departments, it's important to communicate those impacts early and often. For example, if the Accounting department decides to change the way they structure invoicing procedures, the Sales department will need to know this immediately. Accounting may not know immediately that their goal-setting process will lead to a restructured invoicing process, but if their goal becomes "increase paperwork efficiency," this would be a good time to give Sales a heads up about potential impact, not the day the invoicing process changes. Get ahead of the game, and avoid backlash from departments that haven't gone through a goal alignment.

7. Create downstream actions.

Goal setting and realignment within one team or one department can have impacts that reverberate throughout the organisation. Good communication is one way to ensure that the department's positive actions don't negatively impact the rest of the organisation. Another important part of goal setting, however, is to actively drive actions downstream. Helping other affected parties adjust to positive changes is an important part in making sure those positive changes stick. If a manager's team's actions make their team more efficient, but cause havoc in the rest of the organisation, no one wins.

Communicate the "why" of changes, not just the "what". It's unlikely other employees will accept changes that make their work more difficult in the short term unless they know they are doing it for a good reason.

Finally, don't leave anyone impacted by the change out in the cold. Communication is an ongoing endeavour, and there should be processes in place for all affected parties to provide feedback at regular intervals. Avoid a build-up of resentment by keeping everyone informed of developments and the feedback procedures easy and transparent.

Coaching Suggestions
1. Ensure coachee understands organisational vision and higher level goals
2. What goals have been set in the past? Have they been achieved?
3. Coachee to provide collaboration approach for refinement

Training Suggestions
1. Start with vision statement – is it understood?
2. Make sure vision, goals, actions are each clearly defined before commencing work
3. Participants to explain how each goal can be easily measured

Challenge Level: 2 – Difficult
Goal setting in itself can often be a poorly understood discipline, so it's perhaps no surprise that to then align goals across teams and functions is not a simple undertaking.

The key to success in this regard is to apply strong structure and communication across all stakeholders, all the while keeping the overarching purpose of the process front of mind.

This discipline, if mastered, is a key trait of very senior leaders.

4

EXTERNAL RELATIONSHIPS

INTRODUCTION

All organisations must manage external relationships, no matter the industry. At the end of the day, business is about relationships among people, but those people can take on a variety of forms. Managing relationships with clients is different from managing relationships with suppliers, which is also different from handling collaborations or competition with other businesses. Even within these relationships, there is a lot of opportunity for variation and optimisation. But for some businesses, corporate policy can make it difficult to create nuanced understandings of individual relationships, instead forcing everyone in the "customer" category into a one-size-fits-all approach. Instead of seeing all relationships in the same category in the same way, managers should specifically seek to individualise the people they work with. We are all human, and it helps if someone treats us like that is true.

Managing external relationships encompasses a wide variety of tasks and skills, some of which are directed outward, like customer focus and client communication. Many, however, are focused on the relationship between the business and outsiders, like managing suppliers and building trust. In all cases, certain skills, like creating influence or managing tenders are easy to teach as a discrete skillset; others require more maintenance and practise, or a complete overhaul in the way a manager thinks about a problem in the first place. Perspective shift is necessary in dealing with external relationships: it is often the only way to create the necessary empathy to engage with outsiders in a meaningful way.

The most important thing for managers to remember when dealing with external relationships is that they are always in a relationship with someone, which means there is somebody else who is also managing that relationship. In a supplier-business relationship, one business is managing a client and the other is managing a supplier. Both have a vested interest in making the relationship work, and work well. Many organisations end up accidentally torpedoing their relationships with outsiders by remaining too focused on themselves or the other party, and not focused enough on maintaining the relationship between the two.

Red Flags to Look For

Indicators that a manager or an organisation might be struggling:

- **Employees can't say exactly how their work impacts the customer or the client.** This could be a sign that the organisation is not focused on the customer's needs anymore (Demonstrate Customer Focus 4.1). It could also indicate a more surface level problem, in that the manager is simply not communicating well enough with clients (Manage Client Communications 4.6) and their team has followed suit.

- **Supplier relationships are often problematic and heavily contract based.** This could be a sign that suppliers are being managed in a transactional instead of relationship-based way (Manage Suppliers 4.2). If this is a problem that extends beyond suppliers (Deal with Challenging Clients 4.3), and the manager's relationships with outsiders are generally fairly fraught, it could be a trust issue (Build Trust 4.10).

- **Their bids, proposals, and tenders are rarely or never accepted.** Sometimes, this is an issue of skill and following directions – the manager may not have mastered the skill of the application just yet (Manage Bids, Proposals, and Tenders 4.4). However, it could also indicate that the manager has trouble fitting change into their schedule (Display Adaptability 4.9) or that their methods of dealing with clients have led to less-than-positive reviews in the past (Provide Service and Manage Client Relationships 4.5).

- **Clients are constantly getting in touch to check on the status of a project.** Managers should be getting out in front of all client communication (Manage Client Communications 4.6). If clients feel the need to check up on a manager's work properly, they may not be handling external projects with the same degree of transparency of an internal project (Manage Client Projects 4.7). In certain cases, it could also be an issue of managers being reluctant to exert influence effectively (Influence Relationships 4.8).

Preparation

When you start developing talent, it is important to assess where everyone is starting from. What problems and challenges do managers with excellent business understanding exhibit? What skills do they have that can be better utilised? The questions below can help you assess where an employee may experience problems as they move into leadership roles.

Negative attitude	Extremely	Very	Moderately	Slightly	Not At All
1. Sees business relationships as transactional.					
2. Behaves inconsistently with outsiders.					
3. Avoids interacting with clients whenever possible.					
4. Submits problematic proposals and tenders.					
5. The customer is not the focus of their work.					
6. Is inflexible and rigid in their interactions with outsiders.					
7. Seems generally out of the loop when dealing with suppliers or customers.					

Motivating Drivers

Everyone is motivated differently and understanding yourself is the first step towards understanding others. When a leader knows their own motivations, they are then able to explore the individual motivational drivers for each person on the team. This knowledge can completely change how team leaders interact with their teams and drive team success, so this is where we start.

Each motivational driver comes with its own set of "triggers" – concrete ways to jump-start motivation for someone with that driver. Below, we discuss the four main drivers.

People person: A "people person" enjoys dealing with external relationships because of the pleasure of interacting with others. These people consider their conversations and meetings to be the best parts of their business days, and they deeply enjoy this part of their jobs. They tend to be friendly, easy to work with and extremely well connected. However, they can also have a hard time sticking to timelines and often annoy utilitarians, who would rather minimise interaction in favour of efficiency.

Utilitarian: People who approach external relationships from a utilitarian perspective see most of their interactions as a means to an end: the personal interaction just happens to be the most effective way of doing business. At best, these people come across as trustworthy, competent and highly efficient, but they can risk seeming cold, manipulative and transactional in their relationships with others, potentially ruining the "utility" of their calculated approach.

Better together: People who view external relationships as mutually beneficial for all parties believe that what we build together will be better than what we can create apart. These people tend to have an easy time keeping the big picture in mind and are often excellent at treating their business relationships as relationships rather than transactions. However, they tend to get annoyed with people who don't like collaboration or resist transparency.

Problem solver: Problem solvers see external relationships as interesting puzzles to be solved in a way that works well for everyone. The process of working on the relationship is often what is most interesting for them, making them ideally suited to managing problematic clients or suppliers. However, they may get bored if the only goal is relationship maintenance, rather than strategising for relationship improvement.

4.1.

DEMONSTRATE CUSTOMER FOCUS

Overview

It can be all too easy for businesses to lose their customer focus in the day-to-day minutiae of organisational life. Too often customers, without whom most businesses could not exist, take a backseat to shareholders, business partners or even the inner workings of the organisational machinery. All of us have been through miserable customer service experiences, and yet when we are on the business side, we rarely connect those experiences with our work. What makes for a great customer experience or for a terrible one? The answer is deeply important to any kind of long-term success. All businesses have an end user to whom they attempt to provide goods and services. Without customers, the organisation's business model is not sustainable.

Setting the Scene

Scandinavian design is incredibly popular around the world for a reason. From mass market IKEA furniture to upscale interior stores and architecture firms, and even low-end shops marketing cozy socks with the word "hygge," Scandinavian design influence seems to be everywhere. Why? What is so special about "scandi" design, and why do people like it so much?

Scandinavian design's popularity isn't an accident, and it's a good way to understand the power of customer focus. Scandinavian design as we know it today developed during the economic downturn of the 1930s, when people could no longer afford to purchase the heavy, ornate pieces that characterized design during the 19th and early 20th centuries. Functional design became very popular: instead of trying to force people to use a space in a particular way, Scandinavian design works around the way people already use their spaces. The focus on "natural" use of space drives "natural," graceful and simple design that blends in with the environment. Additionally, the Scandinavian countries (Norway, Sweden, and Denmark) experience huge variations in light throughout the year: paying attention to the mood, atmosphere and comfort of a space becomes essential when you can't rely on a regular dose of sunlight. Good aesthetics aren't considered a luxury in these places – they are a human right. It turns out, however, that even those of us with access to year-round sun appreciate affordable, attractive, useful comfortable spaces designed with our needs in mind. Scandinavian design is a great example of customer focus: the ability to orient business activities with customer experience and outcomes at the forefront.

Development Instructions

1. Understand strategic importance of customers.

The first step to understanding how customers are currently being treated by an organisation is to look at the organisation's strategic plan. Where do customers currently sit? How important are they in relation to currently stated organisational goals? Are there any customer goals that are overtly stated? Are there any obvious measures that are missing? Comb through organisational strategic plans to identify missing information and clarify strategic goals in relation to their impact on customer experience and outcomes.

2. Define who customers are (and aren't).

Who are the target customers? What is the target market? Why was this particular demographic chosen? Looking at why customers are customers in the first place can help an organisation better meet those customers' needs.

Even if the organisation is not a traditional for-profit business (for example, an NGO or a government organisation), understanding customer focus is important. In a non-profit organisation, for example, target customers may be two distinct groups: donors and clients. Mapping out the needs of each of those groups to find overlap (or lack thereof) can be useful for streamlining business and avoiding unnecessary work. Help managers work through non-traditional customer arrangements and manage customer needs, even if the business doesn't fit the for-profit model.

What does the ideal customer look like? While a business will likely serve more people than just one idealised type, knowing the exact audience will help managers reach the right people in the right way more quickly. Use those ideal characteristics to determine where to focus marketing and customer service energy.

The 80/20 rule says that 20% of a manager's work is likely adding 80% of their value. This is true of customers as well. Is the business focusing on the 80% of the customers adding only 20% of the value, or has the company honed in on the core 20% of customers? Could the company drop business areas because they simply are not as productive as the core business? Furthermore, are there customers who are taking up too much time for the small return they are generating? Learning which customers to drop is just as important as knowing the customers to attract. Show managers how to prune the customer base so that they can focus on the customers who truly add value.

3. Articulate the value-add for customers.

How does the business add value to customers' lives? Sometimes, it turns out that what customers find most valuable about a business is not what the business thought they were providing. For example, swipe-based picture-only dating apps were originally marketed for people seeking casual relationships only, until it turned out that customers were just trying to meet new people quickly, without being "matched" by an algorithm, regardless of the type of connection they wanted. Help managers learn techniques to answer this question, and ways to increase the business' added value, based on what they learn.

4. Assist customers to navigate the organisation.

What does customer contact with the organisation look like? Create a roadmap to help visualise the ways in which customers interact with the organisation.

Creating a roadmap will not only provide an overview of the entire customer experience, it will show where there are gaps in service, overlapping service or places of stagnation or confusion. These will almost always be experienced by customers as pain points. For example, an airline with an unclear reimbursement policy for delayed flights can not only create pain for customers, it can cost the organisation a significant amount of money. Calculating pain points may seem like a benefit only for customers, but at the end of the day, when business runs more smoothly, employees are able to do their jobs more efficiently as well.

What makes the business stand out from competitors on the customer side? Do people appreciate low prices, convenience or better customer service? Many business models rely on making guesses about what they think customers want without actually bothering to do the research. When a bank in Canada finally surveyed its customers, it found that its assumptions about what would help it compete were completely off – customers didn't want more ATMs, they wanted more personal service. Guide managers through the process of researching customer needs and meeting those needs without making assumptions based on what everyone else in the domain is doing.

5. Understand the customer need.

Let's say a business' ideal customer is a female resident of Sydney in her early 40s. She owns a house in the suburbs and has an office job. She also likes to play sports and is a dog owner. If the customer profile is that specific, it is probably important to go out and profile actual customers – in all likelihood, very few of them will meet that exact description. Creating a composite customer profile based on real data from the best customers can help businesses find the new demographics where they could expand. Perhaps the product actually appeals to all Australian suburban dog owners, but the business has been marketing too specifically.

6. Understand and activate dispute resolution process.

Handling bad experiences comes with the territory of being a customer-oriented business. Adages like "the customer is always right" may help businesses stay customer focused during a complaint or a dispute, but it doesn't help them resolve the problem.

In order to solve a problem, a manager first has to know what the problem is. What complaints has the manager received from customers? At what point does the business commonly see customer disputes arising? Identifying these issues can be especially helpful in conjunction with the customer roadmap – when those disputes and complaints coincide with pain points, the solution is often clear. Developing clear models for managing a dispute with a customer and coming to a mutually acceptable resolution can help.

When a customer has a bad experience, what is the first point of contact? Is this model designed to work best for the customer, or for the business?

Create complaint and dispute roadmaps to understand the customer experience when something goes wrong. These roadmaps can provide deep lessons about how the business is operating, and ensure that the business remains customer focused, even when things do not go as hoped.

7. Leverage customer loyalty.

How does the business reward customer loyalty? Are there existing loyalty programs, and do they reward loyalty from the right kinds of customers? Not every loyalty program has to look like airline mileage and status programs; some highly effective loyalty programs simply consist of lists of high-priority customers who receive special attention. Discuss the various ways to encourage and recognise customer loyalty, and workshop models that might work well for the organisation.

Calculating the lifetime value of a great customer could tell you how much the organisation should invest in ensuring that customer's loyalty. If a great customer potentially brings in millions more than an average customer, isn't it worth spending a little more time, energy and money ensuring that customer returns to the business? Managers should try to balance cost savings with promoting customer loyalty by measuring the possible lifetime value of a customer against any potential costs of keeping that customer on board.

8. Measure customer satisfaction.

The first step to measuring customer satisfaction is defining what it is. What areas of the customer experience are important to measure? Again, returning to the customer for data will be extremely important here: don't be that bank that measured customer satisfaction based on metrics that customers didn't care about.

Decide which methods of measuring customer satisfaction, both formally and informally, quantitatively and qualitatively, would best suit the organisation. Understanding these different types of metrics and when to bring in an expert can help managers avoid spending unnecessary time and energy on measurements that won't provide useful information.

Sometimes, measurements of customer satisfaction can provide unexpected results. Encourage managers to line up data on customer satisfaction with the organisational roadmap in order to find pain points and possible solutions.

Coaching Suggestions

1. Have coachee articulate customer value proposition
2. Review log of happy and unhappy customers
3. Generate plans to improve customer satisfaction

Training Suggestions

1. Start with organisational strategy and goals
2. Have participants bring live complaints to work with
3. Review current customer sat measure – actions to improve

Challenge Level: 2 – Difficult

For any business, customers are the core of success. But demonstrating true customer focus is not simple. Many organisations become trapped in motherhood statements, telling themselves around the boardroom table that they're a truly customer-centric organisation, but not understanding the processes and steps necessary to achieve true customer loyalty.

A thorough top-down review of all customer systems and processes, plus a system of embedding desirable behaviours throughout all customer-facing team members can assist greatly to avoid blind spots and complacency.

4.2.

MANAGE SUPPLIERS

Overview

Developing strong supplier relationships doesn't just make the process of doing business easier – it can support a company's mid-term and long-term goals by grooming the supplier for future success. The more effort a company puts into supplier relationships in the short term, the more benefits it will reap in the long term. For example, if an airplane manufacturer needs a specific kind of computer chip for a new navigation system, they likely have many options to choose from. A large supplier may be able to provide the chip more quickly, but may be less flexible in the services they provide. A smaller company may take more time to create the chip, but because they are more agile, they could tailor the chip and their services to exactly what the airplane manufacturer needs. In the long term, building up the smaller supplier's ability to provide the service may be in the best interest of the airplane manufacturer because they can get exactly what they need reliably, and create a stronger supplier in the interim than they would be able to find with a larger company.

This doesn't mean that supplier relationships should always be lopsided in terms of company size or power. Some suppliers may also be competitors, or equals operating in another industry. In all cases, treating suppliers with keiretsu in mind can help employers improve and deepen their relationships with companies that would otherwise only be seen as direct competitors or strategic allies. With loyalty and trust, suppliers can become essential partners in business, rather than another obstacle to overcome.

Setting the Scene

There are very few companies that do not need to interact regularly with suppliers in order to do their daily business. Large companies tend to have the most extensive supply chains, but this does not always mean they have the best supplier relationships. The Japanese concept of keiretsu, or, informal and deeply connected businesses networks or interlocking systems, can be helpful for companies looking to build better supplier relationships. Organisations that approach supplier relationships from a confrontational perspective risk alienating possible partners in their pursuit of market domination. Thinking about their relationships as being meaningful and mutually beneficial can help companies learn along with their suppliers and ultimately create a better product or service that allows both companies to grow.

Development Instructions
1. Identify key suppliers and their role.
Certain types of supplier relationships are more appropriate for building deeper bonds than others. The nature of the business will have an impact on what kind of relationship should be pursued with each supplier. It can be helpful for managers to first rank suppliers in terms of how critical their product or service is to the organisation's functioning.

Once the level of involvement of a supplier with the organisation has been determined, managers can look at the exact role of the supplier in the supply chain. Does the supplier contribute in an essential way to ensuring the end product is viable? Or do they contribute to the running of the business? Both types of suppliers are important, but the stakes may be different for each. A consultant brought in to fix a management issue will likely have a very different type of relationship with the organisation than the supplier that provides the raw materials for the product.

Understanding why each supplier is critical to the organisation can help managers asses the type of relationship that should be pursued as well. A truly collaborative supply chain will benefit all parties involved, but this only works if everyone is on the same page. Would the supplier in question agree with why the organisation believes they are critical? Understand any discrepancies in perception before trying to improve relationships.

2. View supplier as more than a vendor.
A vendor is someone who sells something to the organisation for a specific purpose – this might be a caterer for an event or a one-time purchase for a specific project. In these cases, a single contract is enough to cover the specifics of the relationship, though the organisation may come back to the

vendor in the future. Relationships with suppliers that provide critical services regularly should not be so transactional. While the traditional Western view of supply chains is to treat suppliers like vendors, relationship management results in more loyalty and trust, and therefore, higher quality business.

Consider how the organisation currently views suppliers. Are integral suppliers treated more like vendors, despite their importance to the organisation's functioning? Who handles those relationships? How is supplier loyalty ensured? Do employees and managers generally find dealing with suppliers stressful? These questions can help managers determine if they need to shift to a more relationship-minded approach when dealing with suppliers.

3. Manage supplier relationships effectively.
The logistics of supplier relationship management are important for making business easy for everyone. Multiple points of contact can be confusing for everyone involved, so designate a clear contact point (whether this is a person or a group of people) so that the company can prioritise human relationships.

The German word *Ansprechpartner* literally means "contact person" in English, but the meaning of the word encompasses more than that. An *Ansprechpartner* acts as an organisational guide to outsiders, helping them navigate the (often extremely complicated) inner workings and politics of German bureaucracy. This is a relationship that many German companies take very seriously, and many people consider their *Ansprechpartner* contacts at other companies to be somewhere between a colleague and a friend, not just their contact at that particular organisation. Allowing these relationships to develop eases the process of doing business with outsiders, because those outsiders can become privy to the relevant inner workings of the company without compromising company secrets. This allows suppliers to better anticipate company needs and interact with companies more appropriately based on their internal knowledge.

4. Maximise purchase spend.
How much is the company currently spending on suppliers? Are supplier relationships disjointed and duplicating work? Managers should look for opportunities to increase value per supplier by examining exactly why each supplier has been retained for a particular service or product.

Consider asking suppliers what else they have to offer the company. For example, a supplier may be excellent at providing value in an untapped area, but the company is currently using their services for something completely different. The supplier knows their product best, and will likely have ideas for how it can be used more efficiently.

Sometimes, a supplier's offerings simply aren't the best value proposition for a company. This can happen because of a shift in the company's business, or because the supplier was hired before the company was able to truly assess its needs or the other options on the market. In this case, it's important to move towards better options sooner rather than later. Keeping a supplier that doesn't offer the company added value for reasons of loyalty only is always a poor choice.

5. Implement effective supplier agreements.

A supplier agreement can be tricky to produce when it isn't clear how long the organisations will be collaborating, or how the relationship might change over time. Avoid agreements that are both too confining or too open-ended, and always keep the relationship at the forefront when constructing agreements. Managers can review their organisation's current agreements for both tone and content to get a picture of how the organisation has dealt with suppliers. If either the tone or content feel problematic, or don't match the relationship that the organisation actually has with suppliers, it is likely time for an update.

6. Manage supply chain risks.

"There's nothing certain but death and taxes," said Benjamin Franklin, and this is true in business as well. No matter how good the agreement or how strong the relationship, sometimes suppliers fall through. Businesses striving for success should keep an index of critical suppliers and contingency plans in case things go off the rails at a particularly bad moment.

Business continuity planning is especially important when dealing with suppliers. If the main contact person for a supplier suddenly became unavailable, who has the knowledge to pick up that relationship? How can a company dealing with major changes ensure it maintains relationships with the respect they deserve? Make sure that important information is always kept in multiple locations and is accessible by multiple people. Processes should be in place to manage handovers, even if they happen at unexpected or inopportune moments. Planning well can make life far easier if the worst actually happens.

Coaching Suggestions

1. Coachee to use existing supplier relationship as case
2. Analyse previous successes and pain points
3. Coachee to build plan to refine with coach

Training Suggestions

1. Use real suppliers
2. Review relationship management principles
3. Work with function-specific scenarios

Degree of Difficult 3 – Neutral

Without an effective and well-managed supply chain most businesses simply can't deliver to their customers, however this is an often-overlooked area of business discipline. Complacency can easily set in which can lead to sub-optimal supplier agreements, or poorly managed supply chain risks.

A periodic review of the overall effectiveness across the entire supply chain and multiple deliverables is essential to ensure maximum reliability and revenue flow for any business.

4.3.

DEAL WITH CHALLENGING CLIENTS

Overview

Fortunately, getting better at dealing with challenging people is a skill that can be learned. Understanding the root of the problem is key, because without knowing what is creating the challenging behaviour, managers can inadvertently end up making the situation worse. This is not to say that all challenging behaviour can be "solved." In the same way that no one would expect to be able to change their boss's personality, changing the way a client relates to the world isn't a reasonable goal.

In any relationship, business or personal, there are solvable and unsolvable problems. Figuring out what problems are solvable and finding solutions is usually the easy part. Identifying unsolvable problems doesn't mean giving up on the relationship however – it simply means that managers need to recognise that they won't find a solution to the problem, but they may be able to find a way to deal with it more effectively. This module will cover solutions to solvable problems, but the primary focus will be on mitigating, managing and working around unsolvable problems to keep the working relationship intact and functional.

Definition

Even if you have pruned your client list following the 80/20 rule, the people who bring you the most business may not always be the easiest to work with. Sometimes, there is a specific reason a client is problematic – the (dis)organisation of their company doesn't facilitate strong relationships with external stakeholders, or maybe the project is important, but it just isn't a company priority. Sometimes, though, it might just be a bad working style or personality match between the manager and the client's contact people. Whatever the source of the issue, it is unlikely that a manager will ever be able to choose to work with only the clients who are on their best behaviour. Even the best relationships can falter under pressure, and a miscommunication can create a challenging situation even when the professional rapport is good. Therefore, learning to work productively and effectively with clients who are behaving in problematic ways is a key skill for all managers.

Development Instructions

1. Separate acceptable from unacceptable client behaviour.

There is a big difference between clients exhibiting "challenging" behaviour (which requires finding solutions or work-arounds) and "unacceptable" behaviour (which requires dropping the client, or worse). Unacceptable behaviour makes it impossible for the working relationship to recover sufficiently, puts the organisation or manager in a compromised position or violates certain norms, rules or regulations that make it impossible for the two parties to legally or ethically work together. Obvious examples might include a lawyer who knows that their client has lied under oath, or a client who has assaulted a member of the team. However, sometimes, the situation is more nuanced – does a company need to fire a client who verbally challenges a team member, or can the company simply change the client's contact person? In this module, managers will discuss where to draw the line on client behaviour, and develop a plan for dealing with unacceptable behaviour swiftly by using prearranged protocols and support networks.

2. Identify different types of challenging clients.

So the organisation has decided it is worth keeping the client, and wants to learn to deal with the challenging behaviour. Now what? In this module, we will workshop relevant scenarios to identify the most common causes of challenging client behaviour.

Is the problem solvable? Solve it! The first scenarios we will tackle are those caused by issues that can be resolved with a little work from both parties. For example, if the client is consistently disappointed in work that the manager thought was top notch, this could be a simple communication gap; taking the time to ask "are you going to be happy with X if we do a, b and c by this date?" can mean the difference between a good working relationship and a poor one. When expectations aren't clear because of insufficient communication, this is a problem that can be solved before it even becomes an issue.

We will also workshop situations in which the problem is not solvable. When there is no easy fix, it can feel easier to just give up and let the relationship deteriorate, but often, there are ways to make the relationship more functional, even if the ultimate problem can't be solved. For example, if a company is working with a client organisation that is undergoing major structural changes, it can be difficult to maintain any sort of consistency through a project, which may present as shifting personnel, unclear deadlines and moving goal posts, poor communication or stressful interactions with people under a lot of pressure. Getting out in front of these situations can be key to maintaining a working relationship in this situation – if the manager can see that a problem might arise, contacting the client first, rather than waiting until the client complains, puts the manager and the organisation in a far better position. The organisation shows its dedication to the client by staying on top of possible issues before they happen, and the client is made aware of issues early, even when it might be hard to hear. These interactions may not always be pleasant, but they will always result in more transparency and understanding, which makes it possible to work towards a better relationship.

3. Communicate effectively.

If an organisation or manager gets similar complaints from a variety of clients, there's a good chance that the client isn't the only problem. The first place to look, in that case, is for communication gaps. Who is learning what information from whom? When are problems communicated? How are they communicated? Hearing employees say "I know I told someone," and "I thought I heard that," is a good indication that your standard operating procedure (SOP) regarding client communication might be lacking.

Before searching for the problems, let's look at the instances where communication did go well. What do those situations have in common? In this workshop, we will discuss past scenarios with positive outcomes in order to understand what is working, and avoid fixing something that isn't broken.

If the organisation has major communication gaps, developing an SOP for communicating with clients is key. Things that may help while developing this SOP are a client communication roadmap, a standard protocol for dealing with certain types of clients or calls, or designated contact people for certain clients. In this module, we will discuss these strategies, and many others, to find the best communication plan for each organisation.

4. Defuse conflict situations.

Conflict resolution strategies are necessary in all parts of business, but can be especially important in client relationships, where the entire relationship may be on the line. In this module, we will cover basic conflict resolution models, as well as how to apply those models in real-life situations.

Arguing rarely results in repaired relationships. Instead, we will workshop a model of conflict resolution that prioritises listening and repeating for understanding. In a client-centred organisation, ensuring the client feels heard is deeply important. In this way, we will move away from an opposition-based model, and towards a teamwork-based model for conflict resolution.

5. Work with deadlines.

If setting reasonable deadlines is the sticking point with a client, it can feel nearly impossible to find a resolution that makes everyone happy. However, there are strategies to adequately manage tight deadlines and reporting methods that ensure the client still feels the work is being taken seriously, even if their deadline expectations are not being met. In the module, we will discuss streamlining the working process to meet tight deadlines as a show of support to insecure clients. We will also cover negotiating appropriate future solutions with clients who routinely set unreasonable deadlines using novel reporting techniques.

6. Manage expectations.

Clear, reasonable expectations on all sides aren't enough to guarantee a project's success, but unclear, unreasonable expectations often guarantee failure. Good communication can help, but sometimes, underlying assumptions can get in the way of even the best communicators. Creating a standard communication plan about expectations explicitly can help.

When confronted with unrealistic expectations, it can be hard not to become defensive, or turn the conversation into an argument. Sometimes, expectations are so unrealistic, it can feel like a personal affront, or even a devaluing of the organisation's work. Letting go of these feelings and operating under a "presumption of innocence" about the client's motives is key to moving forward. Presuming the client innocently came up with these expectations also allows managers to ask the right questions to determine where those expectations come from – often, the problem is simply ignorance of the industry or the working process, not a devaluing of the organisation's work.

7. Maintain emotional state.

People behave unprofessionally in the workplace all the time. Yelling, screaming and name-calling aren't just the domain of school playgrounds – plenty of adults seem to think that these are valid ways to behave in the workplace as well. Dealing with an emotional response, whether someone is screaming in anger or crying in shame, is difficult to do in a professional way because the behaviour being dealt with is inherently unprofessional. In these instances, the key is remembering that we are all human, and that emotional conversations are part of our collective experience. Sometimes, they happen in places where we'd rather leave emotions at the door, but it doesn't mean we get to stop treating other people (or ourselves) with respect and dignity in that moment.

Dealing with high emotions with respect and dignity requires strategising in advance. Remaining calm and collected, even when a storm is raging, can feel confining, but it is usually the best way to diffuse a situation quickly. In this module, we will discuss strategies for maintaining a calm emotional state, while continuing to treat the other person with respect, as well as knowing when to walk away to cool off.

8. Prevent unnecessary challenging situations.

Knowing the cause of the problem in advance might not help a manager prevent the problem from happening, but it will definitely help the manager deal with it when it occurs. Furthermore, understanding where problems tend to occur with a particular client can help prevent or mitigate their impact in the future. In this module, we will create a profile of a particularly problematic client-organisation relationship, in order to troubleshoot the preventable problems before they even occur, and develop strategies in advance for mitigating unsolvable problems before they throw a spanner in the project gears.

Coaching Suggestions

1. Use live case study
2. Explore possible resolution paths
3. Build communication plan

Training Suggestions

1. Group work useful – all participants bring examples to work on together
2. Be careful to respect business confidentiality
3. Build issue resolution model

Challenge Level: 3 – Neutral

To deal with customers is to deal with challenging customers. It's a necessary and unavoidable part of customer service. While everyone in a customer-facing role has had to face this situation, there are greatly varying degrees of skill at handling these situations effectively.

Applying the right process and technique – and then practising these skills in a safe environment is the key to gaining the confidence and skill set to handle any challenging client situation.

4.4.

MANAGE BIDS, TENDERS AND PROPOSALS

Overview

Proposals often have to be written under time pressure, in conjunction with the other work that makes the business run. For many managers, proposals are something they tackle as an add-on to the primary focus of their work-days, even though future planning is what will make the business successful in the first place. Therefore, the ability to communicate clearly, quickly and under pressure could not be more valuable. Managers who find themselves avoiding writing proposals are losing opportunities, not only to generate more business for themselves, but to add a valuable skill to their CVs which will only become more necessary the higher they climb. Luckily, writing strong proposals is a learnable skill, and does not require a masters in English to do well; it does, however, require a variety of subskills, including writing, research and interpersonal acumen.

Setting the Scene

Creating great bids, tenders and proposals is really about great communication. However, for a new manager submitting their first grant proposal or their first tender for a big contract, the process can feel like trying to navigate a supermarket in a foreign language. Some of the shapes and pictures might provide some hints about what is required, but the manager is constantly struggling against a language they simply can't understand. It often feels like the same people win bids, tenders and grants all the time, and perhaps it's because they speak this secret language better than the manager does. The truth is, writing a great proposal has a lot in common with submitting a great job application. Learning the rules of the proposal game can help managers not only improve their proposal strategy, but become better written communicators in other areas of their work lives.

Development Instructions

1. Prepare relevant research.

It is impossible to write a compelling bid without understanding the target company. Therefore, research capability is key. The first place to start is the company's website, because the website is the first face many companies present to the world. What attributes does the company emphasise? How do they present themselves? What are they aiming for in the future, and how is that different from what they have done in the past?

Next, if possible, learn who the key decision makers are. Managers can learn a great deal about the professional lives of key decision makers from online profiles, but sometimes, an in-person approach is best. This is a great opportunity to use personal networks to learn more about the company, the decision makers and what they are looking for in a proposal, bid or tender. What do we know about decision makers?

Finally, look at the past winners of proposals, bids and tenders from that company. Sometimes, information about those proposals is publicly available: this information can be invaluable to a manager who is looking to submit a bid or tender. Past proposals can often provide information with more clarity about what the company is looking for, as well as what they are likely not looking for. If a past winner submitted a proposal almost identical to the manager's, it is unlikely the company will choose the same project twice.

2. Adhere to proposal guidelines.

In some areas, creativity and unusual presentation methods add value. Proposals are not one of those areas. Guidelines are there for a reason, most importantly because it allows the reviewing organisation to compare different proposals and tenders more easily. Any manager that deviates from these guidelines (by providing information in the wrong format, or giving more or less information than requested) is showing that they can't handle basic instructions, not that they are "creative." Help managers follow the unwritten guidelines that apply to all proposal submissions (for example, font choice, deadline adhesion, and proper style for the industry) so that their proposal is not immediately discounted.

Follow written guidelines exactly. For example, some companies will ensure that people do not simply submit the same tender to dozens of organisations by requiring a certain word or phrase to be included: this is a test of whether the manager can follow instructions. When in doubt, ask questions, especially if the written guidelines are unclear.

While submitting too much information is likely to annoy reviewers, leaving out information that is necessary will ensure that the proposal is summarily rejected. Make sure all information in the application is complete, and all attachments are present – there is nothing more annoying than reading a proposal that refers to "Appendix C" and discovering there is no "Appendix C." Dot the I's and cross the T's.

3. Write a compelling tender.
Word count limits for many bids and tenders can be low, so clear, precise and direct communication in writing is key. Help managers solidify their written communication skills if their communication lacks any of these qualities. Proposal presentations should function like elevator pitches: clear enough to be read and understood within a short period of time.

Visually disorganised proposals make it more difficult for reviewers to understand and buy in to the proposal's ideas. White space is a manager's best friend in this case – use it wisely while still conveying the message clearly.

Visually interesting proposals, whether in written or presentation form, are more likely to keep readers engaged. Follow the "rule of thirds", consider colour usage and ensure that the flow of the proposal is dynamic.

Articulate or allude to the unique selling proposition (USP) in every proposal. The manager's USP is their unique edge when pitching – not including it will severely handicap them as they try to pitch. The USP helps the manager brand their presentation and helps the reviewing organisation understand more clearly what the proposal brings to the table.

4. Appropriately address selection criteria.
In a call for proposals, bids or tenders, a good reviewing organisation will clearly include selection criteria in the text of the call. If that criteria is not present, the manager should go back to their original research about the organisation. Help managers discover, even if informally, what the reviewing organisation is looking for before beginning to write the proposal.

If three criteria are listed, it is important to cover each one. Sometimes, the coverage will be a bit lopsided – perhaps criteria one and two receive more attention than criterion three. The important thing is that all are covered seriously and intentionally, and it doesn't look like any points are "throw-aways" when it comes to specifically listed criteria. Read between the lines and address the deeper meaning behind the wording of the selection criteria.

5. Provide accurate information.

Fact check the proposal. Style can be altered or refined later on, but getting information wrong in the first draft will make it much harder to create a good second draft. Managers should ensure that they are seeking information from reliable sources, and create an outline including the information they need before they start writing.

Proofread, proofread, proofread. Spellcheck applications are only so good, and there is nothing more embarrassing than standing in front of a room with a typo on the screen that the spellcheck missed. Avoid embarrassment and show professionalism by proofing proposals and having someone else take a look before they are submitted.

6. Source relevant testimonials.

Testimonials can be helpful when submitting a tender or a bid, especially when the submission is more informal or is not requested directly by the reviewing organisation. Help the manager solicit testimonials from relevant contacts in order to increase credibility and show follow-through, past successes and working process to a potential client.

Including testimonials in the tender process can be tricky. In addition to putting testimonials in an obvious place online (for example, the company website), managers can often find places to include brief testimonials in their bid materials themselves. Look for a way to include testimonials naturally while still adhering to selection guidelines; often a good way to include them is in the summary of the proposed project.

The best testimonials come from the happiest clients, but sometimes, a client isn't comfortable putting their name next to a testimonial. Even if other clients were clearly more enthusiastic, make sure to include testimonials from easily identifiable and contactable clients to increase credibility.

7. Price for competitiveness and value.

There are plenty of online resources to help organisations determine the right price point for a bid in their industry. Generally, the pricing process in most industries should look for the "Goldilocks" price point: not so high an organisation prices themselves out of the competition, but not so low that the work isn't worth doing, or they are unnecessarily limiting their profit.

Going back to the USP can help organisations determine the right way to price their services. If quality and speed are a selling point, it is likely ok to submit a higher price, but if the business is all about volume, a lower price point is necessary to win the bid. Avoid pricing in ways that will feel illogical based on the proposal, regardless of how much money the reviewing organisation says they are offering.

8. Manage timeframes.

While many new managers have had opportunities to practise certain management skills before becoming managers through their experience in the workplace, writing bids, tenders and proposals may not be one of those skills, especially if they were promoted from a technical position. A bid, tender or proposal always has many different components, and the process of submitting one can feel overwhelming at first. Therefore, making a checklist of all the components and the tasks related to each component can help managers plan out workflow and delegate tasks.

The cardinal rule in submitting proposals: meet the deadline. A proposal submitted past the deadline will often not even be considered because it already shows potential clients that the organisation will not take deadlines seriously. Managers should be conscious that submitting an imperfect bid by the deadline is better than not submitting at all.

Coaching Suggestions

1. Have coachee provide previous tenders

2. Use live case

3. Allow coachee to construct bid response time line

Training Suggestions

1. Create bid team and role play tender scenario
2. Test accuracy and ability to adhere to big guidelines
3. Encourage live examples

Challenge Level: 4 – Easy

To gain new projects and therefore revenue, proper management of bids, tenders and proposals is a necessity. In many cases, it is simply a matter of adhering to tender document guidelines and timeframes. In other cases, using a format or template that has worked successfully in the past will also work.

Overall, a structured and consistent approach to learning how to present tenders will assist those newer to this discipline to become effective as quickly as possible.

4.5.

PROVIDE SERVICE AND MANAGE CLIENT RELATIONSHIPS

Overview

Great customer service values clients holistically and intrinsically, rather than viewing every client interaction as transactional. The goal is not to suck as much value out of a client in as short a time as possible, but to cultivate loyalty to the organisation and positive associations among clients so that they want to interact with the organisation in the future. Achieving this balance can be particularly hard for organisations providing services that feel inherently "un-fun": tax accountants, dentists and government bureaucrats all have to interact with clients who are usually stressed out and would rather be anywhere else. However, even if no one likes going to the dentist, a dentist with a great bedside manner, friendly staff and clear, administrative procedures for clients is likely to have more return clients than a dentist who makes the experience even less enjoyable. Customer value should be viewed over their lifetime of potential interactions with an organisation, not in what they will pay for service today or tomorrow.

Setting the Scene

Customer service can feel like a lost art in certain fields. As companies lean into the shareholder profit-based model of success, other stakeholders, like customers, can get lost in the shuffle. For companies with huge numbers of clients, this client-last attitude can grow like a cancer: long service wait times, call centre policies that value volume over quality and poorly trained employees can all contribute to client dissatisfaction on a massive scale. In an age when customer service can be so bad that recorded phone calls go viral (as happened to Comcast in the US several years ago), it can be tempting to treat clients as a given and avoid improving customer service policies that aren't "that bad." However, great customer service and client relationships are key to developing the long-term value of any business, and to maintaining employee morale.

Development Instructions

1. Know the client.

Getting to know the client as an individual will improve customer service almost instantly. A client who feels seen and heard is less likely to be confrontational. This goes for businesses whose clients are other businesses as well: a great interpersonal connection with the manager's counterpart at the other organisation can make the difference between a renewed contract and a phasing out of the relationship.

Trust that the client knows best what they need. Therefore, avoid telling the client what they should want, and instead, focus on learning more about what they say they want. Keeping an open mind is necessary, both in client research and customer service. Great customer service provides something the client asked for, and doesn't attempt to funnel them into the business' idea of what would be best for them.

2. Respect clients' time.

Wasting client time leads to exasperated clients. Giving clients too little time leads to confused and lost clients. So how can a business achieve balance? Ensure that there are robust client time protocols in place so that everyone who interacts with clients is aware of goals for key elements, like wait times and quality of service. If goals can't be met, this is not the client's fault: it's a sign that the business needs to spend more time and resources on customer service and management.

Create simple guidelines for external communication. Large companies may include these with the style guide on their intranet; smaller companies should keep their guidelines somewhere easily accessible. Guidelines should include information that must be communicated to all clients, as well as information that should stay private, and the method of communication for different types of information (for example, some communication may need to be done in writing to maintain a record, while other information is best handled in person or over the phone). Include tone and style information in guidelines as well.

Clients are not the experts on the business, so it can be hard to keep expectations realistic in some situations. Always communicate the "why" clearly. For example, make sure clients know from the start how long something is likely to take, and be clear about why it will take that long. Additionally, if a client is requesting something that isn't possible, knowing why it's not possible may help both sides brainstorm another solution that will work.

3. Demonstrate open communication.

Getting out in front of an issue can be key to retaining clients in the long term. Clients should know about anything that will affect their business relationship with the company, and it is best if the business comes to them first instead of the other way around.

When in doubt, be as transparent as possible. If something isn't working, don't try to tell a client it is working: instead, acknowledge the problem and reiterate that the company is working on a solution. With very few exceptions, opaque communication is likely to close up client relationships and encourage more hostility than understanding.

4. Provide follow up.

Client contact should be regular and easily managed within day-to-day business routines. Organisations that don't follow up with clients are likely to lose them – the key is to figure out the frequency and the type of contact needed, which will be different for every business. Look at the happiest clients: how often do they hear from the organisation? What kind of contact do they receive?

Often, the people that clients speak with at the very beginning are not the people they end up contacting in the long term. Providing a single point of contact after the first stage can help keep clients in the loop and make them feel valued, but this isn't an option for all businesses. Even if the point of contact changes each time, the customer service experience should be predictable and easy to follow.

5. Enact an ongoing service model.

How does the business currently handle ongoing service? Create a map that shows how current clients can get in touch with the business, how long those interactions usually take and outcomes. Managers can follow the flow of customer interaction to find pain points and opportunities for improvement.

Businesses should never wait for clients to tell them what they need to be doing better. Therefore, empower employees to follow up on client issues.

If employees think of themselves as humans helping other humans, rather than cogs in a corporate machine, they are more likely to act as problem solvers for both the business and the client. Employees who can say, "Let me see what I can do," instead of spouting a pre-fabricated response to a client issue will build a better client relationship.

6. Demonstrate value.

Just because something is expensive doesn't mean it is good value. Certain brands can get away with exorbitant pricing because of name recognition, but most businesses need to consider exactly what kind of value their product or service adds to customers' lives. If that service or product is high quality, a higher price might be justified, but businesses should never base their value around what they can charge for a product.

A value proposition shows customers and potential clients three things: 1) How the company/product solves the customer's problems or improves their lives, 2) quantified benefits of the product/company and 3) how the company is different from competitors. A great value proposition can help drive customer engagement by outlining exactly why the company is a great choice for consumers.

A perpetual worry in any industry is being undercut by a competitor who can provide a similar service or product for less. In some cases, notably retail, there are certain costs to doing business in a brick-and-mortar store when buying things online has become the norm. Therefore, one of the best ways for companies that fear low-cost competitors to differentiate themselves is through excellent customer service. The product or service may be identical in quality, but the experience of shopping in a beautifully-designed store with great salespeople is often worth the price for many customers.

7. Exceed expectations.

It is always better to under-promise and over-deliver than to do the opposite and let clients down. At the end of the day, a company is not just selling a product or a service: a company is also selling their word. If a client learns not to trust what a company says it can do, the relationship is broken.

When a project for a client goes particularly well, it's important to communicate those wins. Wins should be communicated to the client in question, but also internally and to other clients and potential clients.

Knowing how the company succeeds makes clients more willing to continue working with a company through inevitable rough patches.

Coaching Suggestions

1. Use a live client scenario of high value
2. Allow coachee to share successes and challenges
3. Pick a specific problem statement and work through

Training Suggestions

1. Understand participants' own service expectations
2. Test existing customer set approaches
3. Use CSAT metrics if available, if not, create goals

Challenge Level: 2 – Difficult

Truly excellent client relationship management and service standards, while spruiked by nearly all organisations, are difficult to achieve. Often this is because the organisation itself lacks a clear understanding of what these standards actually look like, particularly in the eyes of the only person whose opinion counts – the customer.

The pathway to consistent brilliance in this regard starts with an understanding of the clients, which can be used to build a specific and measurable customer service standard. From there a robust and reliable method of measuring customer satisfaction is critical to understanding if the organisation is truly on the correct path.

4.6.

EFFECTIVELY MANAGE CLIENT COMMUNICATIONS

Overview

Elegant and effective communication cannot be achieved between clients and businesses with a few emails when a plan goes off the rails. An active communication plan requires forethought, an understanding of the client's expectations and a multi-level approach, depending on relationship between the organisation and the client. As with feedback for employees, clients should be kept in the loop throughout the working process, rather than being blindsided with new information two days before the deadline. Furthermore, communication should be geared towards the client's understanding: speaking to the client at their level rather than with language that is too technical or detailed, or conversely, talking down to them and overexplaining, will ensure a strong working relationship.

Setting the Scene

Current technology not only allows us to stay constantly connected, it encourages us to never let go. Our phone has made work email available 24/7, but in addition there are also messaging apps, collaboration apps, and social media interrupting us with notifications and alerts. The sheer volume of communication the average person receives in a day has increased to the point that someone who is able to maintain a "zero inbox" can seem as impressive as an ultramarathon runner.

A considerable volume of communication gets lost in the shuffle when messages aren't personalised and urgent. The key isn't to make every message urgent; rather, a business' primary concern needs to be how to cut through the noise to reach clients with information they need to know, and would like to receive. Client communication should be clear, personal and responsive.

Development Instructions

1. Standardise a communication process.

How does the organisation communicate with clients now? Is there a process in place, or is client communication a "sideshow" that gets picked up by whoever isn't busy at the moment? Map out the process for client communication in order to see where there are standardised procedures and where things are being handled ad hoc.

Just because part of the process is improvised doesn't mean communication is bad. Consider where improvisation might be necessary as well as where stricter procedures would make things simpler. An optimal communication process is clear, but that doesn't mean the entire process is regimented ahead of time.

Consider how clients might differ from each other in terms of communication needs. Perhaps one client prefers regular and formal email updates, while another would rather communicate informally with the same team member every time by text message. Staying flexible and accommodating client preferences for communication can help everyone stay in touch more easily. Project constraints may also help define communication parameters; keep in mind that not every project requires the same kind of communication.

2. Set timeframes for updates.

The biggest concern many clients have about communication? Timelines. Regular updates are essential both for keeping clients informed and helping them maintain realistic expectations. Staying out of touch for long periods of time will likely make most clients nervous. The question is, what is the right time frame for communication for a particular client or project?

If anything unexpected happens with the project that could impact the client in any way, managers should get in touch with the client immediately, through an appropriate means, and with a tone that matches the situation, in order to inform the client of the new development.

By communicating as quickly as possible about new information that could impact the client, managers are likely to be able to avoid "reacting" to communication sent by the client. Additionally, keep in mind that if information will not impact a client, but they are likely to hear about it and wonder, the best bet is to communicate first. Businesses will look like they are trying to hide something if clients have to bring potential problems or news to their attention in order to get information.

3. Allow the client to "speak".

Communication is a two-way street. If an organisation is not listening to a client's needs and concerns and taking them seriously, it is unlikely that anything the organisation communicates later will be sufficient. Ensure that a forum in which clients can both voice their opinions and receive a serious response from the organisation is available and checked frequently.

By creating a flexible communication template, organisations will be able to shift with new information that comes from the client. One of the obvious places to create flexibility is in meeting templates. When meeting with clients, ensure that the client's perspective and concerns are front and centre, and that the manager in charge of the meeting is both ready to hear those concerns and able to take action if necessary.

4. Empower team members to deal with external comms.

Advanced planning isn't just for project hand-offs. If the leader of a team is suddenly unavailable for any reason, is anyone else empowered to handle client communication? Leaders that hog all client communication or don't empower their team to deal effectively with external communication are doing their teams and the company a disservice. Great communication plans have contingency plans, and value all team members.

Communicating with external stakeholders can be frightening for some team members, especially if they feel underinformed. Instituting a clear plan for communication with all members of the team, including triggers for calling in a manager, can help even the most nervous team members handle communication on their own. If team members have clear boundaries around what they are and are not expected to be able to handle, they are likely to have more confidence dealing with external stakeholders like clients.

5. Manage timeframes.

Timelines are necessary for the communication and project planning process, but sometimes it becomes impossible to stick with those timelines. If this is the case, managers should assess where the problem is coming from. Internal issues should be streamlined so that they don't interfere with workflow in the future. If process simply takes longer than the manager expected, managers should adjust their timeline expectations.

If the workflow does start to falter, inform the client immediately, especially if it will impact delivery of the end product. The tone of this conversation should reflect the severity of the problem – some level of workflow slippage is understandable, but a larger apology may be necessary if internal issues have created a serious delay. Informing clients sooner rather than later can help them adjust their expectations for delivery well ahead of time. This is especially important in B2B relationships, where timeline slippage can cause problems for the entire supply chain.

Sometimes, the hold-up is actually...the client. A non-responsive client can be aggravating to manage for a business that is trying to act responsibly and professionally. Managers should always give clients the benefit of the doubt, and any concerns should be very gently and politely communicated to the client if the issue is affecting workflow. If the problem becomes severe, organisations should make contingency plans that shift focus and manage workflow adequately so that the company doesn't suffer as a result of client silence.

6. Proactively follow up.
Client relationships don't end at product delivery. Managers should make an effort to follow up with clients. Depending on the industry, project and client relationship, different follow-up methods might be better than others; some organisations can benefit from public reviews or feedback from clients, while others may prefer to follow-up with the goal of retaining the client for future business only.

Following up with clients does not have to be difficult or time consuming. Many clients are happy to hear from an organisation they have worked with and provide quick feedback. Avoid creating a template for follow-up contact that is inherently time-consuming for the client; clients that want to give extensive feedback will do so regardless of the template they are given.

Consider an adequate timeframe for follow-up. Following up immediately after a project is complete can feel too hasty, or as though the organisation is asking for more from the client. On the other hand, following up too late can mean that the project and relationship has faded into the background already. Create a standardised follow-up timeline, and avoid too much contact immediately after the completion of the project when it isn't requested by the client.

Coaching Suggestions

1. Explore current state of comms
2. Have coachee outline personal strengths/weaknesess
3. Help coachee chart a comms timeframe

Training Suggestions

1. Use existing client communication model
2. Test proficiency within existing model
3. When should communication be "BAU" and when should it be proactive?

Challenge Level: 2 – Difficult

Client communication has the ability to make or break a project or relationship. The issue is that while some members of a team or organisation may have great natural facility with communication, others may not. Another potential break point is a manager's preferred communication medium or style may not match the preference of the client or the demands of the situation.

With great communication comes great understanding, and great client relationships. Having a consistent and easily applicable process across the entire organisation is key here, and it is worth investing in a complete organisational review of client communications with an eye on improvement and standardisation.

4.7.

MANAGE CLIENT PROJECTS

Overview

Handling client projects requires a wide range of skills. While internal project managers can sometimes get away with having poorer communication skills or being detail-oriented to a fault, external project managers must be flexible, technically adept and able to communicate effectively with a large range of stakeholders. While they couldn't do their jobs without understanding the project's detail, they must keep a birds-eye-view perspective on their relationship with the client: otherwise, the amount of information a project manager in charge of client projects must process every day would quickly become overwhelming.

Setting the Scene

Project managers are necessary in nearly every industry, making the job title nearly impossible to define precisely. Unlike "bank teller" or "actuary," "project manager" can even mean different things at the same company, depending on the project. However, the skills that make someone a good project manager are often remarkably consistent. Project managers are able to keep both the big picture and the details of their projects in mind as they work. They are responsible for delivering projects on time and on budget, while keeping a clear view on both the day-to-day workings of a project, and the end goals. If a business was a circus, project managers would be both the juggler and the ringmaster: They have many balls in the air at the same time, but they also have to focus on the big picture to ensure the show proceeds smoothly.

Development Instructions

1. Accurately capture project requirements.

It's easy to make big promises early on, especially when trying to woo a client or motivate a team. However, a project manager will only gain the respect of their clients and team through follow-through. If a project manager can't "walk the talk," the project will be unsuccessful in the long run. If something is promised during the initial start-up phase of a project, managers should be prepared to deliver on that "talk," or they may find themselves having to walk back promises at a later date and risk their reputations.

Managers should make every effort to understand all of a client's needs and wants. Without fostering this initial understanding, unexpected (and often unpleasant) surprises are bound to surface along the way.

Managers who are too enthusiastic can get a reputation for overpromising and underdelivering. At the same time, a pessimistic manager can be off-putting to clients and demotivate their team through an assumption that everything will go poorly. The project managers' tone sets the tone for the project: managing tone can help project manager's create realistic, but positive expectations for both their clients and their teams.

2. Develop project management plan.
If the company has a strong project management program, information about planning should be widely available. Looking at similar past projects, how have other managers handled timelines, budgets and other practicalities and moving parts? Project management plans should always be in place at the beginning of projects, even if they change over time. If these plans seem erratic at best and non-existent at worst, it is likely time to start documenting the project management process more effectively.

Sharing best practices, especially internally, should be a given for companies in all domains, but it is particularly important in a flexible field like project management. When a manager learns something that could benefit other managers, ensure there is an easy venue in which they can share that knowledge clearly and concisely with other managers so that everyone can benefit.

3. Manage project delivery team.
A project manager's communication process should convey a sense of urgency without being too overbearing or creating a panic mentality. Project managers are not only responsible for motivating a team: they are responsible for keeping that team operating on time and within budget. Show managers how to help team members stay on track and avoid last-minute crunches through communication.

At the same time, teams need to be able to breathe and use their own reasoning to make choices related to their work. Great project managers know when to step in and when to hold back in order to allow their teams to do the best work possible. Delegating thoughtfully and effectively will allow the project manager to stay focused on the client's needs, without getting too bogged down in the details.

4. Display risk management disciplines.

Old-school project management policies don't work very well in a fast-paced environment. Managers should consider how they can add methodologies to their repertoire that can help them manage risk, as well as agile project management techniques to ensure that risks are not heightened through use of slower, outdated project management.

One plan is never enough. What happens when something goes wrong? Contingency planning should never be rigid, but it must take into account likely scenarios like missed deadlines, new information, budget issues and clients changing their minds. All client projects involve a certain level of risk, and project manger's without contingency plans are sailing into the open ocean without life jackets.

Risk management does not mean that the project manager should become risk averse. Rather, a project manager should be able to reasonably assess the level of risk and decide if the potential pay-off for the client, team or company is worth it. Managers should communicate risks and pay-offs to all of these stakeholders with a level-headed attitude that doesn't downplay or overstate any risks or pay-offs unnecessarily.

5. Monitor progress.

Project management software has proliferated in recent years because there is a renewed understanding that most projects have many moving parts, and that these parts can become difficult to track effectively at the pace of business today, without assistance. Older tracking methods (like Excel spreadsheets) can be effective in certain environments, but if a team needs to collaborate, consider investing in software that actively facilitates project management, and takes some of the hassle out of the reporting process.

A clear monitoring plan that runs throughout the project is important, in part, to track any deviations and re-track the project before any problems surface. In some cases, deviations may actually show project managers a better way to do things: for example, if an employee figures out how to perform a task in two steps adequately that previously took four, that employee could save the entire team time if their work is noticed through monitoring. Frame monitoring as a benefit for both managers and team members: it's a way for managers to understand what's happening with a project, and for team members to document their work and take credit for their accomplishments.

6. Communicate with stakeholders.

A communication plan is key when dealing with clients in any situation. For a project manager, communication should be part of the overall plan for the project, not a side addition that gets little attention until things go wrong. Understanding from the outset what the goals of communication are will help project managers handle outside expectations and deal with clients with aplomb.

Communication plans should be clearly laid out to the entire team, so that everyone understands and abides by guidelines for good communication. When dealing with clients, proactive versus reactive communication is always the goal: when in doubt, disclose.

7. Work within budgetary constraints.

Project managers need to have the business acumen to deal with budgetary constraints. A manager who understands the source of those constraints is more likely to be able to solve problems in inventive ways that don't make budgetary problems worse. Encourage managers to keep their eye on the big picture, not only for their team or the project, but for the entire organisation, when it comes to handling budgets. Managers should deepen their knowledge of finance if they consistently have issues staying within budget, and search for solutions that do not require extra funding.

Maintaining a certain level of flexibility is key when setting a budget. Allocating funds too early can result in a siphoning off of necessary resources when the project takes an unexpected turn; at the same time, waiting until the last minute to make key purchases can result in higher fees and prices. Encourage project managers to set goal posts for spending funds, to ensure that funds are not tied up to early or held onto for too long.

Always keep a contingency buffer in the budget. A project manager who has allocated every penny of their budget to current project needs will have no wriggle room if anything changes. Instead, managers should assume they are working with 90% or less of the actual budget from the outset, in order to provide a buffer for additional needs later on.

Coaching Suggestions
1. Test previous client project experience
2. Examine existing plans
3. Help coachee create their own comms and leadership plan

Training Suggestions
1. Provide project management example templates
2. Seek input on current methodology
3. Work through success and areas for improvement and build on

Challenge Level: 3 – Neutral
The key disciplines outlined here would be considered the basics of a project managers' role. However project management skills are useful in so many management roles – and many managers are thrust into this role without it being a formal job title.

Excellent systems and processes combined with experience are valuable for keeping projects running to expectations. While experience can't be taught, the lessons learned by experienced project managers can, and are worth filtering through all relevant parties in an organisation.

4.8.

INFLUENCE RELATIONSHIPS

Overview

Generating influence at a business level works somewhat differently than at a personal level. For the "kale juice influencer", that rapport is built through perceived intimacy with their followers: They show more of their personal lives, so that followers feel that they are seeing real preferences, not an ad for kale juice. At the same time, they communicate a clear brand: beautiful photos of beautiful people, which really have nothing to do with kale juice, but is the reason why followers are willing to listen when they post a photo of green smoothies. Social media influencers can generate thousands in revenue just from this skill: clearly, being able to influence relationships adds a great deal of value to any business, especially where no direct line of authority exists. This kind of power should not be underestimated, because it can allow a leader to have far more pull both inside and outside of the organisation than their position would ordinarily allow.

Setting the Scene

"Influencer" is a relatively new job title, but it isn't a new concept in the business world. When many people think of an "influencer," they think of beautiful young people selling kale juice through photos of themselves lounging around in Scandinavian interiors on social media. While this image is a bit reductionist, there are some key traits that social media influencers display which are useful for anyone looking to improve their business-level influence. A great leader doesn't have to be fabulously beautiful or an excellent photographer in most fields; however, they do have to be able to use influence at a wider level to create the kinds of business opportunities that will benefit not only themselves but the organisation they work for. Often, those opportunities can be best generated through informal influence.

Development Instructions

1. Create rapport.

In individual relationships, personal rapport can be built through casual contact over time; at a larger scale, rapport has to be developed specifically in relationship to a particular project. The problem for many social media influencers, as shown above, is generating the perception of intimacy on a larger scale.

While most of us will not derive any business benefit from posting photos of ourselves drinking our morning coffee, we can learn something from the social media influencer: that a certain degree of public vulnerability can generate rapport on a wide scale. The artful staged photos of domestic scenes on social media are usually only a small part of the real story, but it is enough to convince social media followings that this person is authentic. People in other areas of business can do this by strategically using their struggles and moments of doubt as part of their public story. Help managers work through their own histories to generate these kinds of stories.

2. Practice active listening.

Social media works because of a constant feedback loop. Unlike regular media, in which there is limited contact between the consumers and the producers, social media allows consumers to interact directly with producers. The best producers then use this interaction to improve their business. Managers should practice active listening to ensure they are talking with the people they want to influence, rather than at them.

A good way for managers to ensure they are actively listening is to continuously communicate their understanding in specific terms. This can be done both implicitly, by building on others' ideas with a "yes, and..." attitude (instead of a "no, but..." attitude), or by repeating what they have understood back to the speaker. Many times, the most important part of a conversation is that both people feel they have been heard; after understanding has been established, it becomes easier to find a workable compromise.

3. Use appropriate body language.

Great social media influencers thrive on perceived intimacy, and therefore eschew any posts or photos that might negatively impact that perception.

If a photo distances them from their viewers (because they are very dressed up, or posed in a formal way), they will often use the caption to generate that intimacy instead. Leaders should consider the way their body language or style is likely to distance themselves from the person they are trying to influence.

The first step to understanding body language is self-awareness. Managers can try walking around the room, noticing what parts of their body they move or use as they walk. They can take a day to simply observe their own bodies in interaction without trying to change anything. Do they stand far away from people, cross their arms a lot, keep their hands in their pockets or position their head downwards? Open postures, as opposed to closed postures, tend to be more inviting and appealing. Furthermore, people who physically present as confident have an easier time encouraging others to trust them. Work with managers to help them find ways they can move in a more open, confident manner.

Mirroring can help leaders unlearn bad body language habits while simultaneously generating unconscious empathy in their conversation partner. Managers can mirror their conversation partner's body language while they talk, in order to help the other person feel more at ease, and avoid the manager accidentally closing themselves off inappropriately. This can include mirroring closed off poses. Guide managers through these exercises by helping them practice.

4. Apply consequence management.
Sometimes, efforts to influence on a larger scale can backfire. This can happen when a key project goes awry in a way that impacts a manager's credibility with others. Other times, efforts to generate influence can create problems in other areas of work life. It is important for a manager to get out in front of the issue before they lose the careful rapport they've built.

Displaying consistency in these instances can help managers reinforce their influence even in the face of adversity. For failures that go "against brand," managers should have a contingency plan for how they will incorporate those failures into their story. Thoughtful responses that do not minimise the impact of the failure will be important when moving forward.

Reinforce the story through the use of failure. For this reason, a story that emphasises perfection in any aspect of work life is unlikely to be tenable for very long. Managers should frame their attempts to influence in human terms that allow for flexibility and problem solving, rather than emphasising only the ways in which they are better than average.

5. Communicate clearly.

When everything can live on the internet forever, it becomes ever more important to ensure the image an influencer projects is an image that works for them in the long term. For leaders seeking to influence people via social media, considering all communication a potential opportunity can help frame their interactions. If an influencer only has 140 characters, how can they convey their message clearly and concisely? Similarly, leaders should watch for being too wordy or overbearing in their interactions. Ask questions, rather than giving orders. Create opportunities for conversation.

Social media influencers sometimes work across a variety of platforms; leaders seeking to increase their influence should plan to use many media to make their message heard. Many leaders get in their own way by avoiding personal or phone interactions because they are more comfortable with email; some leaders would rather avoid new technology developments and work only with "old-school" methods. Different communication media should be viewed as different rooms in a house – sometimes, the real conversation is happening in the kitchen, even though the party is technically happening in the living room. Leaders should strive to become confident using a wide variety of platforms and media to exert influence: otherwise, they risk being left out of important conversations, because they weren't in that particular room.

6. Display empathy.

Empathy is the ability to put oneself in another person's shoes in order to experience what they are feeling. Sympathy is the ability to understand what someone is feeling. Emotional agreement is feeling the same thing as someone else because one is in the same circumstances. Great leaders should always strive for empathy in their interactions. Operating purely on sympathy will usually lead to pity, but not action. Waiting until moments when feelings are aligned can make leaders seem callous and unfeeling, because they lack the ability to project themselves outside of their own experiences.

In one respect, social media influencers have a much harder time generating influence than people in other areas of business: empathy can be hard to demonstrate effectively through social media to a wide following. While there are certainly examples of people accomplishing this, leaders who are seeking influence have a distinct advantage by doing so in a variety of venues.

7. Focus on the stakeholder.
One problem with influencing? Focusing too much on gaining influence at the expense of a leader's relationships. True influence runs deep and is built over time. A leader's influencing ambitions should never take precedence over their ability to accomplish their work or maintain good relationships with stakeholders, because the most influential people are perceived as authentic at their cores. Influence building should happen on top of these other activities, not instead of them.

Multi-level marketing schemes (in which friends are encouraged to sell products to friends) are often criticised for the ways in which they corrupt friendship. Rather than continuing to see their friends as friends, multi-level marketers often reduce their friendships to potential sales opportunities. People in other areas of business can risk doing this even with their business-based relationships if they focus too much on influencing people and not enough on the people themselves. People want to feel special, not like a means to an end or another opportunity. Leaders should therefore focus on their relationships as primary and influence as a derivative of those relationships, rather than the relationships as a means to an end.

Coaching Suggestions
1. Use relationship that coachee would like to influence more effectively
2. Explore examples
3. Create action plan and test

Training Suggestions
1. Seek examples of challenging relationships from group
2. Apply influencing methodology
3. Work on case studies in teams

Challenge Level: 1 – Very Difficult

Many people we work with believe the ability to generate and leverage influence among colleagues, clients, suppliers and other stakeholders is a trait that a lucky few are born with. It can certainly appear this way, and there's no doubt that some people seem to be more naturally influential.

The above said, the natural influencers we know are simply practising certain techniques and skills very effectively in order to achieve the outcomes they want via other people. Often times highly skilled influencers are not even aware of how they are doing it.

But these techniques can most definitely be learned and applied by anyone willing to attempt to try doing things differently from what they've attempted in the past.

4.9.

DISPLAY ADAPTABILITY

Overview

At its core, adaptability is having an appetite for learning. Adaptable leaders see opportunity where others see only problems, and are not only willing to meet changing needs, they are excited to figure out how to do so. Helping a manager improve their ability to learn and think in new directions will help them adapt to uncertainty and unexpected developments. All organisations must manage a certain degree of uncertainty – a manager who is able to do so confidently will be a valuable asset to any organisation.

Setting the Scene

When asked to be more adaptable or flexible, it can feel to some people like they are being asked to give up on their own goals and ambitions. These people see adaptability as being at odds with achievement. In their minds, the only people who are able to be flexible are those who don't have to lead: to them, adaptability means that the original plan wasn't very good in the first place.

However, people who are truly adaptable are not rudderless – in fact, it's exactly the opposite. They have a direction and solid goals. They are simply more flexible on the details. The business world is increasingly devoid of jobs where it pays to be rigid, and as needs change, managers need to be able to adapt to those needs quickly and easily, without losing their sense of direction. Managers who are adaptable are able to respond to and thrive in rapidly changing internal and external business environments.

Look for the following:

1. Ask relevant questions.

For some people, change can feel so overwhelming that it becomes difficult to understand what is happening in the first place. The only question they know to ask is, "Why is this happening?" If this is the case, the manager is missing the point. Learning to ask more relevant questions about change that focus on the "how" of the change: how is the change going to impact their team? How can the manager implement the change? How can they break down a big change into smaller parts?

The best learners ask probing questions early on in the process, and they ask for clarification the minute something doesn't make sense. They assume there is something to be understood, rather than an arbitrary decision. They do not stymie the process with questions designed to slow things down, but instead, try to deepen their own understanding so that they can do their part more effectively. Most importantly, they see their "obvious" questions as important: instead of assuming someone else has asked, they assume that a question that might be obvious to them might not be to someone else. They support their own learning, and allow others to do the same.

2. Identify opportunity in changing environments.
While focusing on the "how" of change can help leaders gain insight into the core of their part of the change, understanding all the dimensions is important as well. Leaders should be able to identify exactly what has changed, why it has changed, who the change affects (and who instigated the change), as well as when and where the change is taking place.

It can be tempting to focus only on what is lost rather than what is gained at an organisational level through change. Instead, managers should aim their focus on the barriers removed and the opportunities that have opened up. For example, in a massive organisational restructuring, many people may decide to retire, leaving the organisation with a dearth of experienced workers. However, this leaves opportunities for hiring that would have otherwise been impossible: the organisation can seek new talent with qualities that are different from the retiring cohort (for instance, more technically-savvy, more diverse or harder-working may be qualities that an organisation hiring new employees may seek in this case).

3. Apply solutions-focused thinking.
Adaptable people see the issues caused by change as a puzzle rather than an added stressor. They do not try to keep doing the same thing, while managing the change on top of their normal routine – rather, they change their routine to incorporate the change.

Solution-oriented thinking encourages people to look at the bigger picture, rather than the details that will cause issues along the way. Rather than focusing on barriers, they focus on pathways around (or over, or under) the barriers. Avoid being that person in meetings who simply spouts off all the reasons why something won't work, without offering solutions to the problems they see.

Multiple, possible solutions are always better. For adaptability, diversity in thinking is an asset to be fostered in a team. This way, if one possible solution doesn't work, there are always more options to try.

4. Understand external environment.

Change that happens in the external environment can feel deeply unpredictable, but that isn't always the case. Hindsight is 20/20, but sometimes looking backwards is the best way to make notes for the future. Were there signs this change was coming that were ignored or missed? Take note of these warning signals for the future.

Responding to warning signals is important for managing change, because the sooner a change in the external environment is predicted, the more easily an organisation can adapt in time. For arts non-profits, funding streams can be deeply unreliable. While this fact can be incredibly challenging to deal with on a day-to-day basis, arts non-profits were actually able to weather the 2008 financial crisis more effectively than other non-profits with more reliable (but financially-susceptible) funding streams. They were able to adapt quickly to the change because their funding structure has always been uncertain. Consider what the organisation can do to better prepare itself for changes in the future.

5. Use all available resources to best advantage.

Avoid using the same ideas over and over again. Many organisations are remarkably homogeneous, mostly because people like to hire people who look like themselves. While this can make working together feel frictionless in the short term, in the long term, it will leave an organisation without the resources to handle unexpected information well. Diversity in thought process and perspective is essential for dealing with change. Managers should use all their available resources by seeking opinions from team members and other stakeholders in order to gain a broader perspective and new ideas.

If the change process felt mildly traumatising to everyone involved, it's clear that new tactics need to be implemented. Use outside perspectives not only for ideas about managing a particular change, but for improving the general process for handling change.

6. Build flexibility into planning.

For Type-A planners, it can be hard not to construct Plans A-Z in an attempt to mitigate any need to improvise. This is a mistake, because it is rare that a situation can ever be fully predicted. Some improvisation opportunities must be built into the plan in the first place. Empower team members to think creatively about solutions and construct an approach that allows everyone some leeway to improvise if things don't go as planned.

Adaptable plans stay focused on the big picture, but remain flexible on the details. Rather than mapping out every possible step, keep the outline strong and clear, but leave room in the details for different scenarios to play out more naturally.

7. Apply advanced contingency planning.

As noted above, planning for all possible contingencies is usually a waste of time because most of the time, the ways in which things deviate is unpredictable at the beginning of the process. However, advanced contingency planners are able to assess many possible scenarios and allocate resources to these possible scenarios accordingly. This doesn't mean they plan exactly how those resources will be used. Instead, they note that it will likely be important to have extra funds on hand in the event X, but if Y happens, they may need more support from upper management to find a good solution. Allocate resources rather than tasks in advanced contingency planning.

If the manager was suddenly unavailable for weeks on end, who would be in charge? While no one likes to plan for worst case scenarios, ensuring continuity is part of being adaptable. Many people have trouble letting go of the idea that they are indispensable to a company; however, acknowledging that someone else can do the manager's job if necessary is a hallmark of a great leader.

Coaching Suggestions

1. Have coachee provide previous examples where adaptability was key
2. Test methods used
3. Work on current change issue

Training Suggestions

1. Move past theory into practical examples
2. Create live adaptability challenges in training room
3. Apply to current organisational situation

Challenge Level: 1 – Very Difficult

The modern hyper-connected business world exists in a highly dynamic external and internal environment. The ability to display flexibility and respond to shifts in the landscape can be a key determinant in the success or failure of any organisation.

The irony here is that people form habits easily, and tend to stick with "what works", even though it may be patently obvious that it's not working any more!

This natural intertia can make any change process challenging, and the need for managers to display flexibility important, but often very difficult, to embrace. A caring organisation will give its leaders the opportunity to learn how to react to the constant change in the modern business age with flexibility and open-mindedness. With this hard-won skill, their ability to cope and lead in the business environment will increase exponentially.

4.10.

BUILD TRUST

Overview

Because it is impossible to have full transparency in any business relationship, trust is critically important. Many businesses conduct their affairs in a highly contractual and transactional matter, specifically as an attempt to get around this problem. Unfortunately, while a contract can help protect both parties in a worst-case scenario, no contract can ensure that trust will be built between them. In business relationships where people don't trust each other, every step of working together becomes painful, and often, the work will stall because managing the problem becomes so overwhelming. It is important that stakeholders can trust each other to behave in predictable and reliable ways. Rebuilding broken trust can be difficult, but it is always worth the effort in the end because a business relationship cannot function without it.

Definition

It can be hard to pin down exactly what creates trust, and part of that is cultural. For some people, trust must be built over time; for others, it is based on someone's history of action; for others, it's created through credentials and hierarchy. Despite global cultural differences, however, trust is always deeply important to a manager's ability to lead. If it is lost, the consequences can be dire. Regardless of exactly how the trust is built, a leader who is trustworthy engenders confidence that they will behave consistently, ethically and authentically in their interactions with all stakeholders. Trust, on a certain level, is based on faith: the faith that someone will act in a way that is reliable and not exploitative of the other person.

---

66 To earn trust, money and power aren't enough; you have to show some concern for others. You can't buy trust in the supermarket.
The Dalai Lama

Development Instructions

1. Display key values.

Regardless of their trust culture, leaders need to display several core values, regardless of the situation, in order earn the trust of various stakeholders. These values include authenticity, compassion, integrity, consistency and humility, among others. These are the qualities that make a person trustworthy in general, not just in business. The question in various business trust cultures is simply, how should these qualities be displayed?

Enacting these values in the real world depends a great deal on the culture of both the business and the external business context. Some cultures show integrity through credentials, while others show it through action. Consider how these values are shown in the surrounding culture and help managers moderate their behaviour accordingly.

2. Behave consistently.

Behaving consistently does not mean doing the same thing over and over again. Rather, desirable consistency allows people to trust that a manager's reactions will follow a certain metric of "reasonableness." This does not mean that all kinds of consistency are good in a leader: someone who is consistently difficult to work with might be predictable, but not in a way that creates trust.

Consistency is usually displayed through actions rather than words. Someone who proclaims that they are reliable is not necessarily reliable – they confirm this self-assessment by showing up on time, being present when necessary and handling things on time and with discretion. When it comes to displaying trustworthy behaviour, it is almost always better to show rather than tell.

3. Act with integrity.

Most people regarded as trustworthy have internal moral compasses that help guide their decisions. Where this compass comes from and how it answers moral questions will vary from person to person. However, a trustworthy person always aims to act in accordance with this moral compass. This doesn't mean that a manager must never make ethical mistakes in order to be trustworthy – however, when ethical mistakes are made, the manager should correct them as quickly as possible.

There may also be outside morality in a given culture or situation that dictates how people should act. Even if this is the case, managers should strive to act in ways that are in harmony with their internal moral compasses, which will give their work greater integrity than simply adopting and adhering to an outside system.

4. Respect confidences.

Trusting someone to keep confidence is at the basis of many business negotiations. Non-disclosure agreements are built around this idea. However, not every secret divulged or sensitive piece of information disclosed is covered by (or requires) an NDA. Furthermore, some sensitive information is sensitive only in specific contexts, but it is ok to disclose with discretion. Managers should maintain awareness of these types of situations and foster a reputation for being able to act with discretion.

Confidentiality at the business level covers everything from human resources knowledge to timelines for rolling out news about the company. Very few people would feel confident hiring an HR person who is a blabbermouth, or promoting a person who has dealt inconsiderately with sensitive personal information of others in the past.

Client confidentiality can be difficult to navigate, depending on the business. Maintaining a certain level of separation between departments can help, but sometimes, it just isn't possible to keep certain types of client information private from people who aren't working on the case. In addition to storing information very securely, managers should avoid sharing client information unless absolutely necessary for the work.

5. Deliver on undertakings.

Trustworthy people tend to also be great time managers. They are able to keep their projects under control so that they deliver what they expect to deliver when they expect to deliver it. Rather than finding excuses later for why a project is running behind, they tend to communicate these worries up front to foster more realistic expectations.

Sometimes, even the best time managers find themselves running behind schedule. To ensure this doesn't hurt their credibility, managers should communicate early and often about any delays, and be as transparent as possible about what caused the delay, even if this shows their work in a less positive light in the short term. Honesty can help avoid crumbling trust when timely delivery isn't possible.

6. Communicate openly.

Trust building communication makes everyone feel safe even when they are vulnerable. Creating or recreating trust depends on having a little trust there to begin with, making it hard to rebuild a relationship once trust is lost. Instead of focusing on the trust that was lost, focus on the trust that remains. For example, if the only thing that remains is a contract, following the contract to the letter (in good faith that this will benefit the other party) can help repair broken trust by establishing the ability to respect boundaries.

Transparency, congruency and competency in communication are all necessary for a leader to be trustworthy. Avoid communicating in ways that do not exhibit these traits, and encourage leaders to be judicious in the way they use communication media. For example, a manager who routinely hits reply-all on sensitive communications may not be trusted with those communications in the future.

7. Actions to match words.

Just because the intent of an action was good doesn't mean the perception of the action was. We define sexual harassment based on the victim's perception, rather than the perpetrator's intention, for a reason: it is the way the action is perceived that affects how the relationship moves forward. If a manager's intentions clearly do not match the way their actions are perceived, it is time for a re-calibration of their workplace behaviour.

Managers need to learn to "walk the talk": if their actions indicate they live by different rules from their team members, they are leading by (confusing) example in ways that they don't intend. If a manager expects their team to arrive on time to meetings, the manager needs to make sure he or she is also on time.

People love stories in which a promise is made early on, and then delivered exactly as expected. Test various scenarios in which this can create results in the workplace. Even in small interactions, this model can be powerfully effective for creating an environment built on trust.

Coaching Suggestions

1. Have coachee devise "personal mission statement"
2. What behaviours give rise to this?
3. Action plan for consistent application

Training Suggestions

1. Start with values
2. Build into actions
3. Roleplay challenging scenarios

Challenge Level: 2 – Difficult

While all managers like to think of themselves as trustworthy, the truth is that many have blind spots in relation to how they are perceived, and the huge influence their behaviours and attitude have on others.

Trust can often take a considerable amount of time to build, but it can be destroyed in an instant through one thoughtless action.

Building and enhancing personal trustworthiness is so valuable to managers who have to lead through challenging environments, and can be achieved through careful planning and communication.

5

BUSINESS

INTRODUCTION

Not all managers come to the position because they were aiming to do "management." In many industries, managers do not have MBAs or a strong business background – they ended up in the position because they were excellent at their jobs before and the job required a talented person with industry knowledge. Unfortunately, this often means that when they enter management, they need to do some work to catch up with their peers who went to business school or retained a sustained interest in the business side of the organisation.

Some of these skills, like finance, process management and human resources responsibilities, may have a steep learning curve at first. In these areas, however, the deficit is usually about lack of knowledge, rather than a reorientation of the manager's thinking about their work. Other skills, like business acumen, strategy and managing other people, are skills that require deep, constant practice and a new understanding of what the point of their work is. This can be a difficult transition for managers who were promoted due to their skill as employees – they may find themselves having to think in new ways or relearn everything they thought they knew about their industry from a management perspective. Some managers handle the challenge with ease and find that they are natural business people; others take more time to adapt. The important thing to note is that, just like the knowledge-based skills, these deeper practice-based skills are also learnable, with the right tools and guidance.

Learning to be an excellent business person is a non-negotiable for managers in all settings. Even if their "business" isn't business, a non-profit manager still needs to understand how internal processes work and how to give feedback well; for example, the principal of a school still needs to have financial acumen and a big picture understanding of how the school and community work together. These skills translate across industry lines because at their core, they are about how we think, not what we do.

Red Flags to Look For

Indicators that a manager might be struggling:

- **They are still operating the way they did before they had management responsibilities.** This could be a sign that they are not seeing the big picture (Gain Big Picture Insight 5.1) or that they find it hard to deal with change for themselves or others (Manage Change 5.7). They could also be repeating old, unproductive processes without questioning their utility (Drive Process Improvement 5.6).

- **They don't seem to be paying attention to certain topics.** This could be a sign that they are uncomfortable with the subject matter and feel out of their league. Subject-specific education can help (Demonstrate Financial Acumen 5.4, Recruit the Right Talent 5.8, Proactively Manage Performance 5.10). However, it could also be a sign that they are not thinking about their new position in terms of the organisation as a whole (Think Strategically 5.5).

- **They are out of touch with current business practices.** Not everyone has the same level of interest in the "business" of business, but that doesn't excuse lack of knowledge. If they lack understanding of how their industry and organisation work as a whole (Display Business Acumen 5.2) or avoid adapting as technology or methods evolve (Demonstrate Agility and Innovation 5.3), it's time for something to change.

- **Their team is dysfunctional.** People management is one of the hardest skills to learn as a new manager, in part because there is both a knowledge and practice gap to fill. Some skills will improve as soon as the manager has the right knowledge (Recruit the Right Talent 5.8), but some require deeper practice and mentorship to learn well (Identify and Retain Talent 5.9, Proactively Manage Performance 5.10).

- **They can't see the forest for the trees.** Good management requires keeping the bigger picture in mind at all times (Gain Big Picture Insight 5.1). Someone who is detail-oriented may have a lot of trouble doing this well, but a manager who gets lost in the details practically ensures that their projects will fail (Think Strategically 5.5). Managers can learn the skills needed to keep their heads in the game (Display Business Acumen 5.2).

Preparation

When you start developing talent, it is important to assess where everyone is starting from. What problems and challenges do managers with excellent business understanding exhibit? What skills do they have that can be better utilised? The questions below can help you assess where an employee may experience problems as they move into leadership roles.

Negative attitude	Extremely	Very	Moderately	Slightly	Not At All
1.Handles change poorly.					
2. Personal goals and organisational goals are disconnected.					
3. Lacks birds-eye-view perspective.					
4. Avoids giving feedback.					
5. Responds badly to criticism.					
6. Holds onto outdated technology or methods.					
7. Has trouble separating the person from the job when it comes to their employees.					

Motivating Drivers

Everyone is motivated differently and understanding yourself is the first step towards understanding others. When a leader knows their own motivations, they are then able to explore the individual motivational drivers for each person on the team. This knowledge can completely change how team leaders interact with their teams and drive team success, so this is where we start.

Each motivational driver comes with its own set of "triggers" – concrete ways to jump-start motivation for someone with that driver. Below, we discuss the four main drivers.

The business of business: People who enjoy the business side of their jobs find the inner workings of companies and industries inherently fascinating. They live for the days when they get to make things work more efficiently or move the company's business activities forward in a tangible way. They tend to have less trouble keeping the big picture in mind but hate getting off-topic in meetings when the conversation doesn't serve a great goal.

Social: People motivated by social interaction appreciate working together with others to create something they couldn't create on their own. These people are more likely to understand the point of meeting with others in person, but are less enthralled by extensive processes and regulations at work. They see relationships as the key to success and approach management in a way that makes the most of their substantial interpersonal skills.

Process: People motivated by process deeply appreciate the mundane. For them, the method of doing something is often more important than the outcome. They believe that a business should operate like a giant machine, which means they can be highly efficient in the right contexts, but may have more trouble with change. They are often quite detail-oriented as well, and can have a hard time seeing the big picture. However, they often have excellent insight into how the pieces of an organisation fit together in order to form the whole, making them the best people to ask when systems management is at the forefront.

Control: People motivated by control often get into management in the first place because they like being in charge. They are comfortable making decisions and managing large groups of people, in part because they feel confidence in their own vision and ability to get things done. Sometimes, this creates issues when they need to work in a team, or the organisational vision is not in line with their personal vision. People strong in control often have a clear vision and sense of direction, and well-developed business acumen, but may have a harder time dealing with change that they did not instigate.

5.1.

GAIN BIG PICTURE INSIGHT

Overview

Managers can become stuck in a bubble where they are only privy to specific types of information. Sometimes this is caused by a values issue (i.e. the manager values quantitative but not qualitative data), and sometimes it's a by-product of being the person at the top (i.e. the manager only hears from a certain range of people and therefore lacks the diverse, grassroots knowledge needed to make a good choice because that information was filtered on the way up the ladder). A good manager is able to work through both personal and structural roadblocks to seek a diverse range of knowledge of internal and external business drivers. The manager can then prioritise and analyse this information, and get a birds-eye overview of the situation to see how each piece connects to the others and the situation as a whole. Learning how to see the big picture is critical to strategic success for the manager's work as a whole.

Setting the Scene

An office manager at a major corporation needs to buy a new printer for the marketing department. If this were 1982, there would probably be one choice, and the office manager would simply buy the only printer available.

Today, we live with an overload of printer choice (and office printer quality is significantly better than in 1982). While this means that a company can print high-quality materials in-house, the office manager needs to do significantly more research to avoid wasting the company's money and marketing department's time on the wrong printer. What does the marketing department need a printer for: full colour marketing materials, or black-and-white photocopying? Does the company have a prior relationship or exclusivity agreement with a specific printer manufacturer? Which printers have the best reviews and ratings? What is the budget for this particular purchase, and is it flexible? Who has final approval of the purchase, and are that person's interests in line with the interests of the marketing department?

When we have so much information, becoming overwhelmed can happen quickly, whether you are buying a printer or making a major business decision. Learning to break down types of knowledge required to make a good choice, gather information from diverse sources quickly and effectively, and prioritise information is essential to strong and strategic management.

HR Trends by importance

Percentage of total responses

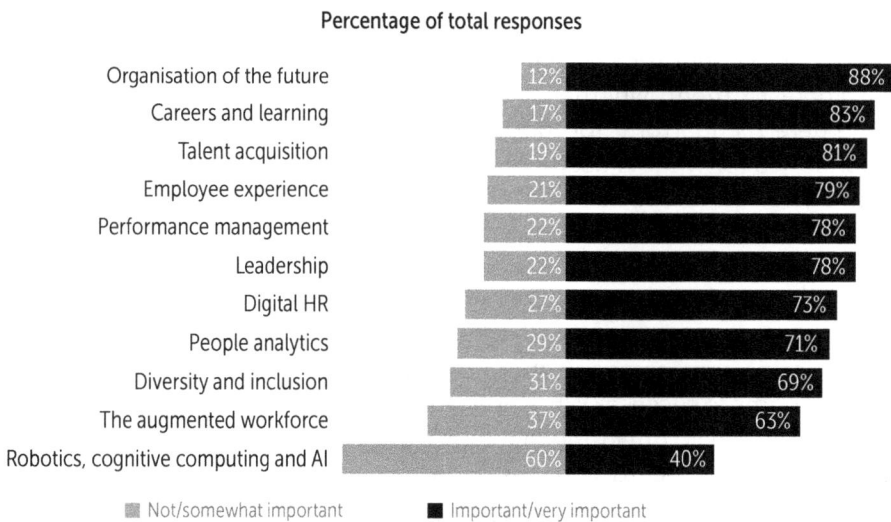

HR Trend	Not/somewhat important	Important/very important
Organisation of the future	12%	88%
Careers and learning	17%	83%
Talent acquisition	19%	81%
Employee experience	21%	79%
Performance management	22%	78%
Leadership	22%	78%
Digital HR	27%	73%
People analytics	29%	71%
Diversity and inclusion	31%	69%
The augmented workforce	37%	63%
Robotics, cognitive computing and AI	60%	40%

2017 Deloitte Global Human Capital Trends

Development Instructions

1. Determine the range, type and scope of information needed.

How wide-reaching is the manager's data? Is there data and information from a variety of stakeholders, or is all information filtered through one or two people?

Is the data quantitative or qualitative? Would some information that is currently expressed quantitatively be more helpful if expressed qualitatively, or vice versa? To understand the problem as a whole, is it better to have more "rational" information (i.e. the annual budget predictions were way off) or "emotional" information (i.e. employees are leaving, and the organisation isn't sure why)?

How much information is necessary? For a small issue, managers may only need a few data points to get an adequate view of the problem at hand, but for a big problem, they may need far more information. How much information needs to be gathered, and from whom?

Rather than considering the three types of information above, many leaders would rather make do with the information they already have because the prospect of gathering and considering more information can feel overwhelming and unnecessarily time-consuming. Therefore, managers should first determine exactly what information is currently available to them, whether it is sufficient and what else needs to be considered important for both expanding the data set and setting boundaries for what is useful and what is not. If data is missing, support managers in learning new strategies for gathering additional information that is appropriate in terms of range, type and scope.

2. Analyse strengths, weaknesses, opportunities and threats.

Consider, current internal and external environment. What environment exists inside that company that creates additional challenges, or eases specific paths to success? What external environmental features loom on the horizon that could affect the manager's plan, such as external stakeholder concerns, governmental changes or developments in technology?

SWOT analysis should be USED: Strengths are Utilised, Weaknesses are Stopped, Opportunities are Exploited and Threats are Defended against. Managers can learn to categorise internal and external environmental factors using SWOT and develop techniques to make sure SWOT is USED effectively.

3. Check validity of information and sources.

Why is this source used? Is this person or source the best possible choice for this particular type of data? For example, a favourite colleague who works in accounting may be a great person to ask about last quarter's numbers, but they may not have the best understanding of the company's strategic vision or the morale problem in HR. Likewise, if a manager is relying on daily news reports to get big picture economics information, they may do better to go straight to the source and read academic papers or professional studies instead.

How accurate/reliable is the data? Rumours are sometimes accurate, but managers should always take steps to verify data that has not been corroborated by a reliable source. Similarly, Wikipedia might be a great place to start research into an issue at the very beginning of the process, but it is not usually an accurate or reliable source for most business information. Managers can be taught how to make nuanced assessments of accuracy and reliability, beyond wikipedia.

What else is available and why is it not used? Is there information the manager has actively chosen to disregard? Why? Is there information they should be ignoring, but are instead giving unearned weight in the decision-making process? Managers should be able to distinguish between valid and invalid reasons for disregarding available information.

4. Develop new sources and maintain existing ones.
Match sources to requirements. A manager who asks their best friend in accounting about the HR morale problem is probably barking up the wrong tree. Developing diverse contacts and sources is essential to obtaining reliable information.

Determine ease of accessibility and backup plans. If the manager's only source of information is their assistant, and the assistant is out on sick leave, the manager is not doing a good job of ensuring strong flows of information. Foster connections and backup options in case the first go-to is unavailable.

5. 5.Understand how insights can support business objectives.
"So what?" Sometimes, the easiest way to determine how information can support strategic decision making is asking this simple question. If a manager can't explain why a piece of information is important in relation to the bigger picture, it probably isn't. Looking at case studies can help because getting specific allows managers to practice this type of analysis and determine which insights will best support business objectives, and which are superfluous.

6. Turn information into strategic action.

It's time to put all of this filtered and analysed information to use. The final step is determining the most valuable data points and coalescing information into a strategic plan. Managers can learn to do this by filling out strategic planning worksheets, brainstorming with others and deploying data organisation systems that work well for their particular data.

Managers can use a variety of strategies to turn each piece of relevant knowledge into an action item that can be completed and measured. If a manager can't see the way in which a data point indicates change is necessary can become an action, it is probably because the data points to a problem are more complex than a to-do item on a checklist. Support managers as they break down data and its implications into smaller actionable tasks.

The strategic plan shouldn't just sit there. As with nearly all managerial tasks, having a method of review is vital to your success: if the manager doesn't know what worked and what didn't, how can they improve the process in the future? Help managers track the output of the strategic plan, and analyse that information to enhance the manager's ability to meet future goals.

Coaching Suggestions

1. Understand what information is currently used
2. Challenge current data sources and explore new ones
3. Test coachee's strategy application tools

Training Suggestions

1. Brainstorm current data sources
2. Look for further sources
3. Conduct live business analysis

Challenge Level: 2 – Difficult

As we observed at the start of this module, many managers rise to their positions through a combination of technical competence, process knowledge and the ability to think on their feet to solve problems. This can make the task of attaining a truly "big picture" view of their organisation and business environment quote a assignment.

Nonetheless, the more any manager can understand the impact of their decisions and output on the business as a whole, the more well-informed and effective their choices will ultimately be. A sharp focus on learning these additional disciplines will pay dividends for any manager looking to add value to their organisation and also their own careers.

5.2.

DISPLAY BUSINESS ACUMEN

Overview

The first step towards developing a strong business acumen is to gain a complete understanding of the company in question. How does the company make and use money? Is the company's internal structures and stakeholder relationships clear, and can managers use that information as necessary? Moreover, how does the company fit into the constellation of companies that surround it as clients, customers and/or competitors in the business environment? People with strong business acumen use an explicit or implicit business framework to ensure completeness and integration as they assess a business situation. The framework links the objectives of key stakeholders, the competitive strategies required for success, and the people and activities needed to produce and sell products and services. Therefore, good business acumen is not just about "rationally assessing" all possible economic outcomes, though this is a major component of the ability. Though the focus is on increasing business profits, good business acumen must combine people knowledge and skills with excellent skills in financial management and strategy.

Setting the Scene

As a society, we are obsessed with the idealised image of the "business person." This ideal type has many qualities we feel must be unteachable: they see opportunities no one else can see, they analyse situations rationally without allowing their emotions to dictate their choices, and they are able to act without hesitation on the decisions they make, despite calculating and knowing the risks. While this "perfect" business person is a fiction, the idealised business person represents several important skills that are, in fact, teachable. Perhaps rather than searching for "business people" to lead us, we should be searching for business acumen and developing the distinct capabilities that make up strong business acumen. Business acumen is the ability to quickly analyse, understand and act towards successful outcomes in a business context. While no one can or should learn to be a perfect, unemotional "ideal business person," it is possible to hone each of the skills that make up good business acumen.

Development Instructions

1. Make decisions that are primarily based upon the business profits.
Managers can workshop test case scenarios to get a sense of how the companies operate on a core level. After getting to know the layout and environment of a new company, managers can act as consultants in designing the most profitable revenue lines for that company, based on a variety of internal and external factors. This workshop can serve as a blueprint for managers' work at within their own (real) company but allows them to explore different scenarios without personal bias.

Understanding profit models, and specifically margin vs volume, is key to managerial success. Does the company operate on a high-margin, low-volume basis? Or is it in strong competition with other companies who offer the same quality of product or service more cheaply? Business acumen can mean different things in these two scenarios. By developing managers' business acumen, they will be in a strong position to keep their company competitive, regardless of the profit model.

2. Deliver results that have the best commercial benefit.
Consider current results measurement: what does the company care about? How do the company's culture and goals affect which results are seen as a commercial success, and which are not?

Desirable outcomes are not always produced by simply following the most commercially beneficial path. The most extreme example would be ethical violations, such as ignoring environmental damage or working conditions in pursuit of profits. But sometimes more subtle problems get in the way as well. How does the company's internal politics affect the possible solutions, and what are seen as most desirable? How do the long-term goals of the company match up with the desire for high short-term returns? Managers can foster their ability to think systemically. By considering the big picture, managers will be able to integrate "softer" types of knowledge with more quantitative-oriented data in order to produce the best possible business outcomes, given the environment in which the organisation operates.

3. Know how the various parts of an organisation functions

No one can fix what they don't understand, and it is impossible to plan without a comprehensive understanding of the systems at play. Managers should work through their organisation's strategic plan and organisational chart to gain a more complete picture of the working environment. What strengths and weaknesses are present? Is change possible? If not, how can managers exploit the company's strengths and minimise interference from weaknesses?

4. Ensure work and actions are aligned with strategic aims of the organisation.

Some organisations explicitly outline their strategic goals in documents published for the entire staff to see. Meetings might be held about these goals, and staff are encouraged to align their progress reports to the organisation's strategic vision. However, many organisations are far less public outside of the highest ranks about primary strategic goals, and some organisations haven't bothered to articulate these goals in a public way at all. Regardless of how open the organisation is, managers can determine the strategic goals of the organisation through direct research. Managers should then align their work with those goals, so that they are always working with the organisational flow, rather than fighting the current.

5. Engage in robust and relevant competitor analysis.

Who is the competition? What is their story? What kind of market share do they have, and how does the manager's company measure up? Defining the company's role in the market can help a great deal in determining both which companies are in direct competition, and analysing those competitors' strengths and weaknesses.

6. Utilise knowledge of company to create competitive advantage and unique selling propositions.

Once a manager has information about their competitors that is relevant, it's time to figure out how to tell their own company's story. Often, this means positioning the organisation in a particular, positive light that takes advantage of the organisation's strengths and minimises weaknesses. For example, Apple uses their "garage start-up" story to keep their image rebellious despite their enormous market share. Use storytelling to shore up weaknesses within the brand. Think about competitive advantages the company can exploit, through storytelling or business action.

7. Keep updated on latest industry and relevant economic trends.
Developing business acumen is an ongoing process. Business acumen is a product of both time and environment – it can't exist in a vacuum. A retailer working for an American department store in 1953 would not have relevant business acumen for a Dubai-based consulting business in 2018. Therefore, keeping business acumen up to date by researching the latest industry developments and relevant economic trends could not be more important. If a manager seems to have fallen behind, it could be that their methods of staying up to date are also old-fashioned. Provide ideas for additional sources of data, and make a plan to cultivate the manager's ongoing business acumen updates, to ensure they never fall out of touch.

Coaching Suggestions
1. Ask relevant questions to gauge current understanding of organisational profitability goals
2. Coachee to conduct competitor analysis for review
3. Review 90 day plan for alignment with organisational goals

Training Suggestions
1. Obtain current organisational strategy as template
2. Have participants build tactical plan to increase revenue
3. Workshop USPs

Challenge Level: 1 – Very Difficult
Business acumen is often spoken of as if it's a mysterious and elusive quality, possessed only by the lucky few who always make the right business decisions. While this is far from the truth, it does speak to the fact that many of the skills that give rise to business acumen take considerable effort and energy to learn.

5.3.

DEMONSTRATE INNOVATION AND AGILITY

Overview

Ballroom dancing, like business, requires a great deal of agility. When working together, a dancing pair must anticipate what is coming next, without losing their ability to improvise in the moment. While technical skill and physical ability is obviously required, the place where great ballroom dancers truly excel is mostly mental: they are able to control their body's response to the music or their partner's motion with great precision. They can adapt their movements gracefully, not only because they have trained their muscles, but because they have trained their minds. Similarly, businesses should always be searching for innovation opportunities and making micro-level adaptations to respond to the business environment, internal shifts and changes in technology or industry. Great managers, like great dancers, are able to notice, understand and process these stimuli in ways that help the business grow responsively. Innovative and agile managers provide high value to organisations by keeping them relevant and adaptable.

Setting the Scene

Innovation and agility are major buzzwords in the business world for a reason. As technology development moves more quickly and revolutionises the ways in which we work, more organisations are finding themselves out of step if they are not constantly looking towards the future. Adaptation is now key to survival in ways it was not 30 years ago: technology changes so rapidly that a business built around a single type of tech will likely fail within ten years if it can't change its business model to reflect technology changes. Therefore, great managers must be able to generate new ideas regularly.

However, these new ideas are only as good as the ability to implement them. If a business is trapped within its own processes and can't either recognise or act upon a good idea, it is likely that someone else will. Managers who can maximise their organisation's ability to adapt and respond to internal and external factors will generate more value for their organisations than managers who stick with the same processes and tired techniques because of "protocol."

The organisation of the future: Old rules vs new rules

Old rules	New rules
Organised for efficiency and effectiveness	Organised for learning, innovation and customer impact
Company viewed as a hierarchy, with hierarchical decision rights, structure and leadership progression	Company viewed as an agile network, empowered by team leaders and fueled by collaboration and knowledge-sharing
Structure based on business function with functional leaders and global functional groups	Structure based on work and projects, with teams focused on products, customers, and services
Advancement through promotion upward with many levels to progress through	Advancement through many assignments, diverse experiences and multifunctional leadership assignments
People "become leaders" through promotion	People "create followers" to grow in influence and authority
Lead by direction	Lead by orchestration
Culture ruled by fear of failure and perceptions of others	Culture of safety, abundance, and importance of risk- taking and innovation
Rules-based	Playbook-based
Roles and job titles clearly defined	Teams and responsibilities clearly defined, but roles and job titles change regularly
Process-based	Project-based

Deloitte University Press

Development Instructions
1. Understand external market trends.
Innovators know their environments well, including the work that is already being done. Avoid duplicating others' work by thoroughly researching both the market and what is already being done in response to market

changes. Often, the most useful innovations piggy-back on existing ideas: one person may see that a response to the market is needed in a certain area, but another person will be able to define what that response should be in greater detail.

Managers need to be able to interpret the data they gain from both market research and investigations into what is already being done. How does a competitor's response to market changes affect the manager's choices? Why did the competitor respond in a certain way, and should the manager's organisation respond differently, or build on the competitor's ideas? Encourage managers to see research as a process that goes beyond the basics of market trends and moves towards a deeper understanding of the industry ecosystem.

2. Listen to stakeholders with regard to current business performance. Having a broad definition of innovation can help managers see where the opportunities for improvement may lie. Start with what is working well: why is it working? What contributes to the success of a particular project or process?

The next step from examining what is working is to look at what isn't doing so well. What do these failing processes and projects have in common with the successful ones? What aspects are different? If managers can identify the differences between successful and unsuccessful projects, it may become clearer where improvement needs to happen. Micro-innovations are often the most important: for example, someone had to invent clickable buttons on screens in order for search engines to become useful. Don't discount an idea just because it seems small at first.

There is a reason so many innovative companies are started by young people. Lack of experience might mean junior staff members have less overall understanding of a problem, but it also allows them to think in novel ways that are often inaccessible to more seasoned professionals. Because they don't know what they don't know, junior members of a team come to problems with a fresh perspective that has not yet been boxed in through deeper knowledge. Including a variety of team members in innovation and agility discussions, at a range of seniority, can ensure that fresh ideas are presented and discussions don't become an echo chamber of professionals with the same depth and type of experience rehashing old, tired ideas.

3. Cultivate and maintains advice and mentoring networks.

Seek out information directly when possible. Everyone is an expert at their particular job – just because someone is more senior doesn't mean that they have more information about the source of an issue that mostly affects lower-level employees or customers. New sources of information often lead to new ideas. Creating a network that includes multiple organisational levels can help avoid echo chambers. Sometimes, the deepest organisational knowledge in a particular area like customer service resides at the lowest levels of the hierarchy.

Make sure that your mentoring networks are diverse. People with a variety of approaches, personal styles and knowledge bases will contribute different ideas. Advice from different areas may allow managers to think about problems in new ways and show where innovation is possible, in ways that a less diverse group may have missed because of a communal blind spot.

Consider what mentoring groups and networks already exist. How can the manager take advantage of the resources that are already in place? How can untapped knowledge be better utilised? Avoid reinventing the wheel and adding to noise where possible: often, pre-existing groups can be built upon to improve innovation and agility without adding to organisational bulk. Help managers seek advice from the right sources and build towards ideas of openness and sharing within these existing groups.

4. Adapt to change.

When managers operate in a vacuum it can be tempting to simply start making changes. Instead, encourage managers to consider their response ideas and then look at how other teams are responding before implementing any changes.

Can the manager initiate a change rather can simply reacting to external forces? Consider how a change can be deepened to prepare the organisation or team for the next round of (inevitable) shifts. Is there a way that a change precipitated by a particular situation can be applied to other issues in the organisation more generally? Encourage managers to take a long view when it comes to adaptability.

5. Develop personal strategic plans.

Innovation is everyone's job. However, everyone will bring something slightly different to the table. When an organisation is attempting deeper change, it can be easy for managers to sit back and wait until it's finished because they don't have "expertise" in a particular area. However, innovation happens when new ideas are applied to existing problems. Help managers consider what their unique perspective can add to an ongoing discussion.

Understanding their particular perspective can help managers decide how to strategise and promote innovation within their own domains. Considering their personal management style, as well as their own strengths and weaknesses, how can a manager create opportunities for innovation? Start with simple changes first. Help managers make 90-day plans to increase opportunities for innovation and agility with reasonable goals that are responsive to external factors and the manager's personal strengths and weaknesses.

6. Encourage collaborative innovation processes.

Dump the "Not Invented Here" mindset. Managers who avoid sharing information with other teams in order to retain credit for their innovations are only shooting themselves in the foot. By keeping information to themselves, managers cut off their best source of great ideas – inspiration from other people. The image of the lone innovator working away silently on their own has always been fiction: true innovation can only emerge in open spaces. This does not mean managers should not claim credit where credit is due; rather, they should encourage others, especially within the organisation, to use their ideas in novel ways, and borrow ideas from others to build their own work.

Managers can start by considering their teams' weaknesses and strengths. Where is there a gap in team knowledge? Perhaps the team is heavy on technical understanding, but lacks project management experience. In this case, the manager should seek help from another team whose skills are in project management, with the goal of combining both types of expertise for great inspiration on both sides.

7. Share best practice.

Best practices work best when widely shared. "But I just cleaned up this mess" is the first thought of a manager who has not shared and implemented best practices. Managers do themselves a disservice when they avoid sharing best practices because of the time it would take to implement widely – they will end up cleaning up the same messes over and over again.

Identify great practitioners and copy them. If someone, either inside or outside the organisation or industry, seems particularly good at something, encourage mangers to copy that practice and adapt it to suit the organisation or team. For example, nurses adopted the practice of checklists into the medical profession from airline pilots, who had a much lower human-error rate.

Catalogue and record best practices. If great practice is only transmitted informally, it can be hard to ensure new team members are acclimatised quickly, or will be willing to adopt the practice, especially if the old way feels easier. Managers should record best practices in formal documents that can be casually referenced for maximum effectiveness.

Coaching Suggestions
1. Look for history of personal involvement with innovative projects
2. Have coachee bring live example of current innovation to session
3. Work on personal strategic plan

Training Suggestions
1. Definition of innovation is key
2. Discuss current feedback loops – are they valuable or "echo chambers"?
3. Innovation must happen at all levels – it's a mindset

Challenge Level: 3 – Neutral
Whether prepared for it or not, all business leaders need to demonstrate the ability to innovate, purely due to the fact that the modern business world is constantly shifting and changing around them. The choice is whether they acknowledge and accept this environment and take steps to move within it, or push back until change becomes inevitable. This is the difference between thriving and struggling for any manager.

5.4.

DEMONSTRATE FINANCIAL ACUMEN

Overview

Successful companies do not rely solely on the finance department or senior leadership to understand, interpret and apply financial information. They recognise the value in developing this critical competency for leaders across every function. For the uninitiated, financial information can feel like it is written in a foreign language. Once the code is understood, learning the basics of finance for business becomes much easier. Most of these principles are probably things you have already seen in your work as a manager. By combining a manager's experience as a business person with a basic financial education, they will be able to grasp the meaning behind data points and point to insights that could be invaluable to their organisation.

Setting the Scene

For a manager who doesn't work in finance, it's easy to think that maintaining a deep understanding of finance or the financial workings of their organisation is not necessary to their job. However, at the end of the day, all for-profit businesses are designed primarily to make money, and even if a manager works at a not-for-profit, they are likely dealing with a wide range of businesses and fiscal reporting measures to support their organisation's work. Developing a broad understanding of financial management principles doesn't mean managers need to go back to business school, or take that microeconomics course they missed at university. Many of these principles can be picked up through experience and short study. Having a basic background in finance can be invaluable to a manager's ability to make decisions that are fiscally sound and responsible. Many people without a formal education in finance find the jargon and culture around finance intimidating or perplexing, but it doesn't have to be that way. At its most basic level, finance is about viewing the world through the lens of profit and loss, which is a skill that anyone can master.

Development Instructions

1. Understand revenue drivers for the organisation.

Which lines of business are most profitable? The general rule for most organisations is that 80% of your profit will be generated by 20% of your business. Is the company focused on those profit-generators, or dividing attention with less profitable avenues?

Are there strategic "loss leaders"? Is there any part of the business that is being used to try to attract customers, but which isn't providing a financial return? Why? Not all loss leaders are a poor financial strategy but understanding their purpose can help managers direct energy appropriately.

Where should maximum energy be focused? Are employees spending most of their time and energy on the least profitable 80% of clients or customers? Or is most of the energy directed towards maximising the top 20%? Taking a hard look at the financial data can help managers decide where to direct their team's energy, rather than allowing their attention to be diverted by whoever is yelling the loudest. Help managers map the financial environment in which the organisation or department operates, in order to gain a clear understanding of the best uses for time and energy.

2. Understand cost drivers for the organisation.

How does the organisation understand and experience the costs of doing business? Analysing the underlying organisational cost structure can help managers gain a clearer picture of where the money the organisation earns is directed, as well as which costs are necessary and which might be reduced. The Pareto Principle will be helpful in analysis and can help managers gain clear insight into the ways costs affect business.

Managers should identify waste and duplication – but what good is identifying waste if the manager can't fix the problem? Help managers learn strategies to reduce unnecessary costs, taking both fiscal and political priorities into account.

3. Trade off volume vs margin.

Unfortunately, it truly is impossible to "have it all" in business, when it comes to volume versus margin. Even managers without a finance background can learn to do basic Cost-Volume-Profit analysis, workshop several test case scenarios and strategise methods for determining their business' optimal volume vs margin trade off. Along with Cost-Volume-Profit analysis, managers can determine the differences between gross margin and contribution margin, conduct breakeven analysis, and learn other quantitative methods to help them determine the best path forward given the specific trade-offs present in their organisation.

4. Demonstrate basic balance sheet understanding.

One of the first steps towards achieving financial literacy as a manager is learning to read a simple balance sheet and interpret the data. Ensure managers have mastered the basics of reading a balance sheet and relevant methods of quantitative data interpretation. If a manager doesn't know what they are looking for, how can they act on important information?

5. Demonstrate Basic P&L understanding.

A profit and loss statement (P&L) shows a company's income and expenses over a specific period and time. Depending on the organisation's core business, this may be one of the most important documents managers can have to help them determine smart financial action moving forward. Help managers learn to read a simple P&L. With so many choices within a company dependent on finance, accurately interpreting a P&L can help ease the decision-making process over the long term and reduce unnecessary stress over whether the choice made was fiscally responsible.

6. Consider performance in financial context.

How well does the manager's job description match up with your organisation's current financial goals? Do their key performance indicators (KPIs) reflect the company's objectives, or are they out of touch with the profit-driven side of the organisation? Discussing the ways in which managers' performance can affect the financial aspects of the company, can provide everyone with the necessary insight to improve.

Sometimes, a manager's position can feel at odds with the organisation's primary objectives. Perhaps they work in a perpetually underfunded department, or they are stuck on a project that isn't bringing in the anticipated revenue. In both of these scenarios, it is still possible to tie the company's financial goals into the manager's performance measurement, which can help remove the roadblocks preventing them from making progress. Strategise methods for realigning managers' goals so that they are in step with the organisation's fiscal reality, rather than constantly fighting the stream.

7. Build plan to increase revenue and decrease costs.
Help managers create personalised 90-day plans to incorporate revenue increases and cost decreases. The final product will take into account the manager's individual situation, and the organisational environment in which they operate. By creating a 90-day plan, managers will be able to effectively test run their newly developed financial acumen in a real-world environment. Provide managers with the help they need to assess the success of the 90-day plan and rework the plan as circumstances change.

Coaching Suggestions
1. Test current knowledge of organisational financial position
2. Set task to read and understand annual report
3. Have coachee explain which lines are most profitable and why

Training Suggestions
1. Use existing financial data from organisation where available
2. Participants to build their own financially based performance goals
3. Quiz to understand typical business financial jargon

Challenge Level: 1 – Very Difficult
A great many business managers did not arrive at their current position via a formal education in finance or accounting. This can make the effort to engage with the financial side of the business daunting and intimidating. Ultimately, though, without a thorough understanding of the financial drivers of the business, it is impossible to make completely informed decisions that will prove to be impactful in the short term and sustainable in the long term.

5.5.

THINK STRATEGICALLY

Overview

We tend to see strategy only with a view of the long term, but strategic thinking encompasses all aspects of decision making, short term and long term. Strategic thinking is a lens we can use to think about, assess and create the future. It helps us take all necessary factors into account before making decisions. While some people demonstrate a knack for strategy before learning the basics, learning to think strategically is a process. This is because good strategists are able to coalesce a plan out of a variety of knowledge types and experiences, with the end goal always in clear sight. Learning to focus on that end goal without sacrificing the details (seeing both the forest AND the trees) is a skill that can be developed over time. Furthermore, the more knowledge and experience a manager has about a variety of situations, the more relevant information can be incorporated into (or edited out of) their strategy.

Setting the Scene

Major conferences choose their keynote speakers for a variety of reasons. Perhaps they want a scientist on the cutting edge of research to talk to R&D teams at major companies; sometimes, it's a golden child of entrepreneurship who is invited to divulge insights about the future of their small corner of the market. In all cases, nearly every keynote speaker at a major business conference can be seen as an expert in strategic thinking. This is the person who can see five moves ahead when everyone else can only see one. They aren't psychic; far from it, most strong strategic thinkers acknowledge that a variety of possible outcomes are likely. Instead, they use their skills to put their company and their vision in the best possible position given each likely outcome. Watching them work, it is easy to think that strategic thinking simply comes naturally to them, and they have innate abilities that can't be taught. The reality is that all strategic thinkers gained their abilities through both study and experience.

They actively develop their ability to come up with effective plans which align with both organisational objectives and economic realities.

Future workforce strategies

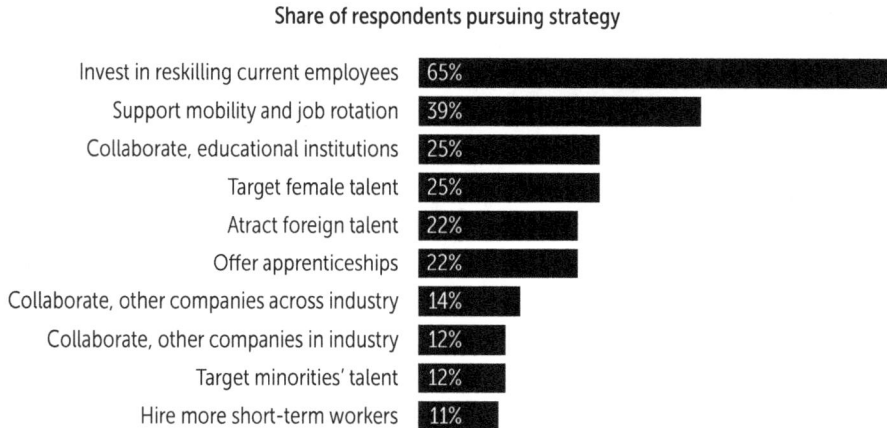

Share of respondents pursuing strategy

Strategy	%
Invest in reskilling current employees	65%
Support mobility and job rotation	39%
Collaborate, educational institutions	25%
Target female talent	25%
Atract foreign talent	22%
Offer apprenticeships	22%
Collaborate, other companies across industry	14%
Collaborate, other companies in industry	12%
Target minorities' talent	12%
Hire more short-term workers	11%

Future workforce strategies
Future of Jobs Survey, World Economic Forum

Development Instructions

1. Develop a clearly defined business and/or personal vision.

Keeping a strategic lens depends on having a vision for the future, Without a lens to focus strategy, it will be impossible to move towards any ideal, imagined future. The first step is for the manager to determine the organisation's vision – sometimes this is explicitly spelled out for employees in an annual report, or in online marketing materials, but sometimes, this process will involve deeper thinking and longer conversations with higher-level members of the company. The manager should then develop blueprints for these kinds of conversations and begin to assess the vision of the organisation.

Knowing the organisation's vision for the future is the first step; the next step is for the manager to figure out their vision for the future and how that vision can align with the organisation's goals. What ideas do they have for their personal and professional life? How can they align those plans with their organisation's vision? Discuss strategies for creating alignment without sacrificing either the manager's vision or disregarding the environment in which they work.

2. Define objectives and break down into specific actions.

Building a living strategic plan is the best possible classroom for learning to think strategically in all aspects of your work life. Does the manager have a strategic plan already? If so, help them work through their current planning process to determine if they have effectively aligned their personal goals with their organisation's goals.

How can a manager tell the difference between a good strategic plan and a poor strategic plan, especially if they have never made one before? Many strategic plans fail, and often for completely preventable reasons relating to writing the strategic plan in the first place. Elements that make up a good strategic plan include how to avoiding bias and subjective judgments, creating clarity of purpose, developing the plan with a sense of urgency, drawing out organisational and personal strengths through the planning process, and creating the organisational discipline to stick with the plan. Help the manager create personalised, pragmatic, strategic plans that can carry them through their work year.

3. Build flexibility into plans via review process.

Many companies goes through regular strategic planning processes. What happened after that process? Did anyone remember the strategic plan or check it regularly once the consultants left? How about after six months? Or after two years? A good strategic plan should be a living document. If the document isn't flexible enough to account for unexpected hurdles or windfalls that come up in the course of business, it isn't a good plan. The strategic plan should operate like a budget; it must be updated regularly, using new data that helps you compare the plan with how things actually turned out. How often are strategic plans reviewed? What data are used to decide whether the plan is still appropriate, if it needs to be modified or if the organisation needs a new plan altogether? Managers should integrate data appropriately, and decide on reasonable timelines for review, based on their organisation's goals and their personal plans.

4. React and respond to internal and external environmental changes.
Once a manager has a flexible strategic plan and strategy for review, how can they use this plan to respond to changes? Strategic plans are designed to provide the insight necessary not only to see the big picture, but to see how to achieve the big picture through thoughtful, measured, clear actions. Managers can use techniques, for example, SWOT analysis to ensure they are able to capture both big overviews and detailed assessments. Managers can increase this skillset by learning to initiate and manage change at the micro as well as the macro level, so that their organisation and their work are still working in service of the vision embodied by the strategic plan.

5. Utilise resources to test strategies.
What resources can a manager use to support their strategic plan? Keeping good tabs on mentoring and advice networks can be crucial when managers are just starting to formulate a strategic plan. As managers improve their strategising skills, checking in regularly with a mentor can help them avoid common pitfalls and issues they did not foresee because of lack of experience. Help managers discover where to seek advice, both within the company and in the outside world.

How can managers tell if a strategic plan is moving in the right direction (or about to fail) without taking major risks? The key is to stress-test the plan with experienced outsiders or stakeholders in the project before putting it into action. No one is unbiased, but it is extremely hard to see where we ourselves are biased and where our blind spots are without outside help. Keep in mind that someone with a different perspective may be the best at spotting weaknesses. Help managers conduct these sorts of stress tests so that they get information they can use, and not criticism without purpose.

6. Be open to new opportunities and ideas.
Strategising is an ongoing process. How does the manager's plan dovetail with events within the market? What about events outside the market? Sometimes, the best opportunities can come from unexpected places; if a manager isn't prepared to accept a different idea, they may miss the opportunity altogether. The microwave oven was invented when a scientist working on military radar applications accidentally melted the chocolate bar in his pocket by standing too close to the device he had created.

At tech conferences, nearly everyone calls their invention "disruptive," though few actually are. How can managers separate the wheat from the chaff? There are tell-tale signs of truly disruptive ideas and technologies, that can help managers avoid wasting time with the wrong development. While not fool-proof, learning what makes an idea truly disruptive can help managers both develop their own ideas and plans for the future, and recognise opportunities within the market when they see them.

Coaching Suggestions
1. Determine coachee's business vision – how does this link to the organisation
2. Review strategic action plans and refine
3. Explore and expand advice networks

Training Suggestions
1. Obtain current organisational strategy as template
2. Have participants build personal strategic vision, aligned with organisation
3. Explore formal and informal advice and mentoring networks

Challenge Level: 2 – Difficult
Strategic thinking comes more naturally to some than others, but the disciplines that give rise to practical and effective strategy outcomes are as learnable as any other business skill.

For many, the ability to improve their big picture thinking relies firstly on a willingness to look at their activities and business from a different perspective than they're familiar with. Once this shift is made, application of specific techniques becomes easier.

5.6.

DRIVE PROCESS IMPROVEMENT

Overview

Sometimes it can be difficult just to see the processes we are using, and if we can't see the process, how can we change it? In many cases, these processes have become so automated in our own minds we barely think of them as processes: the company has been working around a problem for so long that everyone has forgotten what the problem was in the first place. Furthermore, changing ingrained processes requires buy-in from committed leadership and stakeholders throughout the value chain. Therefore, it makes sense that there would be a specific set of tools and techniques to help managers improve processes and create lasting change.

Setting the Scene

Looking at how people handle their email on a normal day at the office can be telling both of the organisation's processes and the person's individual productivity. Does the manager of a team arrive at the office, pour themselves a cup of coffee, sit down at their desk and spend the first hour or so checking their email? Or do they chat with colleagues first, attend a couple of meetings, and then only get to email during the slow period after lunch? Do they respond to emails as they come in, or do they wait to attend to them during a set period of time during the day?

Everyone has a different way of handling email, some of which is defined by the necessities of their positions. However, more and more research points to the idea that handling emails as they come in, for most of us, interrupts our workflow and makes us less productive, even if we are technically more responsive. Email is just one area where reconsidering what is "normal" can potentially help us find better ways of doing business.

By reconsidering the "normal" of our workdays and making it "odd" again (how weird is it that we feel the need to respond immediately to someone who is writing to us online, but not to someone who knocks on our office doors!) we can start to see where we might improve. By improving processes within an organisation through studied analysis, we have the opportunity to make the organisation more efficient and our days less hectic.

Development Instructions

1. Align process improvement objectives to organisational strategic outcomes.

The first step to improving processes within an organisation is to figure out which processes are not working for the organisation or its members. Start by analysing the organisational goals and values known and experienced by the participants at their own companies. If we understand strategic objectives in advance, we have a baseline against which to measure processes to decide if they meet these objectives. For example, if one organisational objective is "client-centric practice," a billing process that requires five signatures and takes weeks to get the final bill to the client probably is not meeting that objective. By using organisational values as the starting point, we can start to make all incongruent processes strange again, and begin asking the questions necessary to jumpstart change.

Sometimes, we can easily see where a process isn't serving us (everyone has a version of the horrible billing process above), but we can't see a better way to do things, because the process was developed specifically to meet certain criteria within the spectrum of organisational needs. Use techniques to uncover easier, smarter paths to achieve the same outcomes, while taking into account the organisational needs that created the dysfunctional process in the first place.

2. Use defined process analysis methodology.

Chart out existing processes to make them visible and easier to understand, including all of the reasons for the different elements in the process. Why does one billing process require five signatures? Are there steps that are outdated, either because technology improved or organisational objectives and realities changed? Noting each step of the process and the reasons for those steps can start to make it clear where the process CAN be changed.

Design desired future processes. Once we can see what we are aiming for, it becomes easier to find alternative methods for achieving the goals intended by the dysfunctional process. Search for the reasons for each of the elements that make the process dysfunctional, and develop new ways of ensuring those elements are not ignored by a more functional process.

Managers should try out different techniques for handling process improvement depending on the size, complexity and nature of the organisation. Process improvement looks very different from improvement in a small start-up or a government agency.

3. Develop process maps and flowcharts.
Encourage managers to use flowcharts to easily map processes and then move elements around as necessary. Like processes, if the diagrams a manager uses to map them are too stagnant, they resist change and end up creating more problems than they solve. By creating a visual aid that works for their needs, managers will be able to facilitate frontline knowledge. Make sure that processes are no longer the obscure, unintelligible domain of upper management, but working knowledge that everyone in the organisation can access and manage as necessary.

4. Understand process interdependencies.
Processes are often deeply interwoven, and understanding exactly how processes intersect and impact one another can be key to making change last. If the new process is more streamlined, but creates problems for a parallel process, it is unlikely employees will stick with the new process for long.

The next thing to consider is who is impacted? If the process will result in a major change in workflow for a specific group of people, how can a manager help them adapt and deal with that? What will have to change upstream or downstream of the process in question, and are the people involved capable of handling the required changes?

Lastly, consider what barriers or roadblocks exist which could prevent the change from being implemented. Roadblocks come in many forms: managers may find themselves up against organisational inertia, or significant financial or technological hurdles.

One barrier that should not be underestimated is the employee who is extremely invested in the current process. Perhaps they designed the process, or maybe their entire job revolves around this one process and changing it could mean they find themselves out of work. Managing people-driven roadblocks is delicate – support managers as they attempt to navigate these issues.

5. **Obtain input to current process and proposed changes.**
One important step for managing roadblocks created by people is to get input from the people affected. Anyone involved in the old process is a relevant stakeholder, and seeking their input is not only an important step to making them feel heard and comfortable with the change, it could provide insights a manager otherwise would not have encountered.

Often, a process change now means a technology change – perhaps better software now exists than when the organisation invented the process, or the company is still using paper records for something because a now-retired manager was uncomfortable going digital. Knowing where to seek relevant technical knowledge, both around appropriate software and implementation concerns, is key to a good transition. Help managers learn to spot strong expertise, even if they aren't "techies" themselves.

6. **Define and communicate process change.**
Change is scary. Developing a transparent change management plan and a strong communication plan is vital to the success of the change, and avoiding drops in morale. Develop a change management plan and ensure that plan is communicated appropriately to different levels of stakeholders. Create personalised communication plans, using language that emphasises the positives of the changes without seeking to minimise the difficulty of change for parties who may find the shift challenging. Finally, institute feedback processes, so that managers can gather information in real time, and ensure that all stakeholders feel heard as things continue to shift and settle.

7. **Implement and test new process.**
Companies rarely roll out new technology all at once; first, they go through a beta test, allowing a small subset of users to test the technology while they observe, with the explicit understanding that the technology may not yet be fully functional. The same holds true for process change. Help managers set up beta tests of the change in order to work out any kinks before rolling it out on a larger scale.

Clearly defined measures for success, with room for unexpected feedback, will give managers the best vision of whether the process is working properly or not. Gaining insight from negative feedback is facilitated by clear metrics for success: If managers don't know what success is, all negative feedback can feel overwhelming. Keep in mind that feedback loops are important for continuous improvement, regardless of whether they speak directly to the metrics for success or not. Help managers set up those loops and metrics to ensure constructive feedback and actionable metrics.

Coaching Suggestions
1. Assess coachee's understanding of business priorities and how this can create a process improvement plan
2. Review and improve existing plan
3. Identify key skills that need to be developed to ensure effective plan implementation

Training Suggestions
1. Best undertaken with live example
2. Organisational goals and priorities must be understood in advance
3. An experienced external facilitator can bring 'fresh eyes' to an existing process

Challenge Level: 5 – Very Easy
With the right mindset, process improvement can be a relatively simple and quite enjoyable journey. All that's required is a willingness to take feedback, step back and look at the big picture, then engage the great ideas of the team, who are probably already frustrated with the process and have some excellent ideas on how it can be improved.

5.7.

HARNESS CHANGE

Overview

Strong change leaders understand that the organisation is counting on their ability to manage change, just as much as they are counting on the organisation to support their work and to make good choices about the future. But it's not simply about "change management". The very best leaders "harness" change and see it as an opportunity rather than an impost.

Setting the Scene

Change is hard for most people. Whether it's moving spaces or changing jobs, all transitions come with their own set of challenges and the process of transitioning can make the person in flux feel like they are experiencing a major setback, even if the transition was supposed to be a big step forward. Maybe that promotion has a steep learning curve or maybe the move to the new office was more expensive than originally anticipated (isn't it always). The frustration of transition periods doesn't mean the change was bad – on the contrary, sometimes these issues are just growing pains, a temporary hurdle before change creates improvement. However, transitional difficulties can feel so overwhelming that most people resist change, even when it is deeply necessary for organisational health, personal growth, or professional efficiency.

Managers in large organisations rarely have control over if and when change is implemented. However, the responsibility of harnessing change for positive outcomes still falls squarely on the manager's shoulders. As a manager, they are not only expected to handle change well themselves – they are required to equip their staff with the skills and knowledge necessary to manage change, and support the entire team through the change process. Strong change management skills could make the difference between a team's ability to thrive in a constantly changing business environment, and drowning in the difficulties created by transition periods.

Development Instructions

1. Recognise when change is required.

If a manager is the kind of person who likes routine and stability, all change can feel like the worst possible option – it would be better to keep working in subpar conditions than to deal with the chaos created by change. Recognise when change is valuable or even necessary. Creating positive associations with change are vital for those in management roles. Between constantly evolving technology and speed at which business moves today, it's inevitable that managers will need to manage change on a regular basis. This gets significantly easier, even for change-resistant people, if they can learn to recognise when change is necessary from an organisational perspective before the change is implemented from above. Help managers learn to spot key drivers for change and implement small scale changes within their control as practise for handling bigger changes with more ease.

Assessing whether change would be valuable starts with understanding what's not working. What processes or situations create friction in the manager's work day? What organisational issues are preventing the manager from being more effective or competitive in their field? Are there any aspects of the team's work that are somewhat dysfunctional?

Even if the manager has no idea how to fix these problems, simply recognising that there ARE problems can help them start seeing change as a positive, and brainstorming ways that the situation could be different. What are the manager's biggest, craziest aspirational goals for their team? What stands in the way of those goals? Knowing what they'd like their ideal future to look like can be a deeply motivating force for handling the unpleasantness of transition periods.

2. Articulate typical responses to change.

Of course, not all change is positive or fully within one manager's control. Maybe the market shifts unexpectedly, or upper management makes a decision to take the organisation in a new direction that they don't agree with, or a vital employee leaves the company. Regardless of whether changes are positive or negative, within or outside of their control, the cycle of adapting to change looks remarkably similar. Help manager anticipate the emotions to expect at each stage of change, deal with feelings of loss and strategise for making the best of bad situations.

It's easy to talk about change in the abstract, but it can be hard to understand what change will feel like without real-life examples. Therefore, workshop real examples in order to recognise the symptoms of change fatigue and change stress more easily. If a manager can't tell when they or someone else is entering the danger zone, it's going to be really hard to manage their own stress.

3. Recognise signs of stress among people.

What happens to the body and mind when someone gets stressed out? Some of us lose our appetites or eat too much, but often, signs and symptoms are subtler than that. Understand common stress behaviours and symptoms, and how to manage them in oneself and in others. This can be especially important because stress is contagious. If one person isn't coping effectively, the whole team could be at risk.

Recognising danger signs is especially important when managing stress in a team setting. Help managers learn to recognise the biggest red flags that should prompt immediate action when observed in themselves or others, as well as appropriate interventions and protocols to neutralise the threat to team health. Destigmatising mental health issues can't be done by a single manager – the cultural issues around stress, anxiety, and depression are simply too complex. However, there are ways that managers can modulate their responses and their teams' environments, so that they and others feel safer discussing their mental state and asking for help when they need it. Brainstorm techniques for creating a safe and open environment, as well as effective coping strategies and additional resources.

4. Support people through change cycle.

Not all change management is just about coping – strong change leaders are able to see opportunities even while managing difficult emotions. The change process might be easily broken down into a standardised emotional cycle, but no two changes are ever exactly the same, no matter how similar the circumstances. Help managers understand that the only thing they can truly control is their own response to the emotions and circumstances created by the change around them.

5. Devise structured change plan.

Once managers understand their own responses to change on a deeper level, it's time to collaborate with others. Create a structured change plan that can be easily understood and referenced by anyone affected by the change, with room for adaptation and flexibility. Change can make people feel like they are on a road to a known destination but without a map or GPS. If it turns out the map isn't leading to the right destination, the manager needs to be able change it so they arrive where they intended.

Successful change management requires the full participation and buy-in from all parties. Change is hard enough without having to actively manage resistance from within. Furthermore, without input from all stakeholders, you risk creating avoidable problems by implementing change in a way that makes things harder for some people involved. Gaining input on the change plan from all stakeholders, both before implementing the plan, and throughout the change process, is therefore vital to successful change.

What does "successful change" mean? The answer will be different for every situation, but defining measures of success means managers are aiming for something – even if the change was not planned or not welcome. "Surviving" is rarely the best someone can do. Help managers brainstorm potential models for success and how to decide what criteria make the most sense in a specific situation.

6. Create impactful meaningful change without fatigue.

Pace is important. Some people have a hard time not doing everything at once – transitions make them feel anxious or behind. They want to "fix" those feelings as quickly as possible. In order to get up and running or "back to normal," they will push themselves to exhaustion, working 14 hour days to get through the change faster. Others procrastinate or delay, unable to make vital decisions, and remain trapped in the transition period far longer than they need to be. Both responses to change can be highly counterproductive and make change harder than it needs to be.

Sometimes, there is a giant gulf between actual change that is happening and the way it is perceived. This is particularly true of large-scale organisational changes that come from top management. Often, the purpose and reasons for the change are related to market strategy or even forces outside the company, the way that people experience those changes is deeply personal. And it is personal, especially when someone has to be let go, even if the reason is that the department's budget was cut. Managing the perceived changes from the perspective of the team is just as important as managing the actual changes from an organisational perspective. The big question is, how can a manager balance those two perspectives and interests? Managers should walk that line by keeping larger objectives in mind while acknowledging the personal impact and perceptions of the change.

7. Create communication plan and implement.
Handling the gulf between perceived and actual change is often the domain of a communication team. A good communication plan is vital during transitions, but many managers don't have a communication plan that is working for them. Either they are delivering incoherent, different messages to different stakeholders (who then talk to each other and realise that their information doesn't match up, which can make them feel lied to and less trusting of the change), or they aren't open and detailed from the start (allowing rumours to fester), or they refuse to acknowledge the perceived aspects of change, focusing only on the explicit detail. Help the manager create outlines for a strong communication plan that avoids all these potential pitfalls and continues supporting and guiding the team through the transition period, without sugar-coating the reality of transitional challenges.

Coaching Suggestions
1. Understand coachee's own experience of and approach towards change
2. Take it back to 'big picture' to gauge understanding of need for change
3. Work through specific key issues of resistance and challenge

Training Suggestions
1. Best undertaken with live example
2. Ensure specific actions arise
3. Must be supported at higher levels of organisation

Challenge Level: 3 – Neutral

All business leaders need to harness change as a large part of their role. This applies not only to large-scale strategic shifts in direction, but also to day-to-day problem solving.

The more effectively a manager can not only cope with change, but use change as an opportunity to guide their teams through to improved outcomes, the more valuable they'll be to any organisation.

Change management can be stressful, simply by its nature. Building skills, and therefore confidence in dealing with and communicating different change scenarios is critical.

5.8.

RECRUIT THE RIGHT TALENT

Overview

Managers outside of the recruiting department often rely on HR to do all of their recruiting for them. However, it is the manager who ultimately needs to work with the candidates who are hired, and therefore, it is in the manager's best interest to do their own recruiting and stay invested in the full cycle HR recruiting process.

When recruiting, many managers make the mistake of thinking that they are the only person doing the interviewing - but a strong candidate is also looking at the company and their interviewer with a critical eye, wondering if this organisation is the right fit for them in the long term. The ability to attract and recruit the appropriate talent is key to the ongoing viability of the organisation.

An expert recruiter is able to ensure great people are placed into the correct roles, while avoiding common pitfalls and traps which end up in a poor fit for the candidate and the organisation. Does the organisation's recruiting process support these goals? Are the best candidates getting the information they need to make a good choice? Is the manager getting the information they need from the candidates to know if the role is a good fit?

Setting the Scene

Anyone who has been through the process of terminating an employee due to poor on-the-job performance will understand it is lengthy, technical, requires significant documentation and can sometimes place great stress on not only the employee, but their manager too. The reason for the lengthy process is the legal requirement to demonstrate that the employee has been (quite rightly) given every opportunity to improve to an acceptable standard.

Of course, this is not the only reason people leave an organisation. Often a business will be more than happy with a particular employee's performance, only to find that the employee themselves decides to leave for reasons of their own.

Now, consider the cost of replacing those people. There's not only the work that has to be temporarily reassigned, there's also the time and expense of engaging in a whole new recruitment, training and onboarding process before a new employee can be brought up to speed.

All of which can be avoided by recruiting well in the first instance. Recruiting judiciously is just good professional practice. Great recruiting can help organisations and employees ensure the long-term career success and development of the recruit, as well as growth in knowledge, skills and effectiveness of the organisation.

Development Instructions

1. Mine recruitment sources.

What is the manager's current approach to recruitment? Do they send a job description to HR and then sit back and wait? If managers think about recruitment as a task that they can completely outsource to another department, they are likely missing valuable opportunities and excellent candidates. Many managers see recruiting as an add-on to their "regular" jobs, not something that is an integral part of their jobs.

Non-traditional sources often yield the best results. Very specific types of candidates come through online recruiting tools. For a manager at a large firm, or one who has heavily outsourced recruiting responsibilities, it's likely the candidates coming through are a deeply filtered selection that may have nothing to do with what the company is actually seeking. For example, what if the recruitment filtering software automatically rejects resumes sent in PDF form, because the software can't search PDFs for keywords? Furthermore, the only candidates who apply via the recruiting software are the ones who found the job advertisement in the first place. These candidates may or may not be well suited to the job – they just happen to be on the same platforms as the company. Help managers use non-traditional recruiting methods to find the right candidates for the job, not the application process.

This isn't to say that managers should ignore traditional recruiting tools, or avoid using recruitment agencies at all. However, sites like LinkedIn, Monster or local tools are only as good as the effort and expertise that goes into them. Learning to use these tools as they are designed to be used and working closely with recruitment agencies (rather than just leaving them with a job description) can help managers make the most of the traditional recruiting methods in which they have already invested time and money.

2. Understand job requirements and competencies.

Bad job descriptions result in bad candidates. Some descriptions are overly detailed or specific, listing minor tasks of little consequence and skills requirements that could easily be learned on the job. Very few candidates apply for these positions, and the ones that do often don't meet the more general requirements of the position, even if they qualify on the minutiae; understandably, these candidates thought that if they fulfilled half of the laundry list of requirements, they'd be considered. Other descriptions give so little detail that it's unclear what the job entails, or so open-ended that nearly anyone who comes across the description will think they are a good candidate. Help managers write an effective job description by toubleshooting real examples of bad job descriptions and clearly defining the core competencies and background necessary to do well in the position.

Too often, effectiveness on the job is relatively unrelated to the criteria on which an employee is evaluated. Because KPIs are often taken directly from the job description, getting this first step right can be crucial. Does the job description really cover the essentials of what it takes to be successful, or is just a list of tasks? Managers should always strive to relate job effectiveness to KPIs by starting off on the right foot with a good job description.

3. Create attractive advertisements, manage applications and screen candidates.

Job ads are like resumes in reverse. Most employers think that candidates are applying for their jobs because the position itself looks interesting, but the fact is, if the employer isn't selling their company in the job ad, they are not attracting the best candidates. Simple, concise language that gets to the essence of who the person is in their professional life makes for an excellent CV and great candidates want to see those same things from job ads. Managers should aim to formulate job descriptions to show off the company so that the right candidates (and not just the ones who will send in a CV for anything) apply for the open position.

Tracking applications is absolutely necessary if a manager is considering more than one person for the job. Hiring is a complex, multistep process, especially if the manager works for a mid-sized company or bigger. While HR usually has tracking tools, it can be very helpful for managers to have their own notes and thoughts on candidates right at their fingertips so that they can remember what they thought of each person they met. There is a wide range of possible tracking systems, from analogue options to a simple Excel spreadsheet to dedicated software, so that managers can choose the tracking system that works best for them.

HR sent 20 applicants who fit the profile requested. All of them meet the job description's criteria; all of them look like potential options. For some managers the process of hiring becomes overwhelming at this point because they feel they need to invite every possible candidate for a formal interview, either in person or on the phone. Doing this is a colossal waste of time. Instead, implementing a casual phone screening protocol can save managers valuable time and resources by weeding out the candidates who just aren't the right fit early in the process. Most of the time, it becomes obvious within the first couple minutes of an interview if a candidate isn't a good fit, and this can happen even if the candidate is a perfect match for the job description on paper. Help managers master techniques to make phone screening feel casual, simple and painless for all parties involved, and allow everyone to move on quickly with their day if it turns out the fit wasn't right.

4. Understand and use selection tests.

If a manager is hiring for a technical position, understanding a candidate's skills is essential. But how can a manager test candidates in a way that doesn't privilege candidates who happen to have used a technology for a specific purpose over candidates who are strong technical thinkers and collaborators? The answer is creating selection tests that do not test technical skills but technical ability. Devising such a test is different for each practice area. Important techniques include using open-ended questions to allow candidates to show their work creatively, conducting tests in a discussion-based format, rather than having a candidate simply turn in a piece of paper, and skills tests that ask the candidate to use the skills they have within a certain framework to create something.

Even if the manager has devised a great selection test, it's important to keep in mind that the test alone cannot determine the best candidate. A candidate may not provide exactly the answers the manager was hoping for, but their out-of-the-box thinking is exactly what the team needs. A test can tell the manager whether a candidate has the skills they claim to have, but it can't tell the manager how well that candidate will work with other team members or anything about their future job performance (unless their entire job is taking tests). Plus, some highly intelligent people are just terrible at taking tests. Basing hiring entirely on test results might seem like an easy short cut for some technical roles, but without looking at the entire person, managers will have no idea what they are getting.

5. Implement a variety of techniques to prepare for and conduct successful recruitment interviews.
A good interview feels like a business meeting, not an exam. A great candidate should be able to speak easily about why they are a good fit for a particular position. A good interviewer should be able to ask the right questions to guide them to provide these answers. Good interviewers are extremely active listeners: they can hear the nuance and undertone of a candidate's answers, not just the literal answer. Great managers know how to create interview flow and use open ended questions and active listening to gain greater insight into a candidate's potential.

Managers also need to avoid asking questions that can be answered by the resume (because this wastes everyone's time). Help managers consider what will help them learn the most about a candidate's day-to-day working style, rather than seeing the interview like an interrogation or extension of the resume. Managers should seek to present their best selves to candidates, and convince the candidate that they are great to work with as well.

Managers also need to avoid biased or illegal questions in the interview. While staying within the law is important, avoiding biased questions is actually more important for the health of the workforce and ensuring the right candidate is hired. Asking about plans to have children, relationship status, and age are all illegal in most places, but more importantly, the answers could bias the manager against hiring the right person for the job because they assumed information that wasn't true. Instead, looking for dedication and enthusiasm in the interview can help managers discern the answer they were looking for through these illegal questions: is this person going to be fully committed to their job if we hire them?

Other questions that create bias but may not be illegal (yet), such as asking for salary history to decide how much to offer, can contribute to low morale in the workforce. A low salary history encourages employers to pay less than what the job is worth, but if the manager low-balls their best candidate, or underpays a stellar employee, not only do they risk the person finding out how badly they are being treated, the manager risks lowering morale throughout the company, leaving themselves vulnerable to poaching by competitors. Help managers find alternatives for these kinds of questions and compensation dilemmas. Usually, this will mean being more direct: why not just ask a candidate what salary they want, and if it's too high for the company, the minimum salary at which they would still consider accepting the position?

Coaching Suggestions

1. Consider past examples – what worked, what didn't?
2. Review current selection criteria
3. Review current interview process and improve

Training Suggestions

1. Obtain current turnover metrics if available
2. Focus on flow efficiency eg:
   a. Early candidate screening: how to manage candidate volume through short phone screenings by asking the right questions
   b. Full cycle recruiting overview
   c. Interview flow and timing practice
3. Use current interview questions to roleplay and coach to what makes for a good interview for ALL parties involved

Challenge Level: 2 – Difficult

Truly excellent recruitment practice is very rare – as the many of us who've personally endured substandard recruitment processes can easily attest.

A comprehensive overview of the entire recruitment methodology, including things often ignored such as elegant communication with unsuccessful candidates, is a necessity to deliver enhanced recruitment outcomes.

Ultimately, new hires and the organisation will achieve far more satisfactory long-term outcomes with a more considered approach to recruitment.

5.9.

IDENTIFY AND RETAIN TALENT

Overview

An organisation is only as good as the people it employs. So, how can managers identify those key team members? And how can the company keep them on board? Competition for the right kind of talent is only becoming more intense, and employers need to learn how to compete for great employees in the same way that employees compete for great employers.

Learning to identify top performing employees is a learnable skill that can be covered in a workshop. Learning to keep those top employees is a little more complicated. When it comes to retaining talent, many employers simply throw up their hands and say things like, "Well, we can't offer a free organic, cafeteria, we'll never compete with the Silicon Valley giants." However, employees do not stay with an organisation because of perks like free food – they stay because the entire environment supports them in their work and their lives. That support can look very different at different organisations, because it is tailored to fit the employees the company wants to keep. Instead of writing off employees who choose to leave, or seeing attrition as inevitable, great managers actively work to keep their employees by focusing on what makes the job worth having.

Setting the Scene

It can be hard to tell from outside of a team who the most talented members are. The work of a good team is greater than the sum of the individual work of each of the members, and that can disguise all sorts of internal workings, both good and bad. However, from within the team, it's often obvious who is pulling more than their weight. Excellent team members often show their greatest strengths behind the scenes by making projects run smoothly and efficiently, supporting their teammates' strengths and managing weaknesses, or providing the emotional centre necessary for group cohesion. How the team worked together is often only known to the team members themselves – and it can be tempting to give the best presenter of the group all the credit. An excellent manager stays involved with their teams regularly, casually and critically. These managers can accurately predict who has great potential based on deep knowledge of their team's internal workings. Additionally, managers who create environments that encourage high performers to remain at the organisation are more likely to keep those people on staff whose substantial talent could easily take them elsewhere.

What does the modern workforce seek in a career

Employees' top needs from employers	Employees' top needs from managers
Opportunities to learn and grow	Job clarity and priorities
A good manager	Ongoing feedback and communication
High-quality management	Opportunities to learn and grow
Interest in type of work	Accountability
Opportunities for advancement	

Re-Engineering Performance Management
Gallup 2017

Development Instructions

1. Define "talent" and "potential" for your organisation.

The first task is always to identify talent. Are measures of employee value based on superficial evidence of hard work? Do the people who stay late and schmooze the management get promoted more quickly than the people who get their work done quickly and efficiently? It may be time to re-evaluate what traits the organisation values. Managers should define "talent" and "potential" based on their organisation's goals and their team's needs, beyond the superficial evidence.

Homogeneity in organisations results in poorer results. A team needs a variety of perspectives in order to do its best work and avoid becoming an echo chamber, and ensure that it balances out any blind spots and weaknesses. This happens mostly because managers like to hire people who are like them – they can imagine a younger version of themselves in the role far better than anyone else. However, increasing diversity isn't about political correctness – it's about staying competitive. Support managers so that they can use a variety of evaluation methods that take into account qualitative as well as quantitative metrics for identifying the most valuable employees.

2. Demonstrate systemic talent identification process.

How does the company currently identify and reward talent? Is it easy to promote employees, or does the process take years? Can a manager give someone a raise or a bonus for good performance? How does the organisation manage the distribution of other benefits? Is the manager focusing too much on measures that don't matter, or are resources directed to the places where they will be most valuable? Map out organisational rewards systems to figure out what's working and what isn't, based on evidence-based models of what actually makes employees more likely to stay.

One of the major reasons that employees leave big organisations is the path to promotion is filled with so many bureaucratic hurdles, it makes more sense to get the promotion they deserve by moving to another organisation. To combat this, managers can focus on building a bi-annual plan to ensure that employees are rewarded regularly on a schedule. This way, bureaucratic processes are not allowed to drag on for years without anyone realising how long someone has been waiting.

3. Understand make or break moments for high potential team members.

Why do top employees stay with the organisation? Great managers can assess what has worked to keep great team members in the past at the organisation, by analysing both employees who stay long term, and employees who almost left but didn't.

Sometimes losing team members is truly inevitable – life circumstances change, or a top employee wants a career shift in a direction that your company simply can't offer. However, many organisations lose team members in avoidable ways. Maybe their life circumstances changed, but they could have made it work if the job was worth it. Maybe they wanted to change careers, but they might have considered staying if the organisation had offered them different opportunities or more flexibility. It could be that many people leave for reasons within your control, even if their departure seemed inevitable. Understanding the reasons that an employee didn't want to try to make it work could be key to keeping top talent in the future.

Exit interviews aren't always the best place to find the answers about why high-quality team members leave. Great employees want to maintain a strong relationship with their former organisations, and if the reason they are leaving would be seen as critical of the organisation, they might be reluctant to be completely honest. Show managers how to read between the lines at exit interviews, how to allow team members to be open during these interviews without losing face, and how to read and act on the warning signs when an employee is considering jumping ship.

4. Map career paths to maximise high potential employee engagement. Are there opportunities at the organisation for upward mobility? Is it easy for employees to move up internally, or does the organisation generally hire from outside the company to fill management-level positions? What barriers stand in the way of employees changing roles as required? Whether or not these problems are solvable by a manager alone, understanding where the gaps and blockages are can be essential for keeping employees.

Part of identifying new routes to successful career paths is imagining what top employees' ideal paths would look like. They probably know what they want – and even if the exact path isn't possible, having that discussion with the best employees may spark ideas for creating better career path maps and timelines within the organisation's existing parameters.

5. Conduct high-quality development discussions. A key management skill is the ability to have high-quality professional development discussions with employees. While these can be linked to feedback discussions, they don't necessarily have to be. Top employees often seek out professional development, but organisational bureaucracy can get in the way. Help managers turn employee requests or needs into actionable development plans and focus on longevity in development planning in order to avoid throwing resources only at short term needs and goals.

6. Employ use of mentors within the organisation.

When employees cite the reasons they stayed longer at an organisation than they originally intended, it almost always comes down to the people. They had great co-workers, or a great boss or better yet - a great mentor. Having a mentor who is truly invested in an employee's progress helps with retention for a very simple reason: they are still learning something from their job.

A mentor is not the same as a coach or a manager. Coaches may help employees solve specific issues or provide advice; managers are bosses who can provide leadership. Both are valuable, but the mentor-mentee relationship goes deeper than that. A mentor not only provides advice and coaching, they act as an advocate for the employee both within and outside of the organisation. They help the employee make the connections they need, and encourage them to become their best professional self through both formal coaching sessions and an informal, professional relationship that often extends outside of the work day.

Coaching Suggestions

1. What is the current talent identification process?

2. Use current hi-po employees to work with

3. Have coachee build career development pathway

Training Suggestions

1. Understand current talent matrix

2. Build talent grid using current team members (where appropriate)

3. Work through organisational roles to develop career pathways

Challenge Level: 1 – Very Difficult

Every large-scale organisation has a talent identification and retention program, but many of these programs fail to deliver due to a lack of clear objectives, overly complex processes and poor implementation. Smaller organisations often do not pay enough heed to talent retention, even though SME's have even more to lose by allowing their top talent to leave.

The right talent process will set any business apart, and make them "employer of choice" as their brand is enhanced by their elegant treatment of their best people.

5.10.

PROACTIVELY MANAGE PERFORMANCE

Overview

All organisations have a need to evaluate and measure performance against specific criteria. Performance management systems can be used to guide the work of individuals, teams and even the organisation itself. Using a set process with clear metrics and buy-in from all parties is crucial. A great performance management system not only ensures that strategic objectives are achieved, it gives team members a framework for understanding their roles, their performance and a way to ensure their everyday work is aligned with the goals of their jobs and the organisation itself.

Setting the Scene

Most organisations schedule twice yearly feedback sessions for all managers with a standard form and basic process for submitting that feedback. Many managers view these sessions as a perfunctory duty they perform to keep upper management happy. If a manager sticks to this schedule alone, they are likely leading an underperforming team. Why? Because performance management is the best tool available to ensure that a team is working at their best.

Performance management is the process of providing feedback, accountability and documentation designed to improve productivity, results and team environment. While many people think of performance management as limited to formal feedback sessions, performance management encompasses a range of comprehensive activities, both casual and formal, to ensure employees are handling their workloads well. Performance management systems should run like the operating system on a computer – the operating system is constantly there while the computer is on, ensuring that all programs work correctly and all tasks are handled well. This is like casual performance management:

daily contact with workers, informal feedback, regular tracking of work and other activities that are integrated so seamlessly into daily office life they become unnoticeable. A couple of times a year, managers need to check the operating system for full functionality and run some updates: this is like the formal check-ins, feedback sessions and documentation required by your organisation. An operating system is relatively useless if it is only using it during update periods, but if it is used it every day, making adjustments as necessary, the system will facilitate all of the other work a computer does.

How often is your performance formally reviewed?

Weekly	2%
Monthly	3%
Quarterly	7%
Every six months	14%
Annually	48%
Less than once a year	26%

Re-Engineering Performance Management
Gallup Survey 2017

Development Instructions
1. Understand what is considered to be "good performance".
The most frustrating feedback usually comes when benchmarks for the reviewee don't align with the benchmarks for the reviewer. In this scenario, reviewees often feel like they've been set up to fail, because they were working with the wrong goals. This is why it is so important to align good performance metrics with organisational goals. How closely do benchmarks for employees match their ideas of what "good performance" means? How closely do those ideas match with the organisation's needs?

Great performance metrics are, by definition, measurable. If something can't be measured reliably, or if the metric is too vague or subjective, it can be easy to turn performance evaluation into a referendum on employee popularity. Managers should create strong, specific, measurable benchmarks for employee performance, based on the needs of both the organisation and the team.

2. Know the key activities that make up an effective performance management process.

Once performance measurement metrics have been clearly defined, it's time to communicate these to employees and transform abstract benchmarks into concrete tasks and timelines. Performance planning gives employees an easy way to understand whether they are doing a good job – they can easily refer back to their benchmarks throughout the following review period to understand if they are on track to meet their performance goals.

What happens if concrete tasks or goals change? Thinking of the performance plan as a living document allows employees and managers to adjust the performance plan together as necessary, without formal meetings. Sometimes, this can be as easy as a quick stop by an employee's desk to mention that a certain deliverable is now lower priority and the employee should focus on a different deliverable. For this reason, performance plans need to be reviewed regularly and informally by both employees and their managers to stay current.

3. Effectively undertake performance planning.

It is rare that an organisation has a performance management system that is fully effective from the macro to the micro levels. This is because so much of performance planning must take place at the team level, and is best done informally so that the team stays flexible and open to new developments. Managers can ensure their team stays on track by creating an environment which allows for these kinds of casual performance plan reviews and updates without sacrificing valuable work time.

Just because something is informal or casual doesn't mean it shouldn't be scheduled. Does the current system allow for both adequate scheduled conversations as well as spontaneous interaction? Create performance plans tailored to the manager's needs, the team's dynamics and the organisation's performance management structure.

4. Establish an effective day-to-day performance management routine.

Establishing a routine is the best way to prevent performance management from becoming a topic loathed by managers and feared by employees. There are many different ways to do this well, but the most important thing for de-mystifying performance management discussions is to make them routine. Sometimes, setting regular weekly or bi-weekly meetings or phone calls is the best way to ensure those conversations take place at all in busy offices. Some managers have open office hours; some employees know to check in with their manager about performance under specific circumstances. Team huddles and group check-ins can be highly effective to take the temperature of the team; one-on-ones are necessary whenever sensitive information is being discussed. However the manager does it, making sure that team members are experiencing some form of performance management regularly prevents anxiety around performance management and leads to better outcomes in formal feedback sessions. If managers are managing performance well, people should already know approximately where they stand by the time they come to the formal review, and will have ideas for how to improve their own performance based on that information.

5. Understand drivers of unsatisfactory performance.

There are plenty of reasons why a team member may be performing below par. Managers need to determine if the performance issue is fixable, something that can be worked around or a deeper issue that could lead to a less effective team in the long run.

If expectations are low, the team will meet those expectations and consider their jobs done. Creating a high-performance environment with high expectations and strong support allows team members to perform at their best, without creating unnecessary pressure. Managers can implement simple environmental changes to encourage team members to meet loftier goals, without sacrificing morale in the process. The best performing teams work in environments with great morale, because they know they have the support to meet the high bar that has been set for them.

How does the organisation celebrate wins? When one team members drives the entire team to success, does the manager celebrate the individual, the team or both? Making room for wins is just as important to performance management as criticism – both the team and individual employees need to know when they do something well, and feel that their hard work was worth it. Brainstorm possible options for celebrating success, both mainstream and alternative, that can reward team members in a way that aligns with both their success and the organisation's culture.

6. Create strategies to address performance issues.

It can be easy to write off a routinely poor performer as "less talented" or "uninterested." In fact, poor performance is rarely a problem of innate talent, and disinterest in the work usually doesn't happen just because a job is boring. Furthermore, accepting mediocrity can lead to a culture of mediocre performance for all employees – once it's clear that the poor performer can keep doing their job badly, resentment will build among your top employees. Encourage managers to challenge poor performance without reducing the employee's value to the quality of their current performance.

Poor performance is not the same as misconduct. A problematic employee needs to face disciplinary action for their behaviour, not performance management. Misconduct can range from workplace sexual harassment to misuse of company property, which means that disciplinary action needs to be just as flexible. Unfortunately, this also means that even high performers can require disciplinary intervention. Ensuring the disciplinary system is fair, even if it means removing a high performer from their role for misconduct, is vital to maintaining the overall performance and morale of the team.

Having conversations about performance can feel awkward to new managers especially, but they don't have to be. Starting with praise and moving towards constructive criticism is always a good place to start. Consider different formats for all types of performance discussions (informal, formal, disciplinary), and who should be present (The whole team? How about the HR rep?) for different types of performance discussions, based on the tone and content of the conversation.

7. Conduct effective performance appraisals.

Managers should have a plan of action when starting conversations with employees that they know are going to be difficult. Identifying goals for the discussion is important – it can be easy to get off track due to discomfort. Second, imagining how the employee may respond can help managers frame the information in a way that is kind, but firm and clear, avoiding any more hurt than absolutely necessary. Finally, checking for understanding is key. Practising for difficult discussions in a workshop environment can be helpful in order to strategise how best to present information so that it can be heard and processed, and how to use the manager's personal style to their advantage.

Lots of managers become managers because they are thought of as "people people." Usually, this means managers are talkers – it is rare to find a manager who is not a natural conversationalist. The disadvantage of being a talker is that it can be difficult for people with this kind of personality to distill information clearly and concisely. Therefore, using the "less is more" rule in performance management discussions is key. Managers who can make their point in as few words as possible are better able to help their employees to understand what they are really trying to say. The other benefit of talking less is that it gives employees room to ask questions and ensure they understand. Use concise, declarative, conscientious language for performance management, and practise waiting for the employee to speak so that feedback can be processed with maximum effectiveness.

In a formal feedback session, there should be no surprises for either the employee or the manager. If the employee knows that their work on a project has been subpar from informal feedback, they won't be surprised to hear that they've improved, but they aren't quite there yet. Similarly, a manager shouldn't be hearing about barriers to performance for the first time during a formal feedback session. Additionally, all critical feedback should have implications for professional development in the future. This can include scheduling additional reviews, advising sessions, planning mentorships or planning for training.

Coaching Suggestions
1. Where is current performance to baseline?
2. What steps have been already undertaken to maintain or remediate?
3. Use live case study where appropriate

Training Suggestions
1. Consider confidentiality issues when using case studies
2. Address common pitfalls
3. What performance managements systems exist and how are they being utilised?

Challenge Level: 2 – Difficult

Performance management is so critical to business success. After all, what could more directly lead to great business outcomes than the performance of each individual employee?

The challenge lies in the simple fact that the only reliable way to maintain good performance or remediate unacceptable performance is through constant feedback. The process that sits behind this giving of feedback is make-or-break, as is the ability of individual managers to deliver this feedback in a timely, clear and considered fashion, be it positive reinforcement or areas for improvement.

5.11.

DELIVER EFFECTIVE PRESENTATIONS

Overview

The ability to deliver an effective presentation is a key skill that all managers have to confront sooner or later. A "presentation" could be a one-on-one sales pitch, a proposal to a boardroom of 6-12 directors, a team meeting of 30 people, a group of clients of 50 or more, or a conference keynote reaching hundreds of people.

No matter what the scenario, the ability to deliver presentations in a manner that gets the desired message across while holding the interest of the audience can make a big difference in how a manager is perceived. It can also ultimately determine how successful they are at getting what they want. If the presentation is compelling, insightful and believable, gaining the support of the audience becomes so much easier.

It comes down to this: what do we want our audience to think, feel and do upon the conclusion of the presentation, and how effective are we at achieving these aims?

> **"**
> In my opinion, the only way to conquer stage fright is to get up on stage and play. Every time you play another show, it gets better and better
>
> Taylor Swift

Setting The Scene

Imagine a hardworking and competent manager caught up in the middle of a busy work day. They have a staffing issue to deal with, there's a customer they have to meet with in an hour to deal with a complaint, plus they have to get a compliance return in to head office by close of business. They glance at their computer screen and notice an email. In recognition of their technical expertise they've been asked by their manager to put together and deliver a 20 minute presentation on a new product for an "A" client's executive team next week. Their boss considers this a reward and a development opportunity. But our friend now has a horrible feeling of anxiety in the pit of their stomach.

For some people, the idea of undertaking such a task seems like fun. But in our experience, the majority of managers would rather stab themselves in the eye with a fork!

Why is this? For most of the people we've worked with, it comes down to two key issues. The first is a lack of specific skills that they can apply to a presentation environment. Most managers are consciously incompetent when it comes to presentation delivery. That is to say, they are all too aware of the fact that this is a skill set they don't possess (yet). Secondly, this awareness of a lack of skill gives rise to what we can term stage fright, performance anxiety or a general fear of failure. No one wants to fail, and even fewer people want to fail in public in front of an audience.

These are not insurmountable hurdles to overcome, but need to be approached with sensitivity, structure and persistence.

Development Instructions

1. Apply effective research.

The starting point for any presentation is a thorough understanding of the content. There is no room for "winging it", no matter how much of a subject expert the manager may be.

While it is not possible to know everything about a particular topic, nor is it possible to anticipate every question that might be asked, an in-depth knowledge of the subject presented will deliver two great benefits: 1) The manager's knowledge will simply become evident as the presentation unfolds, and 2) The feeling that they've "done their homework" will greatly reduce any potential anxiety they might feel if they were unprepared.

Ensure the manager has had the opportunity to research and understand the topic and has all the information required to convey their message clearly and unambigiously.

2. Understand the audience.

Who will be the recipient of this presentation? It may seem like a basic question, but a prior knowledge of the audience can help any presenter prepare an excellent presentation. Not only will it help them tailor the presentation in a direction most likely to be of interest, it can help them anticipate how the presentation may be received, and the nature of questions or objections they may expect.

Give the manager strategies to increase the knowledge of their audience beforehand. Even simple information like their current job role and how long they've been working at their organisation can be a great starting point.

3. Actively rehearse.

Rehearsal is for anyone and everyone who wants to maximise their chances of delivering a strong presentation, regardless of experience or number of audience members. Many adults feel foolish when asked to rehearse a presentation, but in reality there's nothing embarrassing about practising something you wish to do well. In fact, it's far more embarrassing to make a serious error of fact when presenting, armed with the knowledge that it could have been prevented simply by rehearsing. If it's good enough for professional musicians to rehearse the presentation of their show before embarking on a tour (which they most certainly do), it's good enough for all of us.

Rehearsal techniques to be encouraged would be to practise the presentation in front of a trusted colleague or mentor, in front of a mirror and even non-verbally in the manager's head on the commute to work. If it is practical to use the actual presentation room for rehearsal, this is also very beneficial.

4. Manage anxiety.

As we highlighted earlier, a large part of delivering an effective presentation rests with managing the natural performance anxiety or "stage fright" that often accompanies the task itself.

A good first step here is for the manager to understand that anxiety is a perfectly natural and normal response to being asked to give a presentation. Note that we recommend "manage anxiety" rather than "remove anxiety" as a development action. Normally the stakes are reasonably high (in the mind of the presenter) which means the fear of failure and accompanying symptoms can also be quite intense. A modicum of research will reveal that many professional performers suffer greatly from performance anxiety, yet have learned how to manage this condition to the extent that the audience sees nothing other than an excellent presentation.

Teach the manager specific techniques to help them calm their nerves and bring their symptoms of anxiety under control. Managing one's own emotional and physiological state is key here. Again, we stress that removing all symptoms of stage fright is rarely realistic – the symptoms simply need to managed to a level where they don't prevent a quality delivery of information. Indeed, some presenters suggest that a small amount of nerves simply indicates that the presenter cares, and actually creates the "edge" that leads to a truly great performance.

5. **Focus on message and recipients.**
A mistake many presenters make is to focus on themselves and "being great" at their presentation. A much better approach is to focus not on the self, but on the message one is trying to deliver. If the manager truly cares about ensuring the message is delivered with maximum clarity and care, the pressure comes off themselves to be "amazing".

Similarly, encourage the manager to focus not inwardly, but outwardly on the audience. If one approaches the audience with an attitude of caring and concern that what is being said is truly understood, even more pressure is released from the presenter.

If the manager can legitimately put the message and the audience ahead of their own feelings of inadequacy, the intent will naturally come across, which will increase the empathy of the audience and, in turn, the chance the communication will be understood and accepted.

6. **Add variety.**
Dependent upon the duration of the presentation, some visual and verbal variety goes a long way to ensuring the message doesn't become boring and attention spans are maintained.

Encourage the manager to vary the following to increase variety in presentations:

- Volume/pitch/tone of voice
- Visual aids
- Colour
- Talking/questioning/listening
- Active participation from audience
- Humour (if appropriate and presenter sufficiently competent).

7. Say "I don't know".

This can seem counterintuitive to some, however even the best-prepared presenter will occasionally be asked a question they simply don't know the answer to. The mistake we see many presenters make is placing the unrealistic expectation of "knowing everything" on themselves. These presenters will be caught out trying to "fudge" or "bluff" their way through an answer, where a simple, honest and humble "I'm not sure about the answer to that, but let me find out for you and come back to you [later]" would be simpler, less stressful and greatly win the audience's respect.

8. Conclude Elegantly.

It's critical to know when to finish talking. When a presentation is finished, it's finished. The manager has had their time, now it's time to conclude and see if there are any points that need clarification. At this point, listening, not talking, is the key skill that needs to be applied.

An elegant conclusion also means finishing at the agreed time. Unless they have explicit permission to continue, the presenter should respect the timeframe they were given, and manage their presentation to ensure this happens. Stealing five minutes of 50 audience members' time means you've just stolen over four hours from your audience's business!

Coaching Suggestions

1. Baseline the coachee – what does an "effective presentation" look like to them?
2. Use upcoming presentation as a case study
3. Set tasks relevant to the upcoming presentation

Training Suggestions

1. Understand the type of presentations participants would normally undertake
2. Create practice scenarios to work on in front of the group
3. Take away actions for specific skills to work on as personal assignements

Challenge Level: 1 – Very Difficult

Delivering presentations is frequently reported as the number one fear for many otherwise very confident and competent business people. On occasion, people thrown into this situation without adequate help and support can become highly stressed and physically ill.

When working on presentation skills, it's important to seek advice from experienced professionals who can pass on specific methods and task assignments to raise the competence and confidence of any presenter, no matter what their starting point and experience levels.

CASE STUDY: HELEN'S HEALTH HUT

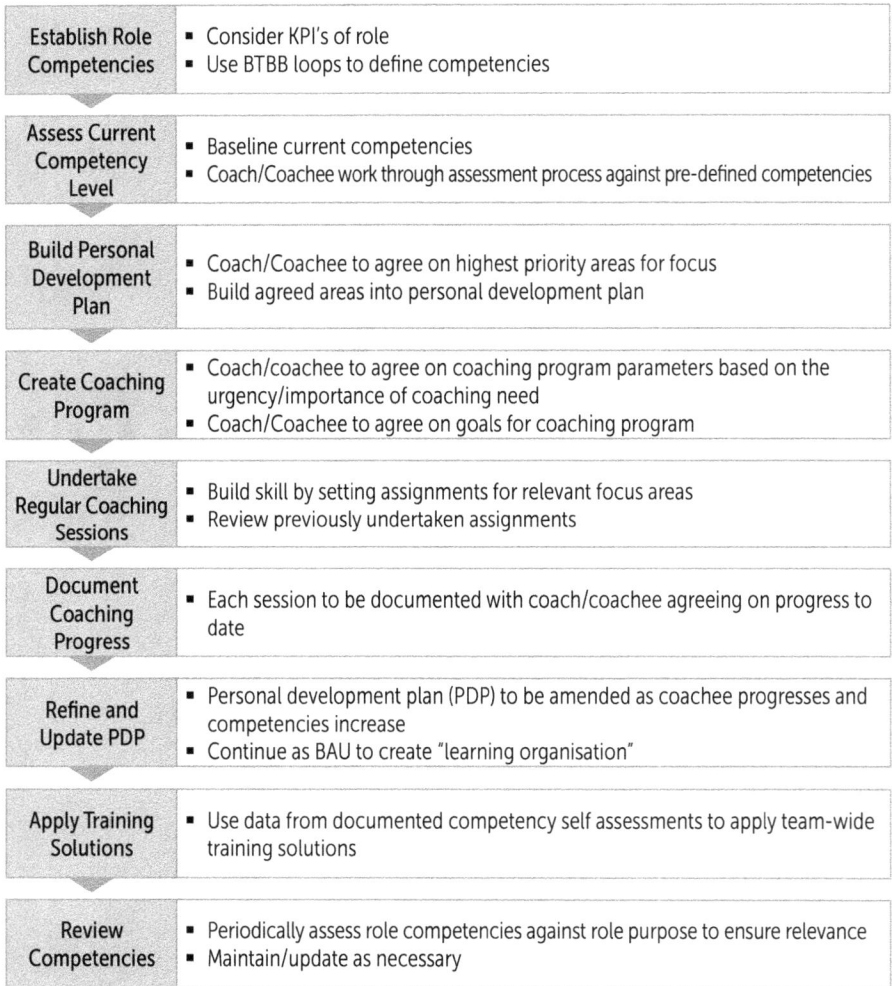

Establish Role Competencies	■ Consider KPI's of role ■ Use BTBB loops to define competencies
Assess Current Competency Level	■ Baseline current competencies ■ Coach/Coachee work through assessment process against pre-defined competencies
Build Personal Development Plan	■ Coach/Coachee to agree on highest priority areas for focus ■ Build agreed areas into personal development plan
Create Coaching Program	■ Coach/coachee to agree on coaching program parameters based on the urgency/importance of coaching need ■ Coach/Coachee to agree on goals for coaching program
Undertake Regular Coaching Sessions	■ Build skill by setting assignments for relevant focus areas ■ Review previously undertaken assignments
Document Coaching Progress	■ Each session to be documented with coach/coachee agreeing on progress to date
Refine and Update PDP	■ Personal development plan (PDP) to be amended as coachee progresses and competencies increase ■ Continue as BAU to create "learning organisation"
Apply Training Solutions	■ Use data from documented competency self assessments to apply team-wide training solutions
Review Competencies	■ Periodically assess role competencies against role purpose to ensure relevance ■ Maintain/update as necessary

BUSINESS HAS BEEN GOOD AT HELEN'S HEALTH HUT

Helen's Health Hut (HHH)* offers a custom design service for retail stores wanting to sell with a healthy image. Sales are steadily increasing and there is optimism in the health and lifestyle market generally. In fact, business has been so strong that Proprietor Helen has rapidly worked her way up to a team of almost 100, simply to meet the demands of her rapidly-growing enterprise.

This growth has happened organically and Helen has been very pleased with her ability to find people to work in her new and exciting business. This said, Helen herself acknowledges that her onboarding process has been something of a 'scramble' to keep up with ever-increasing workload. This now means she has 31 salespeople who have come to the role internally and with no training or coaching. Helen is starting to gain a sense that her sales force is struggling. Results are beginning to plateau – and with the increasing demands of professional selling her team are enjoying the role less and less. It has now come to a point where HHH is struggling to retain anyone in a sales role for longer than 18 months.

Helen reached out to us and posed the most fascinating question: "How difficult would it be for me to create an environment that would allow my sales team to perform at the 90th percentile globally regardless of size or industry?"

Our simple answer was: "Not difficult at all".

The obvious next question from Helen was: "If it's so easy why isn't everyone doing it?"

This was where we used her own business as an example. We asked Helen the following question: "We all know that a nutritious, balanced diet and regular exercise are important to a happy and healthy life. So why is it that media reports tell us that obesity and associated health issues are an ever-growing problem?"

Helen explained to us that there are two issues at play. Firstly, one must know what a healthy lifestyle looks like. Secondly, armed with this knowledge, they now must possess the discipline and structure to bring healthy habits into their daily activities.

And this is exactly what our extensive research over the past decade shows in relation to sales teams. Time and again they are caught in the inertia of "just getting through" each day. Very little or no time or energy is devoted to stepping back, reflecting and planning to be the best. Even when an organisation attempts proper strategic planning it is often limited to a one or two-day strategy session followed by a week of wrap-up emails, before the business-as-usual treadmill of mediocracy creeps back in to daily activities.

So how to break this cycle? Well, to paraphrase Helen, one must know what a healthy sales force looks like, then one must have the structure, process and discipline to enable and maintain this top-performing state.

After this discussion, Helen emerged determined to have a "healthy" sales team.

Helen's goal was to ensure her entire sales force was constantly striving to be the best they could be. In short, she wanted to ensure her people did not end up failing, fleeing or being fired.

This is her story.

The 9 Step Plan to Success

With our assistance, Helen's Health Hut undertook nine steps to envigorate her people management and development approach. She decided to start with her three Sales Leader roles – each leader having responsibility for the outcomes of approximately ten Sales Agents. An opportunity immediately presented itself as Helen was in the midst of hiring for a Sales Leader vacancy.

Step 1: Establish Role Competencies

Before Helen hires anyone, her first step is to consider the Key Performance Indicators or KPI's that will measure the success of this new role. If this is done well, it will create clarity and motivation for her new hires, plus ensure that the new team is working towards personal and organisational success. It's important that the KPI's for this role are clear and measurable.

When recruiting, it's critical to ensure that the new hire has the ability and aptitude to either demonstrate or learn key competencies that will allow them to successfully achieve the job's stated KPI's. Competencies are the skills that underpin role performance. Helen uses her copy of *Be The Best Boss* to deepen her understanding of the competencies that will best align to her Sales Leader Roles. This handy reference, combined with Helen's analysis of high and low performers, determine that the non-sales related competencies relevant to success in this role are:

- Plan Effectively and Manage Time
- Solve Problems Effectively
- Motivate Others
- Influence Others
- Proactively Mentor.

Now that Helen has determined the correct KPI's and competencies for the role, she can use these measures to inform her recruitment strategy.

Potential risks:

- Misalignment of KPI's to role
- Misalignment of competencies to KPI's
- Poor understanding of relevant competencies
- Unsure of which recruitment criteria match role
- Lack of properly structured interviewing questions
- Lack of targeted psychometric testing

Step 2: Baseline current competencies

HHH has undertaken a comprehensive and rigorous recruitment process, including pre-screening, psychometric testing and structured candidate interviewing. The business has chosen their new recruit for the Sales Leader role, Anne.

Anne is a bright, enthusiastic and energetic new employee. She is not overly experienced in leadership, however testing has revealed a great aptitude to learn and an attitude aligned with organisational values. As part of her induction process, her line manager Helen will undergo a "baseline" process to see where her current proficiency lies in relation to the stated job role competencies. Helen uses *Be The Best Boss* to guide her in determining which baseline questions fit intuitively with which job role competencies.

Due to the efficiency of the system she is using, Helen spends just 30 minutes with Anne asking her a series of structured questions which help her self-assess her current level of proficiency. The process is consultative and driven by Anne with guidance from Helen. When the process is complete both parties have a clear understanding of job aspects that Anne feels quite comfortable with, and also other areas of her role where she would benefit from further assistance to maximise her performance.

Potential risks:

- Unsure of best baseline questions to ask
- Lack of structure in discussion, resulting in unclear areas of strength and potential improvement
- New hire unable to articulate personal areas for growth
- Line manager not competent in drawing out strengths and improvement areas
- Line manager not confident in one-on-one discussions of this nature.

Step 3: Coach/Coachee Agree On Highest Priorty Areas Of Focus

Now that Helen has successfully baselined Anne's proficiency in relation to key job competencies, she knows it's time to have her enter into a coach/coachee relationship which will be ongoing for her whole time in this role. Given that HHH is a small company, Helen takes on the role of coach to help coachee Anne achieve her full potential in this role.

Although Anne has great potential, she is new to both the organisation and this role. There are many areas she would like to work on to become a successful employee of HHH. Helen and Anne engage in a one-on-one discussion to determine which competencies she'd like to focus on as a priority to maximise her on-the-job performance. Here Helen uses *Be The Best Boss* to gain handy suggestions on coaching approaches, linked to the specific competency being improved.

Once this is done, Helen and Anne jointly agree on a Personal Development Plan (PDP). This is a simple plan that gives Anne a pathway towards achieving maximum results in all of her KPI's through systematic coaching on each identified competency. The PDP is structured, is signed off by coach and coachee and contains measurable goals. The PDP is a flexible, living document which is regularly updated and amended as skills grow and new learning and improvement priorities emerge.

The PDP sets the initial framework for regular coaching sessions which are built into the easy-to-track system that Helen is using.

Potential risks:
- Coach may lack skill, experience and confidence
- Coach unsure of how to work through competency prioritisation discussion
- Coach and coachee unsure of how to build simple PDP
- PDP does not contain simple learning goals related to desired competencies
- PDP not measurable
- PDP in complex format and difficult to work into BAU process for all employees.

Step 4: Coach/Coachee Agree on Coaching Program Parameters
Now that Helen and Anne have put their PDP in place, it's time to agree on parameters for the ongoing coaching that Anne will receive. Here Helen refers to *Be The Best Boss* to set the framework for appropriate coaching goals.

Helen and Anne spend some time in an initial session working through the following points:
- Goals for the coaching program
- Frequency of coaching interventions
- Who will drive which actions in the coaching relationship
- Governance of coaching progress.

Anne emerges from this initial discussion motivated and confident in the purpose of the coaching program, her role and her coach's role, the outcomes she is working towards and a clear view on the next steps.

Potential Risks:
- Coach unsure of appropriate goals to put in place
- Lack of understanding of how to move coaching process along
- Poor management of frequency of coaching interventions
- Ad-hoc tasks taking priority over scheduled BAU coaching interventions
- Disengagement from coachee if coach becomes distracted or coaching interventions drop off in frequency or relevance.

Step 5: Build Skill

Helen and Anne have started their coaching program. The program is regular, structured and both parties are demonstrating commitment towards each other, and ultimately achieving great outcomes for Anne in her role.

This has been achieved by Helen allowing Anne to drive each coaching interaction by bringing specific and relevant scenarios to the session. Coach and coachee then work through each scenario with an exploratory mindset to assist Anne in her journey of improvement. Helen has been using *Be The Best Boss* to ensure Anne's coaching scenarios remain relevant to the overall development of her chosen skill.

At the end of each session Helen and Anne agree on a series of assignments which Anne undertakes to build her skills and close her identified competency gaps. The assignments are relevant, achievable and Helen and Anne are both comfortable that they will assist Anne in increasing her confidence and competence in relation to her job role.

At the start of each new coaching session, Helen and Anne review her progress on previous assignments. Sometimes Anne completes her assignments with ease, allowing her to move on to a coaching extension which will further enhance her competency. On other occasions, Anne may struggle to complete an assignment. If this happens her coach Helen works with her to understand and remove any roadblocks which may have caused her to have difficulty.

Each coaching session is conducted consultatively with all outcomes mutually agreed, and the coachee's learning progress as the only priority.

Potential Risks:
- Lack of understanding of how to bring structure of coaching sessions
- Coach unsure of appropriate assignments to set
- Coach sets assignments which do not appropriately place work effort on coachee
- Coach not confident in review of previous assignments
- Coach and coachee unsure how to deal with non-completion of assignments
- Coach unsure how to provide appropriate extensions to move coachee towards competency achievement.

Step 6: Documentation

During each coaching session, Helen and Anne work together to ensure all results and new coaching assignments are documented in a central database. This helps Helen and Anne keep track of her progress, but also has the collateral benefit of providing clarity for all when considering Anne's on-the-job performance.

The system Helen and Anne use to document her progress is simple, user-friendly and available on-line. They work on this together while the coaching session is happening, which allows both coach and coachee to completely engage with progress made and new assignments. It gives both Helen and Anne a sense of satisfaction they are making tangible inroads into Anne's coaching goals.

As Helen has three Sales Leaders, this system will also allow her to measure her leadership team's progress to the agreed role competencies and identify trends across the business.

Potential Risks:

- Difficulty of documenting during session without wanting to break engagement during conversation
- Illegible scribbled hand-written notes
- Coaching notes not filed simply and not consistent in approach over period of time
- No central repository of coaching notes
- Lack of continuity for coachee if new coach appointed
- Difficulty of relating documentation consistently across different coaches in same job role
- Documentation put off until later and becoming memory dependent.

Step 7: Refine and Update PDP

Helen and Anne have been working together as coach and coachee for three months now. Anne is thrilled with her own progress, which she has been able to view via the coaching system that she and Helen have been working with. Helen is also very pleased with her new employee's quick progress.

Together, they have been able to complete several coaching goals and Anne has already achieved proficiency in three of her coaching competencies.

As Anne has continued to learn and grow, she and Helen have worked together to refine and update her Personal Development Plan (PDP). What Anne has realised is that learning is an ongoing part of her life at the HHH company, which she has found exciting as her results against her KPI's have been steadily improving from week to week. As each coaching goal has been completed, Helen has referred to *Be The Best Boss* to help determine the most appropriate next competency to add to the PDP, plus design new coaching interventions. This has made the overall process simple and stress free for Helen, and also very rewarding for Anne.

Anne is looking forward to achieving proficiency in all of her job role competencies, and she's particularly excited because Helen has promised her that even when this is achieved, her coaching will continue as she can then work towards even higher levels of success in her current role, or potentially career progression within HHH.

Potential Risks:
- Overall PDP purpose lost amid daily BAU tasks
- PDP not simple or flexible enough to amend as coachee works through competency achievement
- Coach unsure how to shift focus to various job role competencies
- Coach unsure how to extend coachee once all competencies proficient
- Coach not confident in having career progression discussion with coachee.

Step 8: Use PDP Data to Discover Team-Wide Training Opportunity

Helen has been using the above approach not only with Anne, but with her other two Sales Leaders for 12 months now, outstanding results. Anne is still highly motivated and successful, and she has enthusiastically adopted the coaching methodology practiced by Helen with her own team.

Due to the consistent application of a simple on-line PDP and coaching system, combined with a clear and confident coaching approach by Anne, her whole team is engaged with regular and helpful coaching sessions. This has allowed Anne to build a quality database of coaching progress for her entire team. A quick glance at the reporting shows Anne that a common area of challenge for her Sales Agents is a competency called

"Negotiate Effectively". Anne's peers from the coaching and PDP reports also show a similar gap with their Sales Agents – a glaring company-wide issue has been uncovered through a consistent and caring application of a rigorous coaching methodology.

Helen is easily able to use *Be The Best Boss* to understand which elements are causing this specific competency gap. This allows her to quickly determine which skills are currently lacking in the team.

Anne and her peers discuss this with CEO Helen, as they feel this skills gap needs to be addressed urgently, and is beyond their skill-set to deal with effectively across the company. Helen agrees and gives approval to bring in expert external assistance, as the potential benefits are clear. The whole sales team is thrilled to be working for a company that invests in their development – and Anne is thrilled to be able to add value to her team, knowing this is a training session that is directly relevant to their learning needs.

Potential Risks:

- PDP's not consistent across team
- Time consuming and challenging to glean meaningful information and reporting from multiple unstructured PDP's
- Training not undertaken because of challenge to discover clear need or direction – employees feel they are not being invested in
- Money invested in training without proper analysis of need
- Participants feel they are wasting their time.

Step 9: Reassess and Update Role Competencies

HHH has now grown in size and profitability, and provides a home for over 700 employees. New CEO Anne is reflecting on her 15 year tenure, and how proud she felt when Helen retired and the board unanimously voted her in as new Chief Executive. She still views Helen as her mentor, and she still receives coaching from her, albeit informally these days.

Although in her time HHH has grown from a 100-person business to an industry and nationally admired company employing 700 people, Anne has never forgotten the "learning organisation" that she started with.

HHH's internal sales structure has grown in scale and subtlety reflecting the many new markets and opportunities they have been able to leverage over the past few years. HHH now employs Key Account Managers, Business Development Managers, Relationship Managers and Telephone Sales Agents. Each sales team has specific competencies, PDP's and coaching plans tailor-made to their specific job roles and individual learning needs. Although as CEO Anne now has responsibility for Sales, Manufacturing, Finance, Marketing, Human Resources and Operations, she has never forgotten the value of that initial clarity of role provided from her first days as one of 31 sales people on the team.

Being a progressive and intelligent leader, she also understands that as businesses must move with the times to stay competitive, so must job roles and their associated competencies be constantly reviewed.

To this end, Anne has ensured that her Head of HR has, as their first marketplace. the on-going task of continually improving the development structure and competencies to ensure they're relevant in a rapidly changing internal and external environment. Using *Be The Best Boss*, Anne's Head of HR is able to ensure a consistent and sustainable approach to applying the correct competencies to the correct job roles; maintaining currency and flexibility, but within a structured and proven framework.

Anne is confident for the future of Helen's Health Hut, and so are the company's investors.

Potential Risks:
- Overly comfortable with status quo
- Unsure how to review and modify competencies
- Unsure which competencies are relevant in current marketplace

* Names have been changed for confidentiality

BIBLIOGRAPHY

Ancowitz, N. (2009, September 18). Introverts: Manage your perfectionism and reduce your agita! *Psychology Today*.

Bailey, E. P., Jr. (2007). *Writing and speaking at work (4th ed.)*. Upper Saddle River, NJ: Prentice Hall.

Baldoni, J. (2005). *Great motivation secrets of great leaders*. New York, NY: McGraw-Hill.

Bates-Ballard, P., & Smith, G. (2008). *Navigating diversity: An advocate's guide through the maze of race, gender, religion, and more*. Charleston, SC: BookSurge.

Branden, N. (1995). *The six pillars of Self-Esteem*. New York: Bantam.

Charan, R. (2012, June 21). *The discipline of listening*. Harvard Business Review Blog Network.

Cope, K. (2012). *Seeing the big picture: Business acumen to build your credibility, career, and company*. Austin, TX: Greenleaf Book Group.

Covey, S. M. R. (1989). *The 7 habits of highly effective people: Powerful lessons in personal change*. New York, NY: Simon & Schuster.

Covey, S. M. R. (2006). *The speed of trust: The one thing that changes everything*. New York, NY: Free Press.

Curtin, S. (2013). *Delight your customers: 7 Simple ways to raise your customer service from ordinary to extraordinary*. New York, NY: AMACOM.

Davidson, J. E., & Sternberg, R. J. (Eds.). (2003). *The psychology of problem solving*. New York, NY: Cambridge University Press.

Davila, L., & King, M. (2007). *Perfect phrases for perfect hiring: Hundreds of ready-to-use phrases for interviewing and hiring the best employees every time*. New York, NY: McGraw-Hill.

Dweck, C. (2006). *Mindset: The new Psychology of Success*. New York: Random House.

Ferrell, O.C., Freadrich, J., & Ferrell, L. (2006). *Business Ethics*. New York: Houghton Mifflin.

Gerzon, M. (2006). *Leading through conflict: How successful leaders transform differences into opportunities*. Boston, MA: Harvard Business School Press.

Handley, A. (2013, August 7). *Build a better understanding of customers, get a competitive advantage*.

Harrison, C. (2007, December). *Who's your audience?*

Harvard Business School Press. (2006). *Leading teams: Expert solutions to everyday challenges*. Boston, MA: Harvard Business Review Press.

Harvard Business School Press. (2008). *Delegating work*. Boston, MA: Harvard Business Review Press.

Harvard Business School Press. (2009). *Harvard Business Review on developing high-potential leaders*. Boston, MA: Harvard Business School Press.

Hayman, S. (2010). *Be more assertive: Teach yourself.* New York, NY: McGraw-Hill.

Hoenig, C. (2000). *The problem-solving journey: Your guide for making decisions and getting results.* Cambridge, MA: Perseus Publishing.

Kahnemen, D. (2013). *Thinking fast and slow.* New York: Farrar, Straus and Giroux.

Katz, J. H., & Miller, F. A. (2013). *Opening doors to teamwork and collaboration: 4 Keys that change everything.* San Francisco, CA: Berrett-Koehler Publishers.

Kegan, Robert and Lisa Laskow Lahey (2009). *Immunity to change* Boston: Harvard Business School Press.

Keough, D. R. (2008). *The ten commandments for business failure.* New York, NY: Penguin Group.

Kerpen, C. (2013, February 25). *Why "hire slow, fire fast" is a better idea than you think.* Fast Company.

Medina, J. (2008). *Brain Rules.* Seatle: Pesar Press.

Millbower, L. (2000). *Training with a beat.* Sterling: VA Stylus Publishing.

Osterwalder, A., & Pigneur, Y. (2010). *Business model generation: A handbook for visionaries, game changers, and challengers.* Hoboken, NJ: John Wiley & Sons.

Pink, D. (2003). *A whole new mind.* New York: Riverhead Books.

Quinn, Clark (2005). *Engaging Learning.* San Francisco, Pfeiffer Co.

Samov, P. (2010). *Present perfect: A mindfulness approach to letting go of perfectionism and the need for control.* Oakland, CA: New Harbinger Publications, Inc.

Teece, D. J. (2009). *Dynamic capabilities and strategic management: Organizing for innovation and growth.* New York, NY: Oxford University Press.

Thiederman, S. (2008). *Making diversity work: 7 Steps for defeating bias in the workplace.* New York, NY: Kaplan Publishing.

Thomas, K. W. (2009). *Intrinsic motivation at work: What really drives employee engagement* (2nd ed.). San Francisco, CA: Berrett-Koehler Publishers.

Travis, T. (2007). *Doing business anywhere: The essential guide to going global.* Hoboken, NJ: John Wiley & Sons.

Waitzkin, J. (2005). *The art of learning: A journey in the pursuit of excellence.* New York: Free Press.

Watanabe, K. (2009). *Problem solving 101: A simple book for smart people.* New York, NY: Portfolio Hardcover.

Wilson, H. J. (2012, April 2). Employees, measure yourselves. *The Wall Street Journal.*

INDEX

www.ingramcontent.com/pod-product-compliance
Lightning Source LLC
Chambersburg PA
CBHW071326210326
41597CB00015B/1364